MAURICE MAETERLINCK

MAURICE MAETERLINCK
Camera portrait by E. O. Hoppé

MAURICE MAETERLINCK

BY
EDWARD THOMAS

WITH EIGHT ILLUSTRATIONS

University Press of the Pacific
Honolulu, Hawaii

Maurice Maeterlinck

by
Edward Thomas

ISBN: 1-4102-0767-6

DEDICATED TO

IRENE AND HUGH McARTHUR

NOTE

I CAN here only express in the usual manner my indebtedness and gratitude first to M. Maeterlinck himself for his kind permission to quote from his books, and to M. Paul Lacomblez, *Mercure de France*, and M. Eugène Fasquelle for confirming it; also to Miss Laurence Alma Tadema, Messrs. George Allen, Methuen & Co., Duckworth & Co., William Heinemann, and Hodder & Stoughton for permission to quote from the English translations. The following list will make clear the details of my indebtedness.

Published by M. PAUL LACOMBLEZ:

"Serres Chaudes," "La Princesse Maleine," "Les Aveugles," "Les Sept Princesses," "L'Intruse," "Trois Petits Drames pour Marionnettes" ("La Mort de Tintagiles," "Intérieur," "Alladine et Palomides"), "Les Disciples à Saïs et les Fragments de Novalis," "L'Ornement des Noces Spirituelles de Ruysbroeck l'Admirable," "Pelléas et Mélisande," "Aglavaine et Sélysette," "Ardiane et Barbe Bleu," "Sœur Béatrice."

MERCURE DE FRANCE:

"Le Trésor des Humbles."

M. Eugène Fasquelle:

" Joyzelle," " Monna Vanna," " L'Oiseau Bleu," " Le Trésor des Humbles," " La Sagesse et la Destinée," " La Vie des Abeilles," " Le Temple Enseveli," " Le Double Jardin," " L'Intelligence des Fleurs."

Messrs. Walter Scott, Ltd.:

" Pelleas and Melisanda " and " The Sightless," translated by Laurence Alma Tadema.

Messrs. George Allen:

" Aglavaine and Selysette," with an introduction by J. W. Mackail, translated by Alfred Sutro; " The Treasure of the Humble," translated by Alfred Sutro, with introduction by A. B. Walkley; " Wisdom and Destiny," translated by Alfred Sutro; " The Life of the Bee," translated by Alfred Sutro; " Sister Beatrice," and " Ardiane and Barbe Bleue," translated by Bernard Miall; " The Buried Temple," translated by Alfred Sutro; " Joyzelle," translated by A. Teixeira de Mattos; " Monna Vanna," translated by Alfred Sutro; " The Double Garden," translated by A. Teixeira de Mattos; " Life and Flowers," translated by A. Teixeira de Mattos.

Messrs. Methuen & Co.:

" The Blue Bird," translated by A. Teixeira de Mattos; " Mary Magdalene," translated by A. Teixeira de Mattos; " The Disciples at Saïs, etc.," translated by F. V. M. J. and U. C. B.

Messrs. Duckworth & Co.:

" Three Little Dramas " (" The Death of Tintagiles," translated by Alfred Sutro; " Interior," translated by William Archer; " Alladine and Palomides," translated by Alfred Sutro).

MR. WILLIAM HEINEMANN :

> "The Princess Maleine" and "The Intruder," translated by Gerard Harry, with Introduction by Hall Caine.

MESSRS. HODDER & STOUGHTON :

> "Ruysbroeck and the Mystics," translated by Jane T. Stoddart.

Among critical and biographical studies of M. Maeterlinck which I have read I must express my particular indebtedness to the following :

> JULES LEMAÎTRE : " Impressions de théâtre," 8ᵉ série.
>
> REMY DE GOURMONT : " Le Livre des Masques."
>
> GEORGES LENEVEU : " Ibsen et Maeterlinck."
>
> EDOUARD SCHURÉ : " Precurseurs et Révoltés."
>
> RENÉ DUMIC : " Les Jeunes."
>
> GERARD HARRY : " Maurice Maeterlinck."
>
> MADAME MAETERLINCK : " Maeterlinck's Methods of Life and Work " (*Contemporary Review*, November 1910).
>
> WILLIAM ARCHER : " Study and Stage."
>
> ARTHUR SYMONS : " The Symbolist Movement in Literature," " Plays, Acting, and Music."
>
> A. B. WALKLEY : " Frames of Mind."

I have also had the help of Mr. Gordon Bottomley, Mr. A. Martin Freeman, Mr. H. Hooton and Mr. A. D. Williams.

EDWARD THOMAS.

CONTENTS

LIST OF ILLUSTRATIONS

xiii

MAURICE MAETERLINCK

I

INTRODUCTION AND BIOGRAPHICAL OUTLINE

MAURICE MAETERLINCK, Tolstoy, and Ibsen are read in England by men and women who care little or nothing as a rule for the literature of the Continent, because all three make appeals which are not solely artistic. Maeterlinck is the youngest, and his appeals are the most numerous and diverse. He is a moralist, and we like moralists; and there is a special reason why he should reach English ears as a moralist. He knows our literature; he can read Chaucer; he has admired Shakespeare and been his disciple; he has translated a play of John Ford's; above all, his circle of influences as moralist includes Coleridge, Carlyle, Emerson, and Ruskin. His " Life of the Bee," again, attracts us because it appears to reconcile Science and Poetry, which is a reconciliation we have long discussed, foreseen, doubted, and desired. His essay on riding in a motor-car pleases for a similar reason; we like to see that mechanical inventions do not destroy adventure and romance, and we applaud this essay as we do Mr. Kipling's "McAndrew's Hymn" and "Traffics and Discoveries," etc. "The Sources of Spring," "Old-fashioned Flowers," and the like flatter our fondness for writing about the country. He gets home upon us also with his praise of boxing. Then his "Blue Bird" allows itself to be so presented on our stage that it rivals the celebrated "Peter Pan," and even resembles it ; it is also sentimental, indefinitely mysterious and significant. Even his early plays have a melancholy, a romance of unreality, a morbidity, combined with innocence, which piques our indulgence. He has no irony to put us on the defensive. Translated into English, he never astonishes us, and we have an admirable and almost complete series of translations by Messrs. Sutro, Archer, Teixeira de Mattos, Bernard Miall, and Gerard Harry.

Maurice Maeterlinck, or Mooris Maeterlinck, as he spelt it in 1886, was born at Ghent on August 29, 1862. He came of a Flemish family which had been settled in the neighbourhood for six centuries, and the name of Maeterlinck is said to have been first earned and taken by a bailiff who in a year of famine gave corn to the poor. As a child he lived at Oostacker, on the bank of a canal connecting Ghent with Terneuzen ; so near was the water that the ships seemed to be sliding through the garden itself. His formal education he had at Ghent from the Jesuits of the College of St. Barbe, whose seven years' tyranny, says

Madame Maeterlinck, marred the sweet hours of his youth. There he met his friends, Charles van Lerberghe and Grégoire Le Roy, who became poets, and with them he subscribed and even contributed to *La Jeune Belgique*, a new and nationalistic literary review. According to the wish of his family he read for the Bar, and at the University came into contact with Émile Verhaeren, a man seven years older, now a notable poet and " the most eminent, along with Maurice Maeterlinck, of those modern authors who feel in Flemish, and write in French." But like Rodenbach, says M. Edouar Schuré, Maeterlinck had dreamed alongside the sleeping waters of Belgium and in the dead cities, and, though his dream did not become a paralysing reverie, thanks to his vigorous and healthy body, he was already troubled in such a way that he was unlikely to accept the conditions of the Bar and the bourgeois life. He had already written triolets and prose when he went to Paris for the first time, at the age of twenty-four. This visit, made professedly in the interest of his legal studies, but in the company of Grégoire Le Roy, confirmed his literary avocation and ambition. The two men entered the artistic and literary life of Paris, and met Villiers de l'Isle-Adam and others of the very modern writers. It was Le Roy, now turning from art to poetry, who read to some of these men " The Massacre of the Innocents," a prose tale, and afterwards introduced Maeterlinck, the author. From such meetings grew *La Pléïade*, a short-lived review, which printed " The

Massacre of the Innocents" and some of the poems
collected in "Serres Chaudes," and is otherwise
unforgotten for its part in the history of symbolism.
The law-student returned to Ghent after little more
than six months and began to practise at the Bar.
But Rodenbach had introduced him to *La Jeune
Belgique*, and he had contributed more poems to
it.   The year 1889 saw inseparable events—the
publication   of   Maeterlinck's   poems,   " Serres
Chaudes," and his farewell to the Bar.   Madame
Maeterlinck mentions " a very accurate mind and
a special gift of practical good sense " among his
qualifications for the legal profession.   The enthusiastic Gerard Harry says that he lost with
" triumphant ease " the first and last cases in
which he pleaded, and gives as one reason the fact
that his voice was impracticably harsh and thin,
and as another his excessive shyness and solitary,
taciturn habits of meditation.

He had now apparently nothing before him
but authorship.   He was far less a journalist then
than he is to-day.   He continued to live at Oostacker, and turned from his writing only to tend
his bees, to work at a lathe, to walk, row, skate,
or cycle.   Madame Maeterlinck says that he
lived at home because he was indifferent to his
material surroundings, Gerard Harry that he was
there surrounded by reproductions of pictures by
Burne-Jones, Odilon Redon, and Georges Minnè.
At intervals he was even compelled to attend to
material surroundings, as a member of the Civic
Guard of Ghent : but he allowed his musket to rust

until the night before an inspection.   From his window, at least, he could see a country which could easily suggest the scene of his early play, " Les Sept Princesses " : " A dark land of marshes, of pools, and of oak and pine forests. . . . Between enormous willows a straight and gloomy canal, on which a great ship of war advances."

In the same year as " Serres Chaudes," 1889, appeared " La Princesse Maleine," after having been privately printed, to the number of thirty copies, by the author himself on a hand-press.   A Belgian critic announced that the play made an epoch in the history of the stage.   A French critic in *Le Figaro*, Octave Mirbeau, said that no one could be more unknown than the author, but that his book was a masterpiece, " comparable—shall I dare say it ?—superior in beauty to the most beautiful in Shakespeare."   In opposition to this heavy-handed compliment a sting was easily added to the phrase, " Belgian Shakespeare," and some one explained that the play was Shakespeare because it was made with scraps of Shakespeare.   Gerard Harry retorted that the characters of Shakespeare are marionettes in comparison with Hjalmar and Maleine.   Maeterlinck was disturbed by inter-viewers, became tired and sick of them, and comforted his outraged modesty by himself calling the play " Shakespearterie."   Maeterlinck's modesty or shyness is made impressive by many witnesses. Gerard Harry quotes a letter accepting an invita-tion to dinner on condition that he is received without ceremony, adding : " I am a peasant."

Later on, Georges Leneveu says that Maeterlinck
barricades himself against all indiscretion and
curiosity, detests notoriety, is indifferent to the
representation of his work, avoids the cackling,
the flattery, all the small change of celebrity. At
the end of a first night he was modest, simple,
altogether without display in dress or manner.
His gestures were gentle with reflection, his voice
low and rarely heard. He had no pride of success,
but an air at once uneasy and detached, as if tired
of being there. His deep blue eye was cold and
mournful, like a mirror that retains the images of
indefinite and impalpable things, as Barbey d'Au-
revilly says the eyes always are of those who
look more within than without. His brow was
deep and square and shone pale. He made the
observer think of his own untranslatable words :

> Sous l'eau du songe qui s'élève
> Mon âme a peur, mon âme a peur.

The same writer says, by way of contrast, that
the playwright keeps bees and teaches a dog to
sing ; he calls him a sportsman, a man always
getting about, a great drinker of ale—a great boy,
a good fellow, a Bohemian. Here may perhaps
be discerned the writer in praise of the sword,
the fist, and the automobile, the friend of the
bull-dog, and the creator of Tylo.

After " La Princesse Maleine " came " L'Intruse "
and " Les Aveugles," acted in 1891, and " Les
Sept Princesses." His translation from the
Flemish of " L'Ornement des Noces Spirituelles "

of the mediæval mystic, Ruysbroeck l'Admirable,
also appeared in 1891 ; and his Introduction to
this book first made public his interest in Plato,
Plotinus, S. Dionysus the Areopagite, Jacob Behmen,
Novalis, and Coleridge.   Herein also he proclaims
Villiers de l'Isle Adam and Stephane Mallarmé
as the greatest French mystics of the day.   Four
years later he published a translation of Novalis's
" Disciples at Sais " and the fragments, with an
Introduction where he says that here we find
ourselves, not upon Ruysbroeck's dim blue peaks
of the soul, but in an atmosphere of crystal on
the sharp and often perilous ridges of the intellect, but sometimes in the sweet shade of re-
cesses beneath.   He applies a similar figure to
Emerson, speaking of the irregularly rounded and
more humble claims of the heart in his essays.
Seven of these had been translated into French
by I. Will, and were published in 1894 with a
Preface, full of a feeling of discipleship, by Maeterlinck.   He was himself the maker of the French
version of John Ford's " 'Tis Pity she's a Whore,"
acted in the same year and published in the
next.   Meantime he had written more plays.
" Pelléas et Mélisande " was put on the stage
by Lugné Poe and Camille Mauclair in 1893.   It
was loudly praised.   The play was " absolutely
clever," even to a critic who could say of " Sept
Princesses " only that it was a thin volume published at Brussels by Lacomblez.   The next year
was the year of the " three little plays for marionettes "—" Alladine et Palomides." " Intérieur," and

"La Mort de Tintagiles." M. Camille Mauclair now coupled him, as did the opinion of a multitude, with Ibsen. He had then written the book of poems and the eight plays which are, whether his best or not, of all his writings most purely and decidedly his own, works of a singular trembling intensity, apparently conceived and executed in a solitude without a sound. Five or six years afterwards, referring to these early plays as revealing "the disquiet of a mind that has given itself wholly to mystery," he seemed to apologize for them as representing the "instinctive feelings" of his art rather than the thoughts of "real life." Mauclair even at this date points out the duality of Maeterlinck's mind, which is equally fit for creations at once concrete and arresting, and for abstract speculation. He goes on to say that the great man seems to prefer discursive metaphysics to the creative literature which has given him his fame, and that he will end by giving up plays and works of imagination, taking to the work of a moralist exclusively. What he has already done promises an artistic metaphysician, whose philosophy will be like Carlyle's in its images. He has no intellectual affinity to Shakespeare, but he does make us think of Marcus Aurelius.

Maeterlinck now, in 1896, left his native country for good, and settled in Paris. Gerard Harry tells us that he had hoped in vain for a place in the public service which would waste little of his time, and would make him independent. In spite of

MAURICE MAETERLINCK AS A YOUNG MAN

his promised immortality, and his dangerous proximity to Shakespeare and Marcus Aurelius, he lived a secret, intellectual life in Paris, inaccessible to all but a few.

The year 1896 was in other ways a memorable one in his life, for then were published " Le Trésor des Humbles," his first volume of Essays, and " Aglavaine et Sélysette." Madame Maeterlinck quotes a letter, in which he says that Aglavaine brought him "a new atmosphere, a will to happiness, a power of hope." Henceforth, he continues, Aglavaine's light will direct him in a " serene, happy, and consoling course," away, it may be supposed, from the dim, blue-lit marshlands of the early plays, and from that conception of life which he himself, in an essay in " Le Temple Enseveli," calls " not healthy." Edouar Schuré, seeing a resemblance in him to the sick Rodenbach, author of " Bruges la Morte," sees also " a stronger spirit in a vigorous, healthy body," a fundamentally simple and strong affirmative man under the mask of an exquisite and a decadent. Gerard Harry describes his " sturdy, full-fleshed Flemish body, such as Jordaens loved to paint," and the portraits show us a thick-lipped, thick-necked man, who appears to lack nothing of a virile equipment, unless it be humour. This is the man, the painter obviously of the entirely Flemish scenes in " Le Massacre des Innocents," almost inconceivable as the poet of " Serres Chaudes " and the dramatist of " Les Sept Princesses " and " Alladine et Palomides ": this is the man whom Aglavaine, the first of his heroines with a will, leads out into the twilight—whether morning or evening twilight is not clear.

"Le Trésor des Humbles," it should be noticed, is dedicated to the actress Madame Georgette Leblanc, now Madame Maeterlinck. It marks by no means an escape from the world of "Les Sept Princesses," and no great step from the Introduction to Ruysbroeck's book; but some of its chapters had already been printed in the magazines, and its tone is that of a man who wishes to be heard, and does not appear in public by accident. Here, writes Mr. Arthur Symons, Maeterlinck "dropped his disguise." But, as if to show that he could in safety turn back and look at the enchanted forest behind him, he published in this same year, 1896, another little book of poems, "Douze Chansons," now altered to "Quinze Chansons"—poems in which we see and suspect nothing whatever of the full-fleshed and powerful Flemish body.

"Le Trésor des Humbles" was acclaimed like "Pelléas et Mélisande"; it had not to wait for admiration. It showed Edouar Schuré, for example, one of the most grave and spiritual of critics, that the playwright had a will and an ideal, that he had faith in a transcendent and absolute truth. Towards this truth he saw Maeterlinck travelling undismayed by the horrors of reality or the phantoms of dreams. He points with satisfaction to the essayist's "initiators"—Plato, Plotinus, Porphyry, Marcus Aurelius,

Dionysius the Areopagite, among the ancients;
Behmen, Ruysbroeck, mystics of the Middle Age
(a term very much extended to include Behmen);
Spinoza, Kant, and Schopenhauer, modern philosophers; Novalis, Emerson, Carlyle, Coleridge,
Eliphas Levi, and Amiel, those intuitive thinkers
of the nineteenth century, apostles of the soul and
knights of the spirit, against triumphing positivism
and materialism. Schuré saw in this book and
in " La Sagesse et la Destinée " not only reflections
of these mystics and philosophers, but something
more than doctrine—an experience of the inner life,
proof of a subconsciousness in touch with an invisible world, proof that each man is a little world
surrounded by a magnetic atmosphere emanating
from his passions, his feelings, and his habitual
ideas. . . . " La Sagesse " followed " Le Trésor "
in 1898. It was dedicated to Georgette Leblanc
as the result of her collaboration in thought and
example: he had only to listen to her words and
follow her life with his eyes when he wrote the
book; for to do so was to follow " the words, the
movements, the habits, of wisdom itself." Even
" La Sagesse " caused some distress among those
who had hailed a mystic prophet in the author of
" Le Trésor." He had forsaken the heights, they
lamented, for the sad plains of the earth; he who
saw visions now attended to earthly things.

" La Vie des Abeilles " came in 1901. It was
exquisite and it was precise; it was science and
poetry not only together but allied. This was the
full light of day, of every day. There was no need

to be a mystic, or to know that word, in order to admire this joyous eloquence, this sunny and real world. " Truly," says Gerard Harry, after pointing to the happiness of Maeterlinck's union with Georgette Leblanc, " henceforward he looks upon life less desperately and less fearfully." " I am a peasant," said he, explaining his dislike of cere- mony years before. Among his bees he might seem, to an enthusiastic reader, a solid, meditative peasant to whose serenity has been added curiosity without disturbance. Such a reader would be delighted to see that Maeterlinck is indifferent to opera and lyrical drama. " Pelléas et Mélisande " as a lyrical drama, with music by Debussy, was first played in 1902 ; but he took no interest in it— not only, it would appear, from an objection to the mishandling of his work, but because he knows and cares nothing for music.

The year of " La Vie des Abeilles " was also that of " Ardiane et Barbe Bleue " and " Sœur Béatrice," the first a gorgeous and allegorical rendering of the story of Blue Beard, the second a legendary play which might have been written to illustrate the philosophy of " Le Trésor des Humbles." They are the clear and firm work of the mature Maeterlinck, and they point for- ward to " Joyzelle "; but at the same time, they point back to the period of the early plays, where, with some difference of treatment, a more languid and misty development, they would have been quite in place.

" Le Temple Enseveli " was published in the year

after " La Vie des Abeilles," in 1902. It has been seen that it contains a quiet adult criticism of the early plays. Its subjects are " The Mystery of Justice," " The Evolution of Mystery," " The Kingdom of Matter," " The Past," and " Luck." Obviously they are the work of a man of intellect and much reading. If " Le Trésor " is a book which was at least written deliberately in order that it might be read, " Le Temple Enseveli " might have been delivered in the form of lectures. It is the work of a man who, recluse or not, is in cóntact with the world. It alarmed the more religious of his mystical admirers. Schuré bids him beware ! He is tending to a purely materialistic view and a denial of the divine law, which is to destroy eternal justice, the invisible world, and God, the soul's sun, towards which he was steering his uncertain vessel. . . . It might have seemed that Maeterlinck was advancing towards a social and not a solitary position as a writer, willing to consider whatever might concern his contemporaries, a possible contributor of a weekly or monthly *causerie*; not only able to write beautifully on a broomstick, but perhaps willing to do so, should he be asked.

" Monna Vanna," also belongs to 1902. It is a clear and solid play, relating in the main to history and to this world. Here was no need of marionettes to act the still, drugged parts of afflicted men and women. The play is as intense as it is real ; the single interest exacts from each of the five principal characters the deepest truth and nothing else.   Not more than half, perhaps, is unmistakably the work of Maeterlinck, so free is it from mannerism ; all save the conclusion is unmistakably the work of a master. The most striking proof of his individuality is our feeling that the story could not have been chosen or invented by another man, and that, had it been, the development from the entry of Vanna into Prinzivalle's tent must have been entirely different.

"Joyzelle," a play of 1903, is a picturesque romantic allegory. It belongs to the same class as " Sœur Béatrice " and " Barbe Bleue," and, like them, seems a by-product of Maeterlinck's energy. It has not the enchanted atmosphere of the early plays, or the reality of "Monna Vanna." It is fanciful, and has even a kind of finished hardness, as of a *tour-de-force* which has not been able to concentrate all of the author's powers.

In the next year came "Le Double Jardin," and, after a similar interval, " Life of Flowers," two collections of descriptions, essays, and criticisms which had nearly all been translated in England or America before they were gathered into books. Their subjects include a favourite dog, duelling and boxing, the bank at Monte Carlo, a motor-car, chrysanthemums, immortality, Rome, the psychology of accident, "King Lear," and the manufacture of scents.   They are brilliant, eloquent, and ingenious.   They are always perfectly his own, but show the writer in a public character, always in touch with an audience, and more and more purely intellectual.

"L'Oiseau Bleu" was published in England in 1909 and in France in 1910. Gerard Harry tells us that Maeterlinck, in unmeasured terms, refused to allow Coquelin Aîné to adapt this play "to the taste of a boulevard public." It had already appeared on the stage in Moscow, had made the fortune of the Théâtre des Arts, and has since been played by fifty-nine companies in the provinces of Russia. Except that it is for children, it belongs to the class of "Ariane et Barbe Bleue," etc. "In none of his works," says Mr. Herbert Trench, "has Maeterlinck blended so happily scientific observation with the dream-work of the poet. . . . Maeterlinck has thus put a whole philosophy into a gay fairy-tale, that may be understood and laughed over by a child." It is the work of a master of fancy, of the theatre and of the public.

"Mary Magdalene" appeared in an English translation in 1910. It is the long-expected successor to "Monna Vanna," and, like that, has been refused a licence for the English stage. It has been executed with the whole of Maeterlinck's mature power and its best is his best work; but it is incomplete. He is now nearing fifty, and his popularity has never been greater. Nearly all his books are multiplied and repeated, by new editions and translations, into many languages. Always independent, money could only add ease and opportunities for gratifying minor tastes. He spends the winter at Quatre Chemins, near Grasse, in the south of France; the summer at the ancient Benedictine Abbey of Saint Wandrille, in the

Seine-Inférieure, where there is an inscription
upon one of the walls which Gerard Harry thinks
might be the writer's device :

O beata solitudo !
O sola beatitudo !

There Madame Maeterlinck plays "Macbeth,"
in her husband's translation, while he, it is said,
smokes a pipe in peace as well as in solitude.
The pipe, according to Gerard Harry, contains a
denicotinised herb ; for thus, by a piece of heroism
discovered by his hero-worshipper, Maeterlinck
circumvents his unconquerable craving for tobacco
in his hours of work. "By wise disposition," says
Madame Maeterlinck, "he has reduced his weakness, economised his strength, balanced his faculties,
multiplied his energies, disciplined his instincts."
Yet he continues to write. He is early to rise
and go out to his garden and his bees, for which
his liking is now near thirty years old. Two
hours, always exactly two hours, of work follow.
Then he goes out again, canoeing, motoring, cycling,
or walking. He reads in the evening and "goes
to bed in good time." The work of those two
hours is prepared easily and quietly during the
pleasures and other duties of the day. Madame
Maeterlinck compares him taking up his work to
a child leaving its games and going on with them
as soon as allowed—an innocent and ambiguous
comparison. She implies that his work is sub-
consciously matured and methodically put on paper,
and that his natural tranquillity and the surroundings

LES QUATRES CHEMINS

and conditions of his life have long been felicitously combined ; and she says it might seem that the mysterious powers have woven between him and the world a veil which allows him a clear vision whilst yet himself invisible, as they have favoured him by the gift of a home not less wonderful than the castles which he imagined for Alladine and Selysette and Maleine.

II

WHEN Maeterlinck was a young man of twenty-four he met Villiers de l'Isle Adam and other symbolists in Paris. He became a symbolist himself. His early poems, some of them published during that visit to Paris and collected afterwards with others in "Serres Chaudes," are symbolist or they are nothing ; his early plays were accepted as symbolist. It is not obvious what is here meant by symbolism, but it is not merely the use of symbols. " It is all," writes Mr. Symons, " an attempt to spiritualize literature, to evade the old bondage of rhetoric, the old bondage of exteriority. Description is banished that beautiful things may be evoked, magically. . . ." Writing of the sonnets of Gerard de Nerval (1808–1855) he says that here, " for the first time in French, words are used as the ingredients of an evocation, as themselves not merely colour and sound, but symbol." Probably it is meant that they are used solely as an evocation, and deliberately so. One of the examples, " El Desdichado," has something like the magic

18

of the not quite intelligible song of Taliesin,
beginning :

> Primary chief bard am I to Elphin,
> And my original country is the region of the summer
> stars ; . . .
> I was with my Lord in the highest sphere,
> On the fall of Lucifer into the depth of hell ;
> I have borne a banner before Alexander . . .

for it ends : "Am I Eros or Phœbus ? . . . Lusig-
nan or Biron ? My brow is still flushed from the
queen's kiss ; I have been dreaming in the grotto
of the syren . . . and twice have I victoriously
crossed Acheron playing on the lyre of Orpheus,
sometimes in the tone of a saint's sighing and at
other times of a fairy's cry." It is hardly necessary
to say that the words do not take us farther or
deeper than certain phrases of older poets and
even prose-writers, like :

> And battles long ago ;

or—

> Merry it was in Silver Wood ;

or—

> Visit'st the bottom of the monstrous world ;

or, " The famous nations of the dead " ; or,
" Apame, the King's concubine, the daughter of
the admirable Bartacus, sitting at the right hand
of the King, and taking the crown from the King's
head, and setting it upon her own head " ; or,

"And the world shall be turned into the old silence seven days." We know that the words of poets and of others who can handle words often mean much more than the same mean in another place or at another time. We are almost certain that their words have often come to mean something different from what was consciously present in their minds when they wrote, and often more vast. Maeterlinck knew this, and expressed it in 1890, in a criticism now printed in Gerard Harry's "Maurice Maeterlinck." "Is it not," he asks, "by examining what he has not consciously intended that we penetrate the essence of a poet? The poet premeditates this, premeditates that, but woe to him if he does not attain something else beside!" But the symbolists, having come late into this world, are more self-conscious than men before them, and it appears to be their task to produce consciously the strange echoing and branching effects of magic which came to earlier men straight from the gods. Mr. F. Y. Eccles puts it in this way in the brilliant Introduction to his "Century of French Poets":

"Of the many tendencies imputed to symbolism this is the most characteristic—out of an acuter perception of what all poets have always known, that words are insufficient if their power is bounded by their meaning, emerged an audacious doctrine which branded their representative function as inferior, and sought to shift the poetical interest from what they signify to what they may suggest. In the Parnassian system description was paramount, and feeling sprang from it immediately : the emotion which symbolism pursues bears no constant relation to the objects represented or the ideas expressed ; rather it aims at the recovery of vanished moods by curious incantations, by the magical use of verbal atmosphere. To fashion a true likeness of the material world it holds a vain and illusory undertaking : it values sights, sounds, scents, and savours for their secret affinities with states of the soul. . . ."

It is a little unkind to words to suppose that they can be bounded by their meaning, but apparently the symbolist must insist that his words are not only not so bounded, but have a further significance which is quite precise ; otherwise there were no difference between the old and the new. It is a dangerous difference. For a poem of the old kind has a simple fundamental meaning which every sane reader can agree upon ; above and beyond this each one builds as he can or must. In the new there is no basis of this kind ; a poem means nothing unless its whole meaning has been grasped. Take, for an example of the old, a seventh-century Chinese poem from Mr. Cranmer-Byng's " Lute of Jade." It is called " Tears in the Spring " :

> Clad in blue silk and bright embroidery,
> At the first call of spring the fair young bride,
> On whom as yet Sorrow has laid no scar,
> Climbs the Kingfisher's Tower. Suddenly
> She sees the bloom of willows far and wide,
> And grieves for him she lent to fame and war.

This is explicit enough and amazingly condensed;
but, even so, the many elements in it combine, and
then fall away and leave something more than the
sum of them all, and that something over gives
the poem its great beauty, which we may call
symbolical if we like, but not symbolist. A symbolist might have used the same scene, but
probably with this difference, that he would have
drawn no conclusions from it ; he would have left
it to make its own effect. In the same way a
symbolist poet might have seen the Highland
reaper as a symbol, but would not have interpreted
the symbol like Wordsworth. But, look at "Ennui"
from Maeterlinck's " Serres Chaudes ":

" The careless peacocks, the white peacocks,
have fled ; the white peacocks have fled from the
ennui of waking. I see the white peacocks, the
peacocks of to-day, the peacocks in rows during
my sleep, the careless peacocks, the peacocks of
to-day, arriving lazily at the sunless lake. I hear
the white peacocks, the peacocks of ennui, awaiting
lazily the sunless days."

This is a dangerous poem for those who think
that symbolist poems must be judged by new
standards. There is no meaning upon which all of
them would agree. The first wish of the tolerant
reader seeking for profound and designed significance must be for a dictionary to explain " peacocks," especially " white peacocks." He will be
all the more disturbed by his lack of compre-
hension, because probably he would like to think

of white peacocks; but this the words will not allow. The birds have to be examined like an heraldic device. The most he can do is to think—perhaps upon a suggestion from a remembered picture—of a large grey house with white peacocks on the empty terraces, and over all a Sunday desolation of ennui and silence. Nor is this poem the most difficult—not to understand, but to meet in such a way that understanding is possible. For the poem seems to contain interpretation as well as a symbol; so does "Fauves Lasses," with its "yellow dogs of my sins," "squint-eyed hyenas of my hates," "flocks of temptations." "Chasses Lasses" is a poem written in cypher, and containing a glossary of its own terms :

"My soul is sick to-day; my soul is sick with absence; my soul has the sickness of silence; and my eyes light it with tedium.

"I catch sight of hunts at a standstill, under the blue lashes of my memories; and the hidden hounds of my desires follow the outworn scents.

"I see the packs of my dreams threading the warm forests, and the yellow arrows of regret seeking the white deer of lies.

"Ah, God! my breathless longings, the warm longings of my eyes, have clouded with breaths too blue the moon which fills my soul."

If this method is characteristic of the "decadence" and modern France, it is not new. Is it not upon the same model as the song which Musidorus, in Sidney's "Arcadia," sang to Pamela, "to show

what kind of a shepherd he was." This is the
song :

> My sheep are thoughts, which I both guide and serve ;
>   Their pasture is fair hills of fruitless love :
> On barren sweets they feed, and feeding starve :
>   I wail their lot, but will not other prove.
> My sheep-hook is wan hope, which all upholds :
>   My weeds, desire, cut out in endless folds :
>   What wool my sheep shall bear, while thus they
>   live,
>   Dry as it is, you must the judgment give.

Then Pamela turns to Mopsa and says : " Take
heed to yourself, for your shepherd can speak
well. . . ." This passed in Sidney's time for the
language of emotion, as that of " Chasses Lasses "
does in our own. Both appear to be purely fanciful writing according to a fashion, and more cannot be said of them than that the exposure of the
symbols has given the lines a naive decorative
value.

It is harder to speak of the poems which are
not thus translated for us by the one man who
has their secret, Maeterlinck himself. It would
be simple to accept them all together as a not
obscure symbol of something familiar—youth ; or
to take the words of them as bounded by their
customary meaning, the words that recur, most of
them, many times—sadness, weariness, ennui, melancholy, pallor, feebleness, immobility. These are
truly *mots propres*, the right words not sought
but inevitable and significant, like Shelley's
" wingèd," or Ruskin's " entirely." The poems

seem to represent a weariness, a melancholy, an unrest that belong to the writer only when he writes. These feelings, when they are profound, are not so eager to be quickly told. The pallor and melancholy are parts of the writer's refinement, and are unconsciously chosen, partly, perhaps, out of respect for the pictures by Burne-Jones on his walls, and partly as an easy method of distinguishing himself from a vile world not in the least melancholy and pale, or desiring to be so. If there is anything here to be called sorrow it is no more passionate than wall-paper, and is not due to loss of faith, fortune, wife, health, leg, teeth, or the like, but to this excessive refinement in protest against those whom he despises, and in imitation of the admired. In the absence of information it is impossible to be certain, but it seems likely that most of " Serres Chaudes " is due to Paris and the literary life. The little of his still earlier work which I have seen has nothing of this character: " The Massacre of the Innocents," a perfectly Flemish piece of objective realism, is as unlike as possible, and this may have been written before the visit to Paris, though, whether it was or not, its lucidity and entire lack of display of emotion make it a significant contrast with the languor and confusion of " Serres Chaudes."

When referring, years later, in " The Buried Temple " to his early plays, Maeterlinck spoke of them as the work of " some obscure poetical feeling " within him which believed in a hostile and encompassing fate, and he claimed that, with the

sincerest poets, a distinction has often to be
made " between the instinctive feelings of their art
and the thoughts of their real life." What else
is this than what Keats wrote in the dedication of
" Endymion " when he was at the same age as the
Maeterlinck of " Serres Chaudes "? " The imagination of a boy is healthy, and the mature imagination
of a man is healthy; but there is a space of life
between, in which the soul is in a ferment. . . ."
In a young man of the middle class living an easy,
sheltered existence, chiefly in our modern cities,
as it is so natural and common to do, the brave
fervour of youth is often girt up neither by
experience in the past nor by a sufficient object in
the present ; it must spend itself, and it does so
upon little things, borrowed things, which are
presently seen for what they are, and share with
the fervour the same neglect and even contempt.
The poem called " Serres Chaudes " expresses the
sense of strangeness and vanity which comes to
this state when life is at once too languid and too
difficult because it is all cloistered within the brain :

" O hothouse in the midst of the woods, with
your doors for ever closed ; and all the things under
your dome, with their counterparts in my soul !
" The thoughts of a hungry princess ; the weariness of a sailor in the desert ; a brass band playing
under the windows of incurables.
" Seek the warmest corners ! Such, a woman
fainting on a harvest day. Postillions are in the
courtyard of the hospital; while in the distance
passes an attendant, once an elk-stalker.

" Look closely, by moonlight! How out of place is everything here! Such, a mad woman before the justices; a man-of-war under full sail on a canal; night-birds perching on lilies; a noontide death-knell (there, under those bell-glasses!); a station for the sick in the open fields; the smell of ether during a day of sunshine.

" Ah, God! God! when shall we have the rain and the snow and the wind in the hothouses? "

Here, too, "with their counterparts in my soul," if not a complete explanation, is a timid admission of the need of one. But the piece is hardly more than a catalogue of symbols that have no more literary value than words in a dictionary. It ignores the fact that no word, outside works of information, has any value beyond its surface value except what it receives from its neighbours and its position among them. Each man makes his own language in the main unconsciously and inexplicably, unless he is still at an age when he is an admiring but purely æsthetic collector of words; certain words— he knows not why—he will never use; and there are a hundred peculiarities in his rhythms and group-ings to be discovered. In the mainly instinctive use of his language the words will all support one another, and, if the writing is good, the result of this support is that each word is living its intensest life. The first few words of a work of art teach us, though we do not know it at the time, exactly how much value we are to give to all the rest, whether they are to be words only, or images, or spirits. They admit us, or teach us that we cannot be admitted, to the author's world. Any writer whose words have this power may make a poem of anything—a story, a dream, a thought, a picture, an ejaculation, a conversation. Whatever be the subject, the poem must not depend for its main effect upon anything outside itself except the humanity of the reader. It may please for the moment by the aid of some irrelevant and transitory interest—political interest, for example ; but, sooner or later, it will be left naked and solitary, and will so be judged, and if it does not create about itself a world of its own it is condemned to endure the death which is its element. These worlds of living poems may be of many different kinds. As a rule they are regions of the earth now for the first time separated from the rest and made independent ; they may be lit by the sun of every one, or by another, or by the moon, or by a green lantern : whatever they are, they are stronger than this world, and their light more steadfast than sun or moon. Wordsworth writes a poem in the hope of making it give the same impression as a certain hawthorn-tree gives to him; Keats because he cannot dismiss from his mind the words, "Dost thou not hear the sea ?"; Burns because a girl pleases and evades him. Anything, however small, may make a poem; nothing, however great, is certain to. Concentration, intensity of mood, is the one necessary condition in the poet and in the poem. By this concentration something is detached from the confused immensity of life and receives individuality, and this creativeness brings into my mind the inhuman solitariness of the world at the moment when Deucalion stooped to make the first men out of stones ; and the waste of waters when the dove bore an olive-leaf into the ark out of the monotonous waste. But the early Maeterlinck turned no stones into men, nor found the crest of a tree piercing the dead sea. Nothing in "Serres Chaudes" persuades us to see this creative high value in the words; they give no help to one another. It is as far from the writing of a sloven or a common man as from that of a master, but it says nothing save that it belongs to a school to which it has turned in the confusion of its unrest. Whatever its intention, it has not that quality of style which at once takes and retains possession of the reader.

To give such a poem significance it would be necessary to make a key to it, like St. Melito's key to the Bible, where it is shown that in one place the word "Camelus" stands for Christ, in another for love of this world; that "Leo" means Christ, Mark the Evangelist, the Devil, Antichrist; that "Unicornis" is Christ, but "Unicornes" the proud. But the extreme example of such symbolism is found in a verse by Adam de St. Victor, where the word "dragon" is used three times in three different senses within two lines—Christ, the Devil and something like Antichrist. But this is not literature ; as well might algebra be called literature. It is not deep enough. It was no symbolism of this kind that gave the words, "I believe in the forgiveness of sins" inexorable significance to Luther as if the door of Paradise had been thrown wide open, William James, from whom this example is taken.

gives other examples of persons for whom " Phila-
delphia " and "chalcedony " had "a mighty fascina-
tion," and "the words *woods* and *forests* would
produce the most powerful emotion."

" Most of us," says James, " can remember the
strangely moving power of passages in certain poems
read when we were young ; irrational doorways, as
they were, through which the mystery of fact, the
wilderness and the pang of life, stole into our hearts
and thrilled them.   The words have now perhaps
become mere polished surfaces for us ; but lyric
poetry and music are alive and significant only in
proportion as they fetch these vague vistas of a life
continuous with our own, beckoning and inviting,
yet ever eluding our pursuit.   We are alive or dead
to the eternal inner message of the arts according
as we have kept or lost this mystical susceptibility."

A curious example of this value of a single word
or phrase may be seen in George Herbert's poem,
" My Master," and in the treatise on " The Song of
Angels," by a fourteenth-century English mystic,
Walter Hilton :

" Some man setteth the thoughts of his heart
only in the name of Jesu, and steadfastly holdeth
it thereto, and in short time him thinketh that the
name turneth him to great comfort and sweetness,
and him thinketh that the name soundeth in his
heart delectably, as it were a song ; and the virtue
of this liking is so mighty, that it draweth in all
the wits of the soul thereto.   Whoso may feel
this sound and this sweetness verily in his heart,
wete thou well that it is of God, and, so long as he
is meek. he shall not be deceived.   But this is not

angel's song; but it is a song of the soul by virtue of the name and by touching of the good angel."

This is an example of the extreme and highest symbolism of words. Were it common in this degree there could be no more poetry, or it would be more accurate to say that there could be nothing else but poetry.

It is an old opinion that all visible things are symbols. Sallustius, the friend of Julian the Apostate, says Professor Gilbert Murray, held the world itself to be a great myth, and the myths to be all allegories. Paris, for example, being "the soul living according to the senses," and therefore only able to see beauty, which is Aphrodite. For him the value of a thing lay "not in itself, but in the spiritual meaning which it hides and reveals." Heraclitus of Ephesus "deliberately expressed himself in language which should not be understood by the vulgar and which bore a hidden meaning to his disciples," and he said that "if Homer used no allegories he committed all impieties"—on which Professor Murray makes the illuminating comment that "on this theory the words can be allowed to possess all their own beauty and magic, but an inner meaning is added quite different from what they bear on the surface." Ruskin seems to have held a similar opinion to this of Heraclitus, for he sees a designed significance in the fact that Ophelia's name means "serviceableness," and seriously writes: "Hamlet is, I believe, connected in some way with 'homely,' the entire event of the tragedy turning on betrayal of home duty." But had Shakespeare paused to secure effects of this kind, assuredly he could not have produced so many that are infinitely more powerful. The laws governing æsthetic and spiritual effects are innumerable ; those which can be discovered are probably few in comparison, and if these are deliberately followed it is more than likely that many others will be fatally disobeyed. Maeterlinck, for example, had learnt a few when he wrote " Feuillage du Cœur":

" Under the blue crystal bell of my weary melancholy moods, my dim bygone griefs take gradually their motionless form :

" Symbolic growths ! Brooding water-lilies of pleasures, slow-growing palms of my desires, cold mosses, pliant bindweed :

" Alone among them a lily, pale and weak in rigidity, marks its motionless ascent above the grief-laden foliage :

" And in the glimmer which it radiates, gradually, moon-like, lifts its mystical white prayer to the blue crystal."

But is there anything here in addition which can awaken and gratify the profound receptivity of spirit most fit for communion with a poet ? Mr. W. B. Yeats, in his essay on " The Symbolism of Poetry," rebukes those—the journalists—who, in his opinion, are certain " that no one, who had a philosophy of his art, or a theory of how he should write, has ever made a work of art " and supports himself by the words of Goethe : " A poet needs all philosophy, but he must keep it out of his work." The qualification he half rejects, but when he comes to give examples of potent symbolism he finds them chiefly in writers like Burns, who did not know the word and would perhaps have been astonished and even amused by the theory itself. Even Mr. Symons, loyal critic of the professed symbolists, has to say that "Symbolism, as seen in the writers of our day, would have no value if it were not seen also, under one disguise or another, in every great imaginative writer."

It must now be apparent that entirely conscious symbolism comes very near to being allegory, which of all things is abhorred by symbolists. Mr. Yeats himself is a poet who is far more than a symbolist, yet it is possible to see in his work this danger skirted, and sometimes upon the wrong side. He confesses, in the notes to his "Wind among the Reeds," that he "has made the Seven Lights, the constellation of the Bear, lament for the theft of the Rose, and has made the Dragon, the constellation Draco, the guardian of the Rose, because these constellations move about the pole of the heavens, the ancient Tree of Life in many countries, and are often associated with the Tree of Life in mythology." It was natural that he should have said, after quoting from Goethe, that to keep his philosophy out of his work is not always necessary for the poet; for, had he kept his own out of the notes to "The Wind among the Reeds," the annotated poems must have fallen short of his reader. An example is "Mongan laments the

3

change that has come upon him and his beloved,"
beginning :

Do you not hear me calling, white deer with no horns?
I have been changed to a hound with one red ear ;
I have been in the Path of Stones and the Wood of
      Thorns,
For somebody hid hatred and hope and desire and fear
Under my feet that they follow you night and day. . . .

" I got my hound and deer," runs his note, " out of a
last century Gaelic poem. . . . This hound and this
deer seem plain images of the desire of man 'which
is for the woman,' and ' the desire of the woman
which is for the desire of the man,' and of all desires
that are as these." It may be that a day will
come when the force of Mr. Yeats's genius will have
added to common culture the special knowledge
through which alone the poem is intelligible. At
present the language of it is dead or merely
private, like that of Heraclitus, and the note, so
far from helping the poem, attracts attention exclusively to itself. It is again a question of style.
The poet's words refuse to make any impression
corresponding to his intention ; they speak to the
brain alone, and can reveal only his interest in
mythology. Similar notes to " Serres Chaudes "
must have been extraordinarily interesting ; but if
Maeterlinck does not write them it is doubtful
whether any one else can or will.

The one piece in the little book which is perfectly
intelligible is " Hôpital." It should have been
placed, instead of " Serre Chaude," at the front of

the collection, because it is like that poem and at the same time reveals its own origin, real or imaginary. It is nothing but a series of the fantastic images in a feverish man's brain. Each one of the images, like the hothouse in the midst of the snow, the churching of a woman in a storm, the banquet spread in a forest, the meadow sheep trotting sadly into the wood, may well have come up before one sick man lying in a hospital on the bank of a canal, and many of them are, taken by themselves, at least suggestive. As a whole the poem is neither realism nor impressionism, nor successful in any class, because the parts have nothing to hold them together and to transform them from the state of notes into poetry. Nothing sufficient is done to prepare the way for the procession of fever pictures, and no conclusion is drawn from them; each part is greater than the whole. There are half a dozen other poems—such as "Cloche à Plongeur" and "Âme"—which do not differ essentially from "Hôpital." Instead of the dream of a fever-patient the excuse is a hothouse, a bell-glass, or a diving-bell, and he sets off at once with a catalogue of such bric-à-brac as antediluvian beasts invading towns, all a king's daughters (on a parliament day) wandering in the meadows, crows hatched by swans, a sister shelling peas at the foot of an incurable's bed, a nuptial banquet celebrated in a cave, princesses going to bed at midday, like those in his play of "Les Sept Princesses." The hospital recurs in more than one poem, for example in that on a diving-bell he compares the pallor of those who are going to die with that of patients who listen to the rain tranquilly falling in the hospital garden. A sleeping, swooning, fainting, a feverish condition seems to be the foundation of all. The things seen are remote and solemnly absurd, like things seen very far away in an influenza dream at midday. Evidently Maeterlinck liked this magic of looking through the wrong end of a telescope : he was the amateur looking at a diving-bell and thinking of going down in the green water and seeing "strange" creatures round about. He speaks of "the water of dream" and of the "profound reflections of things"—lilies, palms, roses, weeping under the waters and barred over by "the mournful ennui of reeds." He was perhaps dazed by the seeming depth of reflecting water, and the flowers, seen as it were in the sky, were natural to his soul where things innumerable of different and far climates might blossom together, provided that there were enough hothouses. Many of the poems bring before the mind a man in either a conservatory or a hothouse looking out on a level, watered country with swans and flocks of sheep. Nearly all things affect him through his eyes only, and as if he had seen them by compulsion and not choice ; he does not love any of them ; his eyes have caught his soul in a trap, as he says in "Après-midi," and there again he is lying in bed listening to the hours, waiting for rain to fall on the turf and on his motionless dreams, while his gaze is following lambs in the towns upon the horizon. No wonder that he addressed his soul as "truly overmuch in shelter"—in shelter like the plants under the sweating and misty bell-glass. "Ennui," which has already been quoted in a translation, is, after all, the most perfect of this soul's dreams. He saw white peacocks because he preferred what was less common—a black kingfisher, or a white pillar-box, and so on. But lull the mind and lay it back, as it were, on a pillow of sultry noon, and let the birds, the indolent, careless birds have their way, as they did in the poet's dream. The poem is made of strange birds and beautiful, monotonous words full of nasal vowels:

> Les paons nonchalants, les paons blanc ont fui,
> Les paons blancs ont fui l'ennui du reveil ;
> Je vois les paons blancs, les paons d'aujourd'hui,
> Les paons en allés pendant mon sommeil,
> Les paons nonchalants, les paons d'aujourd'hui,
> Atteindre indolents l'étang sans soleil,
> J'entends les paons blancs, les paons de l'ennui,
> Atteindre indolents les temps sans soleil.

This is the music of words, and nothing but words—words in their barbaric and unintellectual purity, and according to your ear for such will be the clearness, beauty, and significance of the white peacocks which they create. Banish all thoughts of symbolism and of different standards, and it is a beautiful poem of refined and luxurious indolence.

III

IF Maeterlinck's early poems contained any
promise, it certainly was not a promise of
plays. The fever-images—some one being poisoned
in a garden, deer in a beleaguered town, sheep
trotting sadly into the hospital ward—these cannot
have seemed to have in them either the method
or the material of drama. Peacocks, or swans, or
sheep, were unlucky characters for a play, yet they
were as real as anything else in " Serres Chaudes."
The effects were chiefly silent, the poet's attitude
spectatorial even towards himself.

" Serres Chaudes," nevertheless, was closely
followed by a play in five acts, " La Princesse
Maleine." Here there is a clear, and perhaps only
too emphatically clear, material outline ; Mrs. Rad-
cliffe would not have been above it. At the
opening, the betrothal banquet of Prince Hjalmar
and Princess Maleine is being held in the castle
by her father, Marcellos, king of a part of Holland.
A comet and a shower of stars amaze the guards

38

while they talk of how the prince's father, king of another part of Holland, old Hjalmar, is too fond of the exiled Queen Ann of Jutland. The banquet lasts late, and old Hjalmar is very drunk, when a smashing of windows is heard and Maleine runs out. Old Hjalmar has quarrelled with Marcellos and goes away taunting him. But Maleine still loves Hjalmar, though she is not yet fifteen, and her father shows how unreasonable it is, seeing that the two kings are now at war. She will not give up the lover whom she has seen but once. The castle is attacked and most of the defenders killed, but Maleine has disappeared. Hjalmar is now to marry Uglyane, daughter of Ann of Jutland, while Maleine and her nurse are shut up in a tower to be safe until the war's end. The nurse makes a hole in the wall, and their eyes tell them, for the first time, that the whole land is wasted by war and fire.

Going towards Ysselmonde through the forest, with her nurse, Maleine hears that Marcellos and her mother, Godeliva, have perished and that Hjalmar is to marry. The beauty of the princess sets two men fighting in a village, and Hjalmar's friend, Angus, seeing her without recognizing her, suggests her for Uglyane's attendant. In that position Maleine takes Uglyane a false message to say that Hjalmar is not going to keep a promised tryst, and goes herself. Her lover feels her beauty in the dim forest, but only when he has asked her what she is thinking of does she say " Maleine," and reveal herself, to his joy.

Hjalmar tells the old king of Maleine's return. He no longer thinks of marrying Uglyane. A knocking at the door is heard at a feast, and Maleine enters in the long white robes of a bride. The old king faints when he knows that it is the dead Maleine. Queen Ann lets him know that he must choose between herself and the returned princess, who is "greener than if she had been drowned and rotting four weeks in water." A madman points at the princess and makes the sign of the cross. Nevertheless, Hjalmar and Maleine are to be married, and Ann and Uglyane to wait for the event. Nuns come to weave the bride's dresses; bells and the croaking of crows are heard and will-o'-the-wisps are seen; Maleine is chilly and pale. The queen has asked for a poison, but the physician, who sees some mystery hovering about the castle, has determined to make it harmless. The king is a reluctant but helpless accomplice; he would like to go away, but Ann holds him back. Maleine's illness makes Hjalmar think that she should try a different air; but Ann points out that here she is well nourished, and the king can only feebly exclaim, "Oh! oh!" Allan, the little son of Ann, asks if Maleine will not ever play with him again, and disturbs them. The king kisses Maleine. A knocking is heard: for a time they do not open, and it is repeated; but when Hjalmar opens nothing is to be seen.

Ann feels that Hjalmar is suspicious. She is impatient; the poison will "idle on till doomsday."

There is another great storm, and Maleine is left
alone in the night with a large black dog quivering
in the corner of the room. She thinks somebody
is in the room, and calls out—for by the queen's
orders no one has visited her all day. The king
and Queen Ann come to her door ; the old man
would draw back, but they enter together, and the
black dog crawls out. Pretending to do her hair,
Ann twists a cord round Maleine's neck and kills
her. The madman appears at the window, but
is struck back into the moat by the king. They
hear a scratching outside, and the nuns singing.
The nurse outside calls out to ask if Maleine is
asleep, and supposes that she is sleeping soundly.
" Soundly," echoes the king. Hjalmar and Allan
are now outside, and the nurse relates that she
was attracted by the dog sniffing at the door.
Allan, too, listens, and declares that there is a
little boy behind it. When he has gone the king
runs out without waiting to help Ann to put the
corpse to bed.

The fifth act opens in the same storm. A crowd
in the cemetery before the castle sees that there
is no light in the room which is the Princess
Maleine's. The moon is black. Lightning strikes
the castle and a mass falls into the moat. Inside
the courtiers and Hjalmar are inquiring for the
king and Ann. At last the two come in, the
king with bloodstains in his now wholly white
hair. Ann forbids the nurse to enter Maleine's
room ; both murderers say, " No, no, no, no." The
king thinks all are suspecting and staring at him.

Outside Maleine's room the dog is still scratching, and Hjalmar and the nurse long try to get him away. They enter and find the dead. They cry out, and every one comes in, the king dragging in Ann and confessing before all. At this Hjalmar stabs the murderess and then himself. The king babbles, asks the nurse if she will be angry, and if there will be salad for breakfast.

When old Hjalmar bids an angry farewell to Marcellos after the banquet, he mentions Maleine only to speak of her green face and white lashes. These features, the silence and feebleness of the heroine, who has a child's will, hard to break but very easy to thwart, stand out as the most original element in the play. The comet, the shower of stars, the banquet, the storms, the knockings at the door, the black hound, the moat, the madman, the mastery and poison of the queen, the strangling and the blood of the end, seem to be imposing externalities used by one who is impressed by them chiefly because they are alien to him. They come obviously for the most part from Shakespeare, from "Hamlet" and "Macbeth," for example, and however any one of them may for the moment recover its original power, the vast accumulation is rumbling, unwieldy, and without life, and it crushes out the faint lyric interest of Maleine herself. Nor is the king's remark that "There is knocking at all the doors in this place," the only one that has the humour of parody. Twice we can forget everything for the sake of that strange beauty with her white eyelashes, her way of casting down her eyes and crossing her hands. The tower where she is shut up with her nurse to escape the war makes an enchanting scene. Their chamber is high betwixt the sky and the earth, above the tops of the forest, and their groping hands come upon bats and fungi. With her fingers the nurse breaks away the mortar until at last the sunshine touches their flesh as warm as milk, and they are dazzled. They see the blue sky, the forest, the green sea, and a ship with white sails upon it, but not the city, nor the belfries, nor the mills, for all is burnt—and only crows in place of men. The talk of nurse and princess unfolds this scene with perfect precision and an effect beyond anything which Maeterlinck had achieved before it, comparable with that of Tennyson's " Mariana in the Moated Grange "; yet as a play " Princesse Maleine " would lose nothing were it omitted. The second scene is the meeting of Hjalmar with Maleine instead of Uglyane in the wood within the park. The prince wished to discover in the dark wood of autumn whether his betrothed had " maybe a little silence in her heart." The leaves fall about him, and the wood is strange and full of presage. Maleine comes. The eyes of the owls shine among the branches, and Hjalmar throws earth to drive them away. They hear the sound of a mole tunnelling, and sounds of other things which enter the park in spite of walls and moats. She seems to him singularly beautiful, and he knows her. She is sad, and he asks why. It is because she thinks of the Princess Maleine : she is the

Princess Maleine, and the moon shows her face.
But the delicacy of the scene is so slender that it is
all but broken by the bleeding at the nose which
sprinkles the princess's dress with blood ; it is
incredible that such a thing should happen to such
a lady.

Hjalmar is a fit lover for Maleine, and only the
unkindest of fates—or rather of dramatists—could
have forced him to kill a murderess and himself.
He is, in truth, a refined man of our own time,
somewhat curious in sensations, as he shows when
he tells his friend Angus of the evening in the
wood :

"Oh ! strange things happened last evening.
But I would rather not dwell upon them at present.
Go some night into the wood adjoining the park,
by the fountain, and you will notice that it is only
at certain times, and when one looks at them, that
things remain motionless like well-behaved children,
and do not wear a strange and weird appearance ;
but so soon as one turns his back upon them, then
they begin making wry faces at one, and playing
bad tricks."

He and Maleine and the black hound, living
together at the top of the tower above the wood,
with rain or hail to beat on a window, and wind
to sound in the willows, whether of a cemetery or
not, would have been sufficient material for the
dramatist.   The child Allan might have been
added, for, though he alone or the hound alone
would have been more effective than both, he is
a being thoroughly characteristic of Maeterlinck.

So also are the swans in the moat under Maleine's window in the last act. They fly away as the crowd watches—all but one, which has blood on its wings, floats upside down, and dies. This is an escape from " Serres Chaudes," except that its symbolism is clear. There is not a character in the play who could not, if he wished, make a better poem than any in that book. Best of all is that made by two lords standing at a window during the storm in the last act. One says :

" Every one of the beasts has taken refuge in the cemetery. I can see peacocks among the cypresses. There are owls on the crosses. All the sheep of the village are crouching upon the tomb-stones."

The other adds :

" Just as one would picture a festival in hell."

And a maid of honour cries :

" Draw the curtains in ! Draw the curtains in ! "

Maeterlinck showed a great power of self-criticism and self-control in face of the onslaught of admiration which " La Princesse Maleine " provoked. He did not accept the position of a Belgian Shakespeare : he knew that he was more Belgian than Shakespeare. Not once did he repeat the error of handling with antique pomp a long, various tale and a host of characters.

His next play, " Les Aveugles," contains fourteen human characters : but one voice, and that not

a ventriloquist's, could play the parts of all. All
but two are blind, and one of those two is dead and
the other a sucking child. They have less vigour
than Maleine when the owls stared at her in the
wood ; they do nothing, nothing is done to them,
and they hardly move or speak. As in "La
Princesse Maleine," the setting is choicely impressive, but it is essential, and it never changes.
It is a forest on a small island—"a very ancient
northern forest, eternal of aspect, beneath a sky
profoundly starred. In the midst and towards the
depths of night, a very old priest is seated wrapped
in a wide black cloak. . . . His eyes, dumb and
fixed, no longer gaze at the visible side of eternity,
and seem bleeding beneath a multitude of immemorial sorrows and of tears." On the right
are six old blind men seated on stones, stumps of
trees, and dead leaves. On the left, and separated
from the men by an uprooted tree and fragments
of rock, are six blind women facing the men. All
are in sombre and uniform garments, and most sit
waiting without gesture, except three playing and
wailing women. Around them are " great funereal
trees"—yews, weeping willows, and cypresses. These
people are the blind from a Home, and the priest
is the priest in charge. They no longer hear his
voice, and they are afraid of everything : of passing
birds, snow falling, or dogs barking, and they do
not understand anything except the sound of the
sea, and they do not know how near it is. They
have walked thus far with the priest exploring
their island, which has "a mountain that no one

has climbed, valleys which no one likes to go down to, and caves that have not been entered to this day," and now they cannot tell what has happened to him, or where he is. They conjecture, they try to explain what is going on, they recall their memories, they lament. At last a dog drags one of the men to where the priest sits. The man touches "a face"—"a dead man"—and he thinks it is the priest. The others grope their way and recognize the dead. "What are we to do? . . . We cannot wait beside a dead man. . . . Let us keep together. . . . I think that the men from the big lighthouse will see us." Only the infant can see. They hear sounds as of footsteps ; the child cries, and they think it must be something, and so they move towards the sound. But is it, after all, only the sea on the dead leaves? At last the footsteps stop in their midst. " Who are you ? " asks the child's mother. There is no answer. " Have pity on us ! " cries the oldest blind woman. But nothing breaks the silence except the desperate crying of the child.

It is not necessary to the effectiveness of this piece that we should believe the blind to represent mankind bewildered after the loss of religion, their old guide. Whether it is true or not that religion is dead and men blind without it, the thought is so stale that in its nakedness it could be of no value to any piece of writing. But the sight of a blind man sitting still or tapping in the street—for example in fog, when, says the poet W. H. Davies, " only blind men know their

way "—is always impressive ; and to the blind
company in the play are added many elements
of mystery and terror which enhance this im-
pressiveness.   They have at the start little more
humanity than the rocks and trees among which
they sit, except that they are conscious of themselves and one another.   They are like creatures
suddenly made out of the rocks and trees ; and it
is easy to picture beings of equal humanity standing
in the depths of a misty wood when rain falls all
through the day at autumn's end.   Or they are
like personifications, so that we feel no curiosity
with the name of any but that one who says for
Maeterlinck :

" We have never seen one another.   We ask one
another questions, and we reply ; we live together,
we are always together, but we know not what we
are."

And the young blind woman who had seen once :

" I come from very far," she says ; " it is beyond
the seas.   I come from a big country. . . . I could
only explain it to you by signs, and we cannot
see. . . . I have wandered too long. . . . But I
have seen the sun, and water, and fire, and mountains,
and faces, and strange flowers. . . . There are
none like them on this island ; it is too dismal
here, and too cold. . . . I have never known the
scent again, since I lost my sight. . . . But
I saw my parents and my sister. . . . I was too
young then to know where I was. . . . I still
played about on the sea-shore. . . . Yet how well
I remember having seen ! . . . One day, I looked
at the snow from the top of the mountain. . . .

I was just beginning to distinguish those that are
to be unhappy. . . . I can still distinguish them
by the sound of their voices."

This last thought, if not peculiar to Maeterlinck,
is characteristic of him, and the tone of the
speech, the passionless pathos of it, the resentless
suffering, the memory which is everything, are
recognizable as his alone in this combination. And
so of the whole play. On the one hand the
grandeur and distinctness of the forest upon an
island of the sea ; the poor, feeble little human
beings, on the other hand, this helpless band of
mostly aged and solitary blind trusting in a man
who has died in their midst without their knowing
it,—these are parts of a picture which is clear and
simple and powerful, having something like the
significance of trees or any other natural group seen
at a favourable moment. We do not wish to
explain it or fully translate it any more than we do
such a natural scene ; it is a symbol whose strength
is in a simplicity at once clear-cut and vague.
Exaggeration has put a still sharper edge on the
nervousness of the piece ; for the shortest speeches,
especially where they are only variants of one another,
might have been taken down from life, but give no
effect of life except of tiny children. This is the
over-emphasis due to the impossibility of calculating
means and ends. It is all the more noticeable
because it has an appearance of realism, although
we must feel that the piece as a whole does and
could owe nothing to a study of the blind. These are

4

not human characters. They are given the names
and figures of men and women because they cannot
thus fail to move others of the species. A similar
effect, as has been hinted, might have been gained
from trees or stones, but the painter preferred the
more pompous material of humanity. It is the work
of a spectator, and one who is far more interested
in the ideas that go to and fro among men than
in men themselves.

"L'Intruse" is of the same date and the same
kind. The grandfather, the father, the uncle, the
three daughters, are sitting round a table ; a lamp
is alight. In the next room lies the sick mother.
Some one else is expected ; they speak in a low
voice and in short phrases about insignificant
things. But the old man is troubled. The trees
in the park tremble as if somebody brushed
through them ; the nightingales become silent, as
if there were some one in the garden ; the swans
are alarmed, the fish plunge in the pond ; but the
dogs do not bark. The door opens as if pushed.
They hear the sound of a scythe being sharpened.
Then it is as if some one came invisibly and
softly, sat down at the table, and rose up and
went towards the door of the next room. The
dying woman's child now cries and continues to
cry with increasing painfulness until the end of
the play. The sick-room door opens and the
sister of mercy comes out and makes the sign of
the cross to announce the woman's death.

As in "Les Aveugles," the scene is made impressive, but less relevantly. It is an old country

house whose panelled walls and stained-glass windows, the park, the lake, the swans, the scythe-sharpening, make up for the fact that the action takes places in modern times. At the approach of death, a little wind rises in the avenue, the nightingales are stilled, the swans frightened, and the daughter is sure that some one has come into the garden:

Grandfather. Are not the nightingales beginning to sing again, Ursula?

Daughter. I cannot hear one anywhere.

Grandfather. And yet there is no noise.

Father. There is a silence of the grave.

Grandfather. It must be some stranger who scares them, for if it were one of the family they would not be silent.

Daughter. There is one on the big weeping willow. It has flown away!

Uncle. How much longer are you going to discuss those nightingales?

Grandfather. It seems to me that the cold is penetrating into the room.

Daughter. There is a little wind in the garden, grandfather, and the rose-leaves are falling.

Father. Well, shut the door, Ursula. It is late.

Daughter. Yes, father. . . . I cannot shut the door, father.

Two other daughters. We cannot shut the door.

Grandfather. Why, what is the matter with the door, my children?

Uncle. You need not say that in such an extraordinary voice. I will go and help them. . . .

This is in the same nervous manner as in " Les Aveugles." Every one is restless, irritable, and expectant. They are probably not clever people, and they are hardly made to look cleverer than they really are. Some of their talk might have been taken down in a drawing-room or a railway carriage, as when they talk of the strange ways of the old grandfather :

> *Father.* He is like all blind people.
> *Uncle.* They think too much.
> *Father.* They have too much time to spare.
> *Uncle.* They have nothing else to do.
> *Father.* And besides, they have no distractions.
> *Uncle.* That must be terrible.
> *Father.* Apparently one gets used to it.

But these are only the words. The dramatist does not indicate the silences, the tones of voice (though these are supposed to be noticed by the characters), the movement, of reality ; because if he did it would be less easy to make felt the most important quality of the talk—its distracted nervousness, and the superficiality which is in a way more pregnant than anything else could be. He is content to make use of the blankest and baldest reality for the sake of the resulting intensity, which distributes itself to and from words like those of the uncle, describing the old grandfather's state :

> "Not to know where one is, not to know where one has come from, not to be able to distinguish midday from midnight, or summer from winter— and always darkness, darkness ! "

On the stage a degree of realism might well destroy the life of the play. Actors and actresses would be unnecessarily large. For here again the characters are called human, and have something human about them ; and yet do not appear to the reader's imagination as life-size. These half-dozen people are only so much paint used in making a decorative pattern of death. If anything from the living world breaks in it is the baby's crying, and this has in the play a similar use to the knocking at the gate in " Macbeth ": it announces that if death has come life is going on, and must persist and overpower talk about nightingales and the nervous fears of a disintegrated family. This crying thus takes us out into the world from the sombre monotony, the subdued and reduced life, of the sitting-room. If we insist on treating these people, not as half-ghostly miniatures, according to the string of implicit suggestions by Maeterlinck, but as human flesh of the middle class, we must inevitably laugh, and, I suppose, be laughed at in turn by the dramatist.

"Les Sept Princesses" belongs to 1891, the year after " Les Aveugles " and " L'Intruse." The description of the scene gives almost as full a picture as the play, which, like its predecessors, is mainly pictorial. There is a vast hall of marble, divided lengthwise into two by a range of seven white marble steps, and upon pale silken cushions laid on these sleep the seven princesses, with white robes and bare arms. A silver lamp is burning. The huge glass windows reach down to the floor, and outside them is a terrace. In the light of a setting sun can be seen a black marshy country and forests of oak and pine. Perpendicular to one of the windows is a dark and undeviating canal between great willows, and upon it at the horizon a great warship is advancing, just as in "Serre Chaude."

The old king and queen and a messenger step forward on the terrace to watch the ship approaching. At first the king cannot see, and the queen describes the full spread of sail touching the willows, and the oars like a thousand legs. At last the king sees it, as if too large for the canal. Anchor is dropped, and the prince descends. The swans go to meet him. Then the queen turns and looks through the windows at the princesses, asking, "Are they sleeping all the time?" They discuss whether to wake the sleepers, but the doctor has forbidden it. They hear a step and leave the window, bidding Marcellus come up and beware of the old staircase. After embracing, he observes how old and feeble his grandparents are, and asks after his seven cousins. They show him the seven sleeping in the hall. "How white they are!" he says, and asks why they sleep. "Oh how pale, how strange, they are!" He begins to distinguish one from the other. He prefers, he says, the one who is not so clear. "That," says the queen, is "Ursula, who has waited seven years for her lover." A shadow lies across her; she sleeps more profoundly. And Marcellus goes round to another window, but cannot see her face. The queen tells him their names—Geneviève, Helen, Christabel, Madeleine, Claire, and Claribella. Why did not Marcellus come sooner? So long have they watched night and day along the canal . . . it is now black night, and the rain has a sound of crying in the dark. A distant, monotonous song is heard, with the burden, "We shall return no more, we shall return no more." It is the sailors turning the ship. The queen tells Marcellus she has waited long for him, and now "It is not you any more." Looking at the princesses again—the song still in their ears— something has changed, and Ursula's hand is no longer held by her sisters. "She cannot sleep thus," says the queen, "it is not natural; and her hair is not done up. But she said at noon: 'Above all, do not wake us.' How still they are!" She taps on the window, but they do not move, or make a sound. The queen cries: "Oh, my God, save them! . . . they sleep so horribly!" and she sobs wildly against the window. They try to open the door, but neither door nor windows will open, and the king, with Marcellus, have to enter by a sub-terranean passage. Cries of joy come from the sailors, and the ship is lit up. At the appearance of Marcellus all the princesses but Ursula awake. The queen outside cries, "Ursula!" The young prince kneels and touches her bare arm, then looks round fearfully at the pale, silent six. They raise her up stiff, while the king and queen cry and beat on the windows. "She is not asleep," says the queen. "Pour water on her. . . . Open the door. . . . It is too late. . . . Shut! shut!" All cry, shaking the door and knocking at the window: "Open, open!" A black curtain falls suddenly.

Nobody who had read "Les Aveugles" and "L'Intruse" could doubt the authorship of "Les Sept Princesses." Here are the same agitated, helpless people speaking in abrupt, simple, and often-repeated phrases. Here again something is going on which they do not understand, and are impotent to arrest or change. But the matter of both earlier plays was a not improbable incident which was developed, it may be extravagantly, but in a manner that touched human beings. If "Les Aveugles" was extraordinary, while "L'Intruse" was not extraordinary in any way, both were easy to understand. But "Les Sept Princesses" is a picture drawn for its own sake. It has its logic, but the elements in it seem chosen, like those of "La Princesse Maleine," because they are attractive in themselves—the marble hall and stairs, the terrace, the dark land of marshes and forests, the canal and the warship, the seven princesses in white sleeping on the stairs, the swans, the prince arriving to claim one of them and finding her at last dead, the old king and queen shut outside the hall and knocking vainly at the windows ; only, these elements are combined without any of the unwieldiness of "La Princesse Maleine," without interfering with themselves or with anything else. It is simply a picture in Maeterlinck's manner, and this manner has the effect of creating a feeling of helplessness and smallness in the presence of fate and the earth. If any one seeks to explain it as a solar myth he will not lack argument: the princesses are from a warm country, and they are always seeking the light, but the trees are too big and the fogs too lasting; and thus they sicken, and the solar hero, Marcellus, who actually has a name, arrives too late. In life we do not expect to find seven princesses sleeping all through the day by lamplight on the stairs of a palace hall, but no one who has seen the pictures of Burne-Jones will be in the least surprised at seeing them in a picture. The use of a number, seven, should put us into the right key for enjoying the picture for itself. This shows us at once that the princesses are to be used decoratively, like the seven branches of a candlestick, or what not; and their names confirm us. It is a little more difficult not to take too seriously the nervousness of the queen, by which we are repeatedly invited to believe her some trepidant old lady of flesh and blood. But we are helped when the king says: " We are poor little old people," which means, " We are poor little old people, such as M. Maeterlinck loves to harass for an hour, but it really does not hurt as much as it seems." If this does not perfectly reassure, then the words of the prince will:

" Oh! how white they are, all seven! . . . Oh! how beautiful they are, all seven! . . . Oh! how pale they are, all seven! . . . But why are they asleep, all seven? "

These are not the words of mortal man. Further, the queen herself gives us valuable help by saying that the princesses " are not happy; it is not our

fault. . . . We are too old, too old; every one
is too old for them. . . . One is too old without
knowing it." The queen tells the king that her
crying is nothing : " One often cries for no reason :
I am so old to-day " ; and these words, that might
be deeply moving in life, or in another writer, do
not move us too much on this page, which is no
more real than a pastoral. If only these characters
could be quite silent they would be even more
pleasing. Even the water in the moat is "very
old also," and so " it always sleeps." One or two
strange touches of reality mark them : thus the
princesses always wake up thirsty ; also they grow
very tall, " which is perhaps why they are so
sickly "—like tall artist's models of the Burne-
Jones type, who were said to be fed upon crumpets,
capsicum, and warm water ; and then Marcellus
asks the absurdly natural question, " Is this their
bedroom ? " Nevertheless, read sympathetically,
it is a literary picture of charming composition,
with the languid refrain of " We shall never come
back ! We shall never come back ! "

" Les Sept Princesses " was in a sixth edition
in the year of its appearance, but Maeterlinck
did not go on writing little plays of this kind.
Others could do them all but equally well. In
this same year, 1891, appeared his old school
friend, Charles van Lerberghe's, play, " Les
Flaireurs," dedicated to himself. When " Les
Flaireurs " was written I do not know, but Gerard
Harry calls it the " elder brother " of " Maleine."
It is exceedingly like Maeterlinck in all its de-

vices, differing from it chiefly in the atmosphere
which has been freshened by a breath from the
world of everyday. It opens with a funeral march
—a rolling of muffled drums—the far-off sound
of a horn. A sick woman and her daughter hear
a voice outside in the night, and they learn that
it is "the man." But they expect nobody, and
the daughter tells her mother it is the wind, and
asks, "Do you come for me?" "No, indeed,"
says the voice, and in answer to her explains that
he is "the man with the water . . . and the
sponge . . . for washing." He knocks. The girl
is afraid. He knocks again, but she will not admit
him. Very well, he will wait. The women pray,
the rain whips the panes, and ten o'clock sounds.
A dog barks.

Again the drums and the horn, and presently a
knocking at the door. "Be quiet, mother sleeps";
but he knocks again. "I have come," says the
voice, and bursts into laughter. The mother
listens, and hears something under the door, rustling and dragging. "The man with the linen,"
says the voice. "Mother, it is nothing." "But
there is some one," the mother persists, and the
knocking is repeated again and again. The
mother hears horses; she can hear the grass grow,
and she knows that the lovely Lady of the Castle
has come on a horse. Again the knocking. "Why
do you tremble, mother?" "For joy. She is
there." The voice, on the daughter's renewed
refusal, says, "I will wait." The mother has
dreamed that she was in Paradise. . . . "Has she

gone?" They pray for the lovely lady, and eleven o'clock strikes, the dog barks, and the girl puts out the candles. Again the drums and the horn, and a knocking. "You will make my mother die," says the daughter; but the knocking or the voice replies to all she says. Her mother bids her light candles, but her house is "not fit to receive her." Outside the voice says, "I am the man with the coffin"; but the mother says, "Open the door. She can enter." The knocking cracks the door. "I will not open, never, never. Are you come to kill my mother?" while the mother says, "Enter, lovely lady; this is the day, and I am ready." Outside is a knocking and cracking, and voices disputing. The old woman begins to rattle terribly. Horses are heard whinnying. The mother smiles, and folds her daughter to her, while she points to the door. "It is the coach." There is a sound of a heavy carriage, and fragments of talk and oaths. Again a knocking. "Saint Mary, Virgin," exclaims the mother. The door gives way, but the daughter hurls herself against it, and midnight strikes. The voices outside utter a relieved "Ah!" and at the last stroke the old woman gives a loud raucous cry, the girl quits the door, and throws herself open-armed on the bed, while the entering wind blows out the candles. But here the presence of a will, or at least of an active vitality, robs the method of most of the quality which it has in Maeterlinck's hands.

IV

"PELLÉAS ET MÉLISANDE"

INSTEAD of writing another "Sept Princesses,"
Maeterlinck wrote "Pelléas et Mélisande,"
which appeared in 1892, when he was thirty. The
story has fully as much external interest as "La
Princesse Maleine," and it is treated upon a
similar scale, but without irrelevancies. The
characters are of the same vaguely "ancient"
period as those of "Maleine," and the scenery is
the same. Old Arkèl is "King of Allemande."
Golaud and Pelléas are his grandsons, and Geneviève their mother. Yniold is the son of Golaud by
a former marriage. Mélisande is a princess from
a strange land. There is a castle, a park, a forest
by the sea. Golaud is lost in the forest while
following the wild boar, and finds the beautiful,
timid Mélisande sobbing beside a fountain. He
takes her home, half-willing, and marries her. But
upon meeting the younger brother, Pelléas, she is
sad, and would not have him go away from the
castle. She tells Golaud that she is not happy, she
knows not why. But she continues to meet Pelléas,
and the child Yniold sees that they have both been

crying as they sat together in the dark. Golaud comes upon Pelléas kissing Mélisande's hair, which she has let fall from her window. Golaud warns his brother, calling it smilingly only child's play; but is jealous, and, after having caught them together again, he drags her about by the hair, so that Arkël, looking on, says : "If I were God I should have pity on men's hearts." The lovers meet again beside a fountain. Golaud is in hiding, and kills Pelléas and wounds Mélisande, so that she dies after being delivered of a child, "a little puny girl that a beggar would not care to bring into the world . . . a little waxen thing that came much too soon."

Such stories have been told before, but simply as a story. Maeterlinck tells it admirably, with proportions that are original as well as just, so that even those who cared nothing for his peculiar method must recognize a master. The surroundings, the colour, the air are his own, like those of its little predecessors. His choice of an Arthurian name for his hero is not unimportant. It gives the key to the story as a whole. He needed an atmosphere remote from modernity and from all historic time, and, by using an Arthurian name, he gained an antique richness far beyond anything which could have come through a medium of his own imagination like that in "Les Sept Princesses." Whether from its Celtic blood or not, the Arthurian literary tradition has just that unreality which serves Maeterlinck. He comes to us upon the music of—

Lancelot and Pelleas and Pellenore.

but tempers it by a scene, the first, which might have been the opening of a modern play, for he is to make the tradition his own and colour it afresh, as Morris and Swinburne did. "What big forests," exclaimed Mélisande when she came to the castle, "what big forests all around the palace!" Seldom could she see the sun. The well where she sits with Pelléas is "perhaps as deep as the sea." When she and Pelléas enter a cave they see "three white-haired old beggars, seated side by side, and supporting one another in sleep against a ledge of rock." Looking out of a window, Pelléas shows the boy Yniold the dogs fighting. Under the castle there are deep vaults where "the darkness is thick as envenomed pulp," but opening on the sea. On the doors there are heavy bolts and chains, and when Pelléas goes out to his last embrace of Mélisande he hears these shoot behind him : "It is too late, it is too late," he cries, and the words echo like, "We shall never come back." When Mélisande lies on her death-bed the maid-servants come in unasked and range themselves in silence and in spite of Golaud, along the walls.

Golaud first sees Mélisande crying because she is lost, and does not "belong here," beside a pool in the forest, and at a touch from him she threatens to cast herself in. She has great eyes that seem never to shut, and she takes him for a giant. She would rather die than that he should recover her crown, which has fallen into the water. But he takes her home and weds her, though the hair is grey on his chin and temples: six months after he knows no more of her than at first. When she first meets Pelléas he tells her that he is perhaps going away on the next day, and she asks: "Oh! . . . Why are you going?" They sit and talk, not to one another so much as into the silence. She dips her hands into the water because "it seems as if my hands were ill to-day," and, tossing Golaud's ring up into the air, she lets it slip into the fountain, and they cannot get it back. When she reached the castle she was joyous like a child, but now, says Arkél, she stands, "careless perhaps, but with the strange bewildered look of one that was ever expecting a great sorrow, out in the sunshine, in a fair garden." Even the jealous Golaud sees innocence in her eyes so great "they could give lessons in innocence to God"; yet her flesh disgusts him—her hands are too hot —and he tortures her by the hair. When she tells Pelléas, who has just said "I love you," that she loves him too, her voice "comes from the end of the world." Asked if she is lying, she says: "No, I never lie; I only lie to your brother." When he kisses her she is "so beautiful that one would say you were going to die." Forgiving Golaud— "what is there to forgive?"—she dies of a wound that would not have killed a bird; and as she lies in her bed she looks like her baby's big sister.

Compared with his wife, Golaud is a human being upon the ordinary plane. Falling in love with Mélisande is probably his first serious indiscretion, and he knows it is indiscreet. When

SAINT WANDRILLE : RUINS OF THE ABBEY

he sees the flocks being led to town he observes their crying, like lost children—"one would say that they already smelt the butcher"; but goes on to utter words which betray, if anything, a too ironic opinion in the dramatist: "It will be time to go in to dinner. What a lovely day! What an admirable day for the harvest!" He sets his child to spy for Mélisande. Upon her death-bed he seeks from Mélisande a confession of infidelity—"Quick! quick! . . . the truth! the truth!"—and, failing to get a clear statement of facts, he raves because he will die "like a blind man," and will never know.

Pelléas is a brother soul to Mélisande, but not to Golaud, who had a different father. Before he has seen her he seems to his mother weary of waiting so long for Mélisande. He is always agitated, and when little Yniold enters the room after knocking at the door he reproves him: "That is not the way to knock at doors. It was just as if some misfortune had happened." His passion finds open and direct expression but seldom, as when Mélisande's hair inundates him from a window above, and he holds it and winds it about his neck. "Look, look," he cries up to Mélisande:

"Look, look, I am kissing your hair. . . . All pain has left me here in the midst of your hair. . . . Do you hear my kisses creep along your hair? . . . They are climbing all the length of your hair. . . . Every single hair must bring you one. . . ."

5

On the night when Golaud surprises and kills
him he watches the long shadows of Mélisande
and himself and notices how, far away, they kiss,
as if he were enchanted as the child Traherne was
by his reflection in the water : " Our second selves
those shadows be."

As Pelléas is Maeterlinckian in the languor and
acquiescence of his actions, so his grandfather
Arkël is Maeterlinckian in thought.   On reading
the letter in which Golaud confesses his "strange
marriage" and fears that Mélisande's beauty will
not excuse his folly in the old man's eyes, Arkël
says :

" He has done what he probably had to do.   I
am very old, and yet I have never for one instant
seen clearly within myself; how then would you
have me judge the deeds of others ?   I am not
far from the grave, and I am incapable of judging
myself. . . . One is always mistaken unless one
shuts one's eyes."

And he concludes :

" Let it be as he has willed.   I have never put
myself in the way of a destiny ; and he knows his
own future better than I do.   There is no such
thing, perhaps, as the occurrence of purposeless
events."

Arkël, it is evident, has been reading " Le Trésor
des Humbles" and " La Sagesse et la Destinée,"
though these books were not actually published for
several years yet.   When Pelléas wishes to go
away from the castle, and Arkël wishes him to stay,

the old man says: "If you think it is from the depths of your life that this journey is exacted, I shall not forbid you to undertake it; for you must know, better than I, what events you ought to offer to your being and to your destiny." The old man has relatives among the blind in "Les Aveugles" and is at least cousin to the grandfather in "L'Intruse" and the prince in "Les Sept Princesses." He is the intellect of the family, and has thought so much that he is never much disturbed, and can always speak like a philosopher if not like a wise man. When Mélisande has died and Golaud is sobbing—"Oh! oh! oh!"—Arkël says to him: "It is terrible, but it is not your fault. . . . It was a little, gentle being, so quiet, so timid, and so silent. . . . It was a poor little mysterious being, like all the world," and this is the very accent of his microcephalous relatives; but his next words, the last in the play, mark the philosopher again: "Let us go from here. Come; the child must not stay here, in this room. . . . It must live now, in her stead. . . . The poor little one's turn has come. . . ." It is like the end of "L' Intruse."

The doctor also who attends Mélisande has had the same training. "It is," he tells Golaud, "not of this small wound that she could die; a bird could not die of it . . . it is therefore not you that have killed her, my good lord; you must not distress yourself so. . . . She could not have lived. . . . She was born for no reason . . . to die; and now she is dying for no reason. . . ."

Not for nothing does Maeterlinck make his characters royal persons, or at least landowners; or, if not, blind men in the care of an asylum. Such lives could not be supported by any others except, perhaps, priests. It is hard to think of them as performing the simplest functions of men, so sad, languid, and submissive are they. They can lie about beside forest fountains all day and lose a ring or a crown and take sadness or happiness as if it were a sweet drug. Golaud's normality interrupts them from time to time and ends them at last. The child Yniold interrupts them because he is strange, but only with the strangeness of a child among elders, while all the others are strange, meditative children whose elders we do not see. Yniold is perfectly natural. Golaud is asking him about Pelléas and Mélisande, and promises to give him something to-morrow:

"'What, father dear?' asks the child.

"'A quiver and arrows; but now tell me what you know about the door,' says Golaud.

"'Big arrows?'

"'Yes, yes; very big arrows. But why will they not have left the door open?—Come, answer!—no, no; don't open your mouth to cry. I am not angry.'"

This is a domestic conversation from any day. Yniold and Golaud, in fact, and the servants of the opening scene, give scale to the play. They are strong, rough, ordinary members of the human species. Arkël, Pelléas, and Mélisande are of another race. And yet Golaud himself has the trick of these "poor little" people when he says: "Do you see those poor creatures over there who are trying to light a little fire in the forest?—it has been raining. And, round the other way, do you see the old gardener trying to lift up that tree which the wind has blown across the path?—he cannot do it; the tree is too big; the tree is too heavy, and it must lie where it fell. There is no help for it all. . . . "

None of these people is free, and if they were modern or belonged to any time, we could not endure the sight of their servility. They are enslaved to two great powers—to life, like all other men, and to Maeterlinck. He has given Arkël his philosophy, for example. He has made Pelléas's friend say that he knows precisely the day of his death. He has made the grandfather of Pelléas see in his grandson "the sad, kindly face of one that has not long to live." He alone could make Arkël say that he had observed how all young and beautiful beings shape round themselves events that are young, beautiful, and happy. He bade Pelléas say: "We cannot do as we wish"; and Mélisande: "I don't myself understand all that I say, do you see." He delights in the sound of the chains and bolts shutting out the lovers from the castle. He has given the doctor also a copy of his "Trésor." He gave the servants orders to go and form an impressive line along the walls of the death-chamber and to fall down all together on their knees at the moment of death, though it was unknown to the doctor. Maeterlinck

it was who insisted that the lovers should speak as
if they were not speaking to one another, uttering
words that are hollow, solitary ejaculations, not
communion ; and when they sit side by side, as
Yniold notices, they stare not at one another but in
the same direction, without closing their eyes.   And
as he can make Golaud see the "poor little" men
struggling helplessly, so he can make Yniold.   For
when the child is trying to lift a rock to release a
ball he says : " It is heavier than all the world. . . .
It is heavier than all that has happened. . . . I
can see my golden ball between the rock and this
naughty stone, and I cannot reach it. . . . My
arm is not long enough . . . and the stone will not
be lifted . . . I cannot lift it . . . and there is nobody that could lift it. . . ."   Not content with
this, the child is made to see a flock of sheep
coming : " How many there are ! . . .   They are
afraid of the dark. . . . They huddle together ! . . .
They all want to turn to the right. . . . They may
not ! Their shepherd is throwing earth at them. . . .
Ah ! ah ! . . . They are obeying."

   Symbols, symbols ! It is the triumph of Maeterlinck that these symbols, though exaggerated, are
never out of harmony. They are all variations
of one theme—the littleness, the impotence, the
lostness of mankind. The sound is sweet because
the creatures are so small and far away, and unlike
anything known to us. Even so must the giant
have regarded the man whom he caged for the
sweetness of his voice in lamentations. The voices
of Pelléas and Mélisande are sweet. Their gestures

are beautiful, and they move among scenes which are grim or beautiful, such as impress men. We who know ourselves free, or, if we think otherwise, at least always behave at the moment of action as if we were free, we can safely smile upon them, as perhaps we also are smiled upon by them. Yet the symbols, and the beauty of Mélisande, touch as well as amuse, so that our smile ends in a sigh, which again turns to a smile because "it is not real." At least the music of the scene and action is so great that we are no more disturbed by the sadness of the theme than in De Quincey's "Oh, burden of solitude, that cleavest to man through every stage of his being!"

A curious contrast with "Pelléas et Mélisande" may be found in a Portuguese play of the early nineteenth century, Viscount de Almeide Garrett's "Brother Luiz de Sousa." Here the mysterious intelligence of a young girl gives half of its powerful quality to the play, and yet itself remains credible and does not disturb the naturalness, albeit romantic, of the whole. The principal characters are Manuel de Sousa (afterwards Brother Luiz), his wife Magdalena, his daughter Maria, and Telmo, an old servant. Manuel was Magdalena's second husband, and father of Maria. Her first husband was supposed to have perished with King Sebastian at the famous battle of Alcacer (1578), although he had written on the morning of that battle: "Alive or dead, Magdalena, I will see you at least once again in this world." These words haunted Magdalena, and though she had never loved this man, she waited and searched for him for some years. Old Telmo was always at hand, who had known her first husband, and recalled him as a mirror of chivalry, with repeated doubts of his death. He was always talking of King Sebastian, whose return the people expected, as they might King Arthur's. Telmo, too, had a strange hold upon Maria, a delicate and subtle child. Her mother feared lest she should get to know of her obsession. She loved Telmo's tales and songs of the battle, and begged him for the romance of " the hidden island where King Dom Sebastian lives, who did not die, but will come again one thick, misty day. . . . For he did not die, did he, mother ? " She had observed that only Telmo was willing to talk of the lost king. She noted her mother's anxiety, reading her eyes " and the stars in the sky, too—and knew things. . . ." She lay awake whole nights trying to understand. When they were anxiously expecting her father's return from Lisbon it was she who first knew of his arrival—" and he comes affronted," she said, before the others heard a sound. Then it became necessary to move to a new house, to the house which had belonged to Magdalena's first husband. In spite of all, she had to go there to live, and the old house was burnt. Maria saw that her mother was being preyed upon, but she also believed that they were being forewarned. She was thinking too much ; her father bade her play and laugh and enjoy herself, but she recognized, with " a kind of inner knowledge," the portrait of Dom John hanging on one of the walls. She was one to find "marvels and mysteries in the most simple, natural things." Again her father had to go away—on the very fatal day for Magdalena, the anniversary of her first marriage, of King Sebastian's death, and of her first meeting with Manuel. While he was away came a palmer from Jerusalem, and slowly let drop into her soul the news that he was sent to her by one who loved her much, and had been twenty years a captive. After seeing Telmo and learning that Magdalena really had sent messengers in search of her lost husband before the second marriage, the palmer begged the old man to say that his story was a lie. Maria was near physical death from excitement and sorrow. Magdalena was willing to pretend to question the word of a vagabond, but both she and Manuel were persuaded that nothing was left for them but "these shrouds"—the religious habit. It was when they were actually about to take the scapular, and in the presence of the archbishop, that the bewildered Maria burst in upon the ceremony, crying, "What God is this on that altar who would rob a daughter of her father and mother?" The palmer entered at the last scene to try to save them, but Maria fell dead, and Manuel, addressing Magdalena as "My sister," said: "Let us commend our souls to this angel whom God has taken unto Himself." Perhaps no child in drama, after and including the romantic period, is so exquisitely and spiritually revealed as Maria, who is really the heroine of the play; a child of fourteen, who is on the stage

almost from beginning to end, and dominates it
with a vivid and fatal melancholy.   When Magdalena says, " This child is marvellous : she sees and
hears at such distances "; and her brother Jorge,
" True ; it is a terrible sign at that age, and with
that complexion " ; when Jorge says alone, " The
hearts of all seem to have a presentiment of misfortune . . . and the malady has almost taken
hold of me too," *—we seem to be listening to the
words of Maeterlinck's characters.   Their words,
but not their voices.   These are people who were
born and lived and died among men in the six-
teenth, or at any rate the nineteenth, century.
Their words deepen the mystery of this life, which
the words of Mélisande and Pelléas and Arkel
do but delicately embroider with old mysteries of
which they have heard tell.

* " Don Luiz de Sousa," translated by Edgar Prestage (Elkin
Mathews).

V

"TROIS PETITS DRAMES POUR MARIONNETTES"

FROM "Pelléas et Mélisande" Maeterlinck returned to plays of the earlier kind. "Alladine et Palomides" is indeed much like "Pelléas et Mélisande," but it is also much more thoroughly Maeterlinckian. Any one might have used the story of "Pelléas and Mélisande," and would probably have made the outline of it much like Maeterlinck's; it is an obvious problem romantically solved. But "Alladine et Palomides" is far, very far, less external, and has no movement or outline worth mentioning; nor is it conceivable that any character in it could be interested in foreign policy, as Golaud was supposed to have been, instead of marrying the little girl of the forest. It has not, I believe, been acted. "Intérieur" is like "L'Intruse"; "La Mort de Tintagiles" is as clear a picture as "Les Sept Princesses," and is not only mysterious, but intelligible and impressive. Both these plays, "Intérieur" and "La Mort de Tintagiles," have been acted. All three appeared as "three little plays for marionettes" in 1894.

At the beginning of "Alladine et Palomides" Ablamore is leaning over the sleeping Alladine, a beautiful little Greek slave from the heart of Arcadia. Ablamore says she always falls asleep under those trees ; when she is awake she looks at him like a slave ordered to do the impossible. It is sad for him to love too late ; but no adventures ever came to him. Holding back his " poor white beard," he embraces her, and she awakes. She has had a bad dream—some one is coming. There! Palomides enters without his betrothed, Astolaine, daughter of Ablamore. Palomides and Alladine look at one another, and his horse frightens her lamb—a lamb which understands all that happens. Ablamore bids them enter the castle, noticing how much the silent Alladine talks this evening ; she is always restless in the great palace.

Alladine is looking at the park with her brow pressed against the window, and Ablamore can only get monosyllables from her. She will not talk of Palomides, nor go out, and she falls weeping on Ablamore's breast. Going to seek help, he finds Palomides sitting staring at the door. Alladine and Palomides meet on either side of the drawbridge—she with her lamb. She dares not venture over towards the forest side where he is, but her lamb goes to his call and falls into the moat ; and she tells Palomides she will not see him again. At this Ablamore, who has been spying on them, enters and drags her away. He finds them kissing, but tells Alladine that she is obeying laws she does not know. She denies the kiss.

He thinks she fears him as an old man, and cruelly seizes and threatens her, but suddenly falls on his knees and asks pity; she weeps in silence. Palomides tells Astolaine that he loves her, "even more than her whom I love"—that is Alladine, in whom he has found something more incomprehensible and powerful than the beauty of the most beautiful soul or face. Astolaine says that she knows we do not do what we will.

Astolaine now tells Ablamore she cannot love Palomides, whereupon Ablamore bids her come and show him the truth without words; she cannot deceive him. Palomides tells Alladine that he has seen Ablamore ominously rattling his keys. They are prepared to fly, with Astolaine's help. But Astolaine has to tell the sisters of Palomides that he will not fly, and that her father goes about with his big gold keys singing, "Go wherever your eyes may bid you," and has shut up Alladine. While Ablamore is asleep Palomides takes the keys and opens Alladine's room, where her hands are manacled by her hair. There Ablamore locks them both in, after saying that he bears them no ill-will, and that they have done what they must, and so must he also.

The lovers awaken bound in the deep grottos of Ablamore. They set themselves free, and care not so long as they are together. But Ablamore's soul must have told them they were happy; they hear iron blows, and stones are dislodged and light let in upon the cave. The two recoil from the incomers and fall. It is not Ablamore. but

Astolaine and the sisters of Palomides who enter and can see them embracing in the dark water without trying to save themselves. In the water the decomposed body of the lamb is found.

Outside one door, in a long corridor of innumerable doors, are the sisters of Palomides; Astolaine and the doctor talk by another and she tells him how Ablamore had called around him these events, and was now their first victim—for he had fled on the day when he made the lovers enter the grotto. They must forget one another. But presently the voice of Alladine from the one room calls to Palomides in the other, and he replies; nor can those outside the door prevent the feeble voices from reaching one another's ears. The voice of Palomides whispers he does not suffer, but wishes he could see her; and she replies that they will never see one another again—the doors are shut. Her voice seems to him as if she were going away, and the play ends:

Palomides. Alladine!

Alladine. Palomides!

Palomides. Alla—dine!

The characters in this play have Arthurian and similar names: they have such names, but they are not kings and queens, nor kings' sons and daughters, like the people of "Pelléas et Mélisande." Perhaps it was that royal persons, invested by traditional opinion with some grandeur or strength, could not be made sufficiently small and frail to the imagination. The pet lamb of Alladine, although wise, is feebler than Mélisande. Not only

are the characters more frail and miniature, but
the scene is mightier and more terrible, and Alladine is aware of the contrast, and tells it to
Palomides when they first meet :

" I cannot tell why it is that uneasiness comes to
me, each time I go into the palace. It is so vast,
and I am so little ; I am lost in it. . . . And all
those windows that look on the sea. . . . You cannot count them. . . . And the corridors that wind,
and wind, for no reason ; and others that do not
turn, but that lose themselves in the walls. . . .
And the rooms I dare not go into——"

("We will go into every one," says Palomides.)

" I feel that I was not meant to live there, or
that it was not built for me. . . . Once I lost my
way. . . . I had to open thirty doors before the
daylight returned to me. And I could not escape ;
the last door led to a lake. And there are vaults
that are cold even in summer ; and galleries that
twist, and twist, back on to themselves. And
stairs that lead no whither, and terraces whence
nothing can be seen."

Through these vaults the lovers were carried to
the caverns under the palace. Palomides had
heard of them :

" No one ever went into them ; and only the
king had the keys. I knew that the sea flooded
those that lay deepest ; and the light we behold is
doubtless thrown up by the sea. . . ."

And very much more both Palomides and Alladine are able to say about the cave and its majesty
and magnificence, even in the first moments of their

awakening in imprisonment. The cave was beautiful until the rescuers broke open an entrance for the sunlight. But this probably is not a parable, but only one of those symbols of something or nothing which help to preserve our attention. The same may be said of Ablamore's metaphor of truth hiding itself among the rocks—a phrase which is remembered when Alladine's lamb is picked up in the grotto ; and of Ablamore's six fountains in the park which sprang up, one after the other, at the death of his daughters. Some day there may be a key, not by Maeterlinck, to all these things, even to Ablamore's song, as he jingles his keys :

> Unhappiness had three keys of gold—
> But the queen is not yet freed.
> Unhappiness had three keys of gold—
> Go where your eyes may lead.

But they are probably only attempts to give the same effects as traditional tales where mysterious numbers and the like point through the mist to some ancient meaning now lost.

Like "Pelléas et Mélisande," "Alladine and Palomides" has a framework upon which a very different kind of play might have been built. The story of an old man and of a young girl who loves a young man better is not an unfamiliar one ; but here there is no motive and no character. A story was necessary, and so one of the monumental simple stories was used. Maeterlinck gets no farther than the impression that Ablamore is old and Alladine and Palomides both are young. They do what they

do because they must.   They explain themselves to
one another.   Like Arkël, they know that they do
what they must.   When Palomides has fallen in
love with Alladine he tells Astolaine, his betrothed,
in this way: "Fate has stepped out towards me ;
or I, it may be, have beckoned to Fate."   And she
replies by bidding him not to weep; she too is
aware that we cannot always do what we will.   All,
therefore, that is necessary for them all the time is
for them to describe what has happened to them.
They all see themselves as if they were reading
about themselves in a book, and what they see they
speak of in low tones of even sadness that exclude
particularity of passion.   When Alladine and
Palomides lie a-dying, or losing the desire to live,
they seem to be reciting a litany far older than
themselves :

The voice of Alladine.   I had pity on you ! . . .
The voice of Palomides.   They have parted us,
but I always shall love you. . . .
All. I had pity on you . . . are you suffering
still ?
Pal. I suffer no more, but I want to see you . . .
All. Never again shall we see one another, for
the doors are all closed. . . .
Pal. There is that in your voice that tells me you
love me no longer. . . .
All. Yes, yes, I love you still, but now all is
sorrow. . . .
Pal. You are turning away. . . . I scarcely can
hear you. . . .
All. We seem to be hundreds of miles from each
other. . . .

6

Yet how like this is to "Serres Chaudes" in its
sick sense of remoteness, while the neverness, the
lostness, of "We shall never come back" in "Les
Sept Princesses," Mélisande's "They have closed
the doors," and Pelléas's "It is too late," are repeated and concentrated in a perfect phrase of
Alladine's : "Nous ne nous verrons plus, les portes
sont fermées." (Never again shall we see one
another, the doors are all closed.) It is not
the separation of Alladine from Palomides and
Palomides from Alladine that we feel as this scene
passes. It is the idea of separation audibly
presented. Were Alladine a woman, and not a
little Greek slave from the heart of Arcadia, and
Palomides a man instead of an Arthurian wraith,
the scene would be almost intolerable if indeed
it were not incredible. But, on the other hand,
suppose such a dying conversation between as good
a man as Mercutio or Richard Feverel and a woman
his equal, not separation alone would fill the mind.
They would give our sorrow something of their own
opulence and nobility. But here a perhaps entirely
inhuman sense of separation afflicts us, even less
than what may be brought into the heart through the
dying last note of a horn at evening, a door shutting
when there is no other sound for a long time before
and after, or the last of anything. It has a rhetori-
cal effect equal to De Quincey's elaborate description
of his last hours at school before running away, or
that dream in the "Opium Eater" which ends :
"And at last, with the sense that all was lost,
female forms, and the features that were worth all

the world to me ; and but a moment allowed—and clasped hands, with heart-breaking partings, and then—everlasting farewells ! and, with a sigh such as the caves of hell sighed when the incestuous mother uttered the abhorred name of Death, the sound was reverberated—everlasting farewells ! and again, and yet again reverberated—everlasting farewells ! " It is equal, but very different. De Quincey is purple, Maeterlinck is grey ; De Quincey ends with a full orchestra, Maeterlinck with only a solitary voice singing unseen.

The effect of the play is simpler and more con-centrated than that of " Pelléas et Mélisande." The story is much less a story, and could not be read as one. There is no sanguinary Golaud with a sword, but white-bearded Ablamore, who gives the lovers an appropriate end, since life, as the doctor says, had " ebbed very low in their hearts." When Ablamore's reason was shaken after shutting up the lovers and before running away, he climbed to a tower and stretched his arms out towards mountain and sea, " summoning the events that too long had remained concealed in the horizon," as if he were a kind of Maeterlinckian Solness at the topmost of his tower calling upon the Mighty One to hear him vowing that from this day forward he will be a free builder. As Mélisande, coming from afar, is saddened by the dark, huge castle, so is the Arcadian slave by the many-chambered palace of Ablamore. The life of both Alladine and Palomides, like Mélisande's, flickers out slowly, even more slowly and without disturbance. Well did Maeterlinck

know his power when he gave the vigorous name
of Palomides to his ghostly hero ; he knew that his
treatment would destroy everything belonging to
the name except a splendour. For an apathetic
symphony nothing could be more admirable. If
there is one place in the whole where a discord is
risked it is at the end of the second act. Palomides
has told Astolaine his love for Alladine, has wept
and been kissed for it, and has asked if she also is
crying : " These," she says :

" These are little tears . . . let them not sadden
you. . . . My tears fall because I am a woman ;
but woman's tears, they say, are not painful. . . .
See, my eyes are already dry."

It is natural for a woman in one of Maeterlinck's
early plays to refer to her tears as little and to
describe herself to her companion ; but in this
scene Astolaine assumes a womanly height though
still pale and slender, and the pathos of her " See,
my eyes are already dry " becomes a little too real
for the play—the author comes near to asking too
much from his marionettes.

Unlike all of its predecessors, " Intérieur "
depends on nothing conventionally impressive in
scenery and starts with no prestige of any kind.
Except two children the characters have no
names, but are the old man, the stranger, the
peasant, the father, the mother, the two daughters,
the child. The scene is a house standing in an
old garden planted with willows. Three of the
ground-floor windows are lit by a lamp, round

which the family is visible: the father in the
chimney corner, the mother resting one elbow on
the table and gazing into vacancy, and the young
child asleep resting on the other arm, the two
daughters in white sitting over their embroidery and
smiling at ease. The old man and the stranger
come cautiously into the garden. They have to
announce that a daughter of the house has been
drowned, and they are undecided what to do;
meantime they talk of the finding of the body and
watch the unsuspecting inmates of the room. The
old man's grandchild, Mary, arrives and says that
the bearers of the dead girl are now quite near.
The sisters within come to the window and gaze
unseeing into the darkness. Mary thinks that they
are " praying without knowing what they do "; she
says, " Tell them to-morrow, grandfather," and the
two men are losing time. Martha arrives, and,
seeing that the people in the house are not crying,
knows that they have not been told. The murmur
of the crowd is heard; some enter the garden.
The old man goes to knock at the door and
Martha and the stranger watch for the effect
among those within. Now they see the old man
in the room; the crowd press up to the window.
They see the mother beginning to understand—
they know that he has told them; he tries to
prevent the mother from going out. Then, as
they see that the inmates are coming out, the
crowd hurries away, all but the stranger, who waits
a little longer, and having said, " The child has not
awakened!" goes out.

However handled, the idea of this play is perhaps quite original. There is a hint of something like it in De Quincey's "Suspiria de Profundis," in the passage beginning, " Who is this distinguished-looking young woman, with her eyes drooping, and the shadow of a dreadful shock yet fresh upon every feature?" As the crowd looks in unobserved upon the still ignorant, bereaved family so De Quincey seems to stand outside and watch. In "The English Mail-coach" also he does a similar thing when he paints the unsuspecting lovers driving through the silence and solitude of an English road in summer twilight, and the mail-coach, with "Death, the crowned phantom, with all the equipage of his terrors, and the tiger roar of his voice," bearing down upon them. And many before and since, standing out in the dark, must have been fascinated by the seeming charmed life of a family group in a lighted room. But now the mere choice of the subject—the too confident people separated from the enemy only by a window—seems peculiarly Maeterlinck's. "Serres Chaudes," with its vision of things seen isolated under a bell-glass or through the pane of a diving-bell, foretells "Intérieur," and the concluding sentence in the description of the scene recalls "Serres Chaudes." The people are gathered round the lamp :

"When one of them rises, walks, or makes a gesture, the movements appear grave, slow, apart, and as though spiritualized by the distance, the light, and the transparent film of the window-panes."

The old man says definitely that he seems to see them "from the altitude of another world." The whole piece is evidently elaborated from an impression of a lighted interior seen thus detached, and its effect is to sum up and intensify the feeling of a fascinated spectator. In spite of the crowd, the movement, and the talk it remains purely dream-like and lacking in the breath of life. It is a vision of the unconsciousness of life, of its ignorance of what is before and round about it. The old man reflects that the drowned girl was living in the morning and "did not know that I should see her again," and he continues: "You live for months by the side of one who is no longer of this world, and whose soul cannot stoop to it; you answer her unthinkingly. . . . They do not themselves know what they are! . . . Yesterday evening she was there, sitting in the lamplight, like her sisters." They do not know that they are watched: "We, too," he sees, "are watched." As he stands and sees them, thinking themselves beyond the reach of danger, he does not know what to do. The stranger, on the other hand, thinks there is something about them—he does not know what—as if they were not wholly unaware. One looks out into the dark, smiling "at what she does not see." The little girl, Mary, seeing them so peaceful, feels as if she were seeing them in dreams; she begs her grandfather to have pity on them : Martha says, " How patient they are ! " When he goes inside he faces towards the window, but feels the eyes of the crowd and turns away. He speaks, and the bereaved understand ; they rush to the door. All is dissolved, the little undesigned play in the room is over and the enchantment at an end ; the crowd breaks up. The child still sleeps in the arm-chair, as unconscious as the dead girl.

But Maeterlinck is not quite exclusively the spectator, bent upon reproducing his vision. He makes the old man say that he acknowledged something unusual when he last saw the dead girl alive. She was on the point of asking him something, but perhaps did not dare, and, now that he thinks of it, " she smiled as people smile who want to be silent, or who fear that they will not be understood." In the manner of Arkël he says : " What a strange little soul she must have had !— what a poor little, artless, unfathomable soul she must have had ! "—not because she was she, but because she was human. The stranger, seeing the two sisters look out, thinks the eyes of one are full of fear, and the old man bids him " take care ; who knows how far the soul may extend around the body ? " This is the thought of Maeterlinck the philosopher hovering unobtrusive but unneeded about a scene which his feeling alone makes effective.

" La Mort de Tintagiles " is simpler than "Alladine et Palomides," as simple, in fact, as " Les Aveugles." A child, a black castle and a hidden queen, and

death—that is all. Tintagiles has come from over
the sea to an island where dwell his sisters, Ygraine
and Bellangère, and a wise old man, Aglovale. He
has been forced to come, he does not know why,
nor can they tell, except that "the queen wished
it." They are leading him to a house near the
castle at nightfall, and it looks very black, but the
windows are red, and "it is there that the queen
has her throne." She is never seen, and she never
leaves the castle, but her orders are carried out.
Suddenly one day Bellangère, sitting with Aglovale
in the castle, bursts into tears; for she had penetrated
to a forbidden part of the castle and heard voices
of people who were speaking "of a child who had
arrived to-day and of a crown of gold." And
Ygraine says: "She shall not take him without a struggle." Aglovale says that their only
defence is to enfold Tintagiles in their "little arms."
Tintagiles has pain, and when Ygraine bids him
trust in her and no evil can come, he says: "It
has come, sister Ygraine." He notices that Aglovale is sitting on the threshold with his sword on
his knees and that he is wounded. He hears his
sister's heart beat as if bursting, and he cries. "I
have heard," he says; "they ... they are coming."
Aglovale also can hear, and takes his sword.
A key turns in the lock. The door slowly
opens wider and wider in spite of their leaning
against it with all their strength, until Tintagiles,
who has fainted, regains consciousness and gives a
cry of deliverance ; then the door shuts again.
"He is saved," says Ygraine. He is asleep between

his sisters when the servants of the queen go into the room and take him away. He awakes with "a cry of supreme distress," and only when his crying is almost inaudible do his sisters awake and rush out. Bellangère has fallen and Ygraine is alone "before a great iron door in a gloomy vault," holding a lamp in her hand. She shrieks out, she beats upon the door. The voice of Tintagiles is heard on the other side, asking her to open. But she cannot, although the child tells her that "She" is coming. Now "It is too late," he says; "her hand is at my throat." His body is heard falling. But she continues to cry out for him until, after a long silence, she calls: "Monster! . . . Monster! . . . curse you! curse you! . . . I spit on you!" and she "continues to sob softly, her arms outspread against the gate, in the gloom."

In this play the persons are the feeblest and the scene is the most gloomy and terrible. Ygraine recalls how once she felt almost happy, and "very soon after, our old father died, and our two brothers disappeared." She has lived long on the island, "not daring to understand the things that happened." She has wished to escape, but in vain. She has "no confidence in the future," and they have always to be on their guard. Tintagiles has come because the queen wished it, and from the first he is evidently a sacrifice. He has come from far away, to die like Mélisande and Alladine. On the other hand, the castle is enormous and dark, and its shadow always upon their house. It is ruinous, and it is deep down in the valley and out

of the air. It has many corridors and galleries, and
innumerable stairs. There lives the queen—"the
mother of our mother"—suspicious, jealous, mad,
and having such great power that the sisters live
there " with a terrible weight on their souls." She
lies on their souls like a tombstone, and no one
dares oppose her. If she were to send for Aglovale
he would go unlingering, though he knows that none
returns, with eyes unclosed. Tintagiles is soon
crying in the dark castle, he knows not why ; he
sleeps " very gravely, with one hand on his brow,
like a little sorrowful king." At his arrival
the sea has roared and the trees moaned. It is
undoubtedly of him that the hidden voices are
speaking when Bellangère strays in the castle.
The sisters bar a great door, but sitting on their
knee he knows of evil, he hears long before the
others the sound of the enemy coming. All the
sisters can do is to push vainly against the door.
Aglovale's old sword is broken. The child is taken
away in sleep though his hands are plunged deep
down into his sisters' hair, and they are clutching at
one another as if drowning. The stealers see that
one of the sisters wishes to scream but cannot.
Everywhere is a stealthy quiet and the helplessness
of nightmare. These people are powerless, and
yet it is only slowly that they are overcome. The
great door, with Ygraine on one side trying to
open it, and the small Tintagiles on the other
begging to be saved—this is a scene from the
torture-chambers of sleep. At first she can hear
no sound of Tintagiles, and calls in vain. Then

she remembers: "I have climbed steps without number, between great pitiless walls, and my heart bids me live no longer." The door is of iron and very cold, and she sees some of Tintagiles's golden hair between the panels, which makes her shriek and beat frantically against the door and cry out: "Listen! I blaspheme! I blaspheme and spit on you!" The rest is suspense. She is trying to open the door, breaking her nails and numbing her fingers against the iron. On the other side Tintagiles hears the queen coming—is caught by her at the throat—and falls. Ygraine speaks in silence:

"Tintagiles! . . . Tintagiles! . . . What have you done? . . . Give him back, give him back! . . . for the love of God, give him back to me! . . . I can hear nothing. . . . What are you going to do with him? . . . You will not hurt him. . . . He is only a little child. . . . He cannot resist. . . . Look, look! . . . I mean no harm . . . I am on my knees. . . . Give him back to us, I beg of you. . . . Not for my sake only, you know it well. . . . I will do anything. . . . I bear no ill-will, you see. . . . I implore you, with clasped hands. . . . I was wrong. . . . I am quite resigned, you see. . . . I have lost all I had. . . . You should punish me some other way. . . . There are so many things which would hurt me more . . . if you want to hurt me . . . you shall see. . . . But this poor child has done no harm. . . . What I said was not true . . . but I did not know. . . . I know that you are very good . . . surely the time for forgiveness has come! . . . He is so young and beautiful, and he is so small! . . . You must see that it cannot be! . . . He puts his little arms around your neck;

his little mouth on your mouth ; and God Himself could not say him nay. . . . You will open the door, will you not ? . . . I am asking so little. . . . I want him for an instant, just for an instant . . . I cannot remember . . . you will understand . . . I did not have time. . . . He can get through the tiniest opening. . . . It is not difficult. . . . (*A long, inexorable silence*). . . . Monster ! . . . Monster ! . . . . Curse you ! . . . Curse you ! . . . I spit on you ! "

This is something like realism, and the conclusion is unfit for a marionette. This violent impotence of a being who has hitherto offered no resistance to fate would be unendurable unless nature defended herself with laughter. It is an attempt to dramatize a lyric scene like that summed up in the lines :

> There were two kingly children
> That loved each other dearly—
> They could not come together,
> The water was so deep.

But it produces only a lyrical effect, if the effect is not altogether ruined by Ygraine's sudden curses. For here nature seems to interrupt art, as if Shelley had appended to the " Lines written in dejection near Naples " such an expression as, " Good God, what a life it is ! " They have been threatened by a physical evil from the unseen queen, but have taken no care to meet it with physical defence. They have fallen asleep with the child instead of watching, and he is carried away from them. Very well, then ; this is a fitting languor for one of these obsessed, pale women to show in her dream of life; to wake her up and afflict us with real and common horror after the muffled and far-off horror of the earlier acts is perhaps ill-mannered and unfair. "L'Intruse" ends with the baby's crying, "Pelléas et Mélisande" with old Arkël's turning from the dead woman to her child ("It must live now"), "Intérieur" with the stir of the crowd, and the breaking down of the magic wall round the lighted room; and these are unquestionable ends, like "Go, bid the soldiers shoot." But "Monster! . . . I spit on you," is not such a casting off of the spell of the play; it does not appear, for instance, to be a pledge that Ygraine will never again honour death with terror. Nevertheless, as Mr. Sutro has told us, this is Maeterlinck's favourite play.

VI

EARLY PLAYS

WITH 1896 ends the work of Maeterlinck's youth. It begins with one volume of poems, "Serres Chaudes," in 1889, and ends with another, "Douze Chansons," in 1896. Between these the eight plays appeared. These are by far the more interesting part of his early work, and, unlike the poems, they surrender the best of themselves to readers who are not perfect masters of French, and all but the best to those who know them only in translations, the style of the original being unaffected to the point of affectation. They have the one-sidedness and consequent exaggeration of youth, but also an intensity which may prolong their life beyond that of later work. In his poems he dwelt confessedly upon curiously isolated images of fever and the select life of a hot-house or a bell-glass or a dream of the day or night. His plays do the same without acknowledgment of any similar source. But in some of them the dream character is strong. The play of the seven princesses asleep on the marble stairs, if not taken or adapted from a picture, might have come from

an inexplicable and inconsequent dream ; while
the frenzy, without power or hope, of the old
king and queen at the end, when they strive to
enter the death-chamber and beat upon walls and
windows, is perfectly dream-like, and has a parallel
in the scene where Ygraine tries to break through
the impassable iron door behind which her brother
is being murdered. "L'Intruse" and "Intérieur,"
are studies of a motionless interior, commonplace
in itself but made intense by the hidden form of
death, by isolation, and by a nervous monotony of
manner. In "L'Intruse" the words hardly break
the silence which they accent and mysteriously
fall into and expound like stones dropped into deep
waters. Had Maeterlinck read James Thomson's
"In the Room"? It is a poem made entirely out
of the silent voices of motionless things in the
room of a suicide—the mirror, the curtain, the
empty cupboard, the glass, the table, the fire-grate,
the little phial which had been emptied of its
"cold wine of death," and the bed which thrilled
the gloom with tales—

> Of human sorrows and delights,
> Of fever moans and infant wails,
> Of births and deaths and bridal nights.

"L'Intruse" is equally still and quiet, the room
is equally "silent and aware," while the dramatic
form persuades us that the mystery is that of life
itself, and not of an indomitably sad poet's heart
like B.V.'s.

The other six plays are full of the external

sublime. They take place on islands, in the neighbourhood of the sea or of immense forests, in high towers or in castles or palaces honeycombed with innumerable chambers and corridors, and built upon rocks that are hollowed into great caves and lakes reached by many stairs. The water, the gloom, the labyrinthine complication may well be a dream elaboration of the canals, the bridges past counting, and the vast buildings of the ancient city in which he was born. The castles are in perpetual shadow, are damp, and without any ordinary coming and going of life. They are inhabited by a brutal king's son, an old man who loves an unwilling young girl, a dotard who is the slave of a poisonous mistress, a hideous and cruel queen unseen but irresistible. To these castles and such masters and mistresses come the frailest of creatures : a beautiful, homeless princess whose rival's mother is omnipotent, a lost princess in rags who sickens at once in the dark places, a slave from the heart of Arcadia and her pet lamb, a single child sent from far over the sea for an unknown purpose. All miserably perish, not by sudden violence, but by long days of anticipation and fear and dungeons, ending in poison, a strangling cord, a knife, a sword, and a separation worse than death. All of them love, and have little joy of their love because they have a stronger rival or unrelenting tyrant. This they know full well, but cannot escape ; nor, as a rule, can they even try to escape. Thus the vastness and complication of the world, the power of fate and of cruel men, the littleness and feebleness of women and children and many men, are expressed in clearly visible symbols. Though marionettes in size, they are also humanity. The people are not individuals, but types or personifications of mankind, or a class, or age, or sex. They are an old man, a young man, a sister, a solitary maiden from a far foreign land, a child, an old servant with a rusty sword. Sometimes they take part in a tale of unfortunate or forbidden love, but the romance or the problem is no part of the interest of the play. For these are not men and women, but tragical and small simplifications of them. The plays are bloodless, but not lifeless epitomes; little miracle plays, each with a new variation upon the one great tale of the suffering of man and the majesty of fate. The characters speak either in simple, short phrases, often repeated, which suggest that they are half awake or thinking of something else, or in far-reaching, symbolic phrases like "We have never seen the house in which we live," "One would say we were always alone," "It is too late," "We shall never come back," "We shall never see one another again; the doors are shut." Separation, fear, helplessness, or consciousness of what must happen, love that is always crying and never abandoned, prevail. The men and women have many of the refinements of the most modern tea-drinking, scented, cloistered members of the middle class, yet we are as little drawn to sympathy with them as we should be if they took after their Arthurian names, Palomides, Aglovale, Pelléas, and so on.

" They belong," Mr. William Archer thinks, " to the far future rather than the past." What they do touches us because we are mortal and they have a mortal frailty and sadness, but here is nothing of the tears of things. Life in this drama is a dream of a dream of a dream, refined, reduced, grey and remote, and very quiet. This is how we have come to see ourselves. Like gods we look down from an altitude of dream or trance, and behold ourselves crawling uncomfortably about eternity and infinity.

Long ago men said that mankind was like an ant's nest, but they did not believe it. Only a theologian said it, and, for joy of an ingenious invention, they repeated it as if it were a reality. But now we can see mankind so. It is not the spaces of the stars that terrify us, but the spaces between one lover and the other, between a child and the dead that bore him. Maeterlinck's people are pismires, Arthurian pismires. Their tragedy does not disturb or purge, but dignifies us through creating us at once Brobdignagians, in relation to these Lilliputians on the stage. De Quincey has already been mentioned in comparison or illustration ; and, looking back upon the early plays as a whole, a passage of the " Opium Eater " has more than once returned to my mind as giving a picture like that left by the plays. I refer to De Quincey's recollection of Coleridge's description of Piranesi's " Dreams." He says :

" Some of these (I describe only from the memory of Coleridge's account) represented vast

Gothic halls ; on the floor of which stood mighty engines and machinery, wheels, cables, catapults, etc., expressive of enormous power put forth, or resistance overcome.   Creeping along the sides of the walls, you perceived a staircase ; and upon this, groping his way upwards, was Piranesi himself.   Follow the stairs a little farther, and you perceive them reaching an abrupt termination, without any balustrade, and allowing no step onwards to him who would reach the extremity, except into the depths below.   Whatever is to become of poor Piranesi ? At last you suppose that his labours must now in some way terminate.   But raise your eyes, and behold a second flight of stairs still higher, on which Piranesi is perceived, by this time standing on the very brink of the abyss. Once again elevate your eye, and a still more aerial flight of stairs is descried ; and there, again, is the delirious Piranesi, busy on his aspiring labours ; and so on, until the unfinished stairs and the hopeless Piranesi both are lost in the upper gloom of the hall."

And De Quincey adds that in the early stage of his malady the splendours of his dreams were "chiefly architectural," and that the architecture was succeeded by "lakes and silvery expanses of water."   In drama it is a new sensation. We have had shadow-shows and puppet-shows before ; but they were deliberately ironical or even farcical. These are serious, and share only the unconscious irony of nature.   Probably they were "all made out of the carver's brain," and the author retired into the wilderness, far from men, to dream of them. Their foundations in experience are not obvious nor perhaps very deep. It needs no experience to discover the meaning of "Farewell" or "It is too late." Along with this discovery, to make the plays possible, went the power, and the will to exercise it, of seeing things with the detached, sunless remoteness of dreams. It is said that the sun never appears in dreams; if it did the scale of life would return, and the dream either disappear or come true. There is no sun in Maeterlinck's plays; the forest or the castle walls or the dungeon roofs exclude it.

It is a new sensation for the intellect, for it is to the intellect that works of such length and design must appeal. But it is not wholly new. Lyrics and lyrical narratives have done the same before in a more instant way. To give only one example, Poe's "Annabel Lee" does it, and does indeed twice as much; for it has also human passion, something different from the solicitude of Ygraine or the faith of Maleine and Mélisande. The "kingdom by the sea," "many and many a year ago," the love of the two children, the envy of the seraphs of heaven, the chilly wind blowing out of a cloud upon the girl, and the "highborn kinsman" bearing her away to "shut her up in a sepulchre," are all elements that might have made a play by Maeterlinck, and to these are added strength of love—

> Stronger by far than the love
> Of those who were older than we,
> Of many far wiser than we;
> And neither the angels in heaven above
> Nor the demons down under the sea
> Can ever dissever my soul from the soul
> Of the beautiful Annabel Lee.

This rebelliousness, equal to that of Ygraine, and also essential, changes the poem, but the resemblance to Maeterlinck remains in the definitely vague time and place, the intense love, frail but everlasting, assailed by a death out of heaven, and even perhaps in the sepulchre by the sea where Annabel was 'shut up.' But far stranger is the general resemblance in Maeterlinck's sad castles of death to the same poet's "City in the Sea." There may be no connection between the two, in spite of Poe's prominence in France, yet it is worth noticing that the feeling most like that of Maeterlinck's scenery as of his people, is to be found in a lyric:

> Lo! death has reared himself a throne
> In a strange city lying alone,
> Far down within the dim west,
> Where the good and the bad, and the worst and
>   the best
> Have gone to their eternal rest.
> There, shrines and palaces and towers
> (Time-eaten towers that tremble not!)
> Resemble nothing that is ours.
> Around, by lifting winds forgot,
> Resignedly beneath the sky
> The melancholy waters lie.
> No rays from the holy heaven come down
> On the long night-time of that town;
> But light from out the lurid sea
> Streams up the turret silently. . . .

This is pictorial lyric. Maeterlinck's plays are not lyrical drama, but lyric dramatized. He could dramatize—

> Golden boys and girls all must,
> As chimney sweepers, come to dust.

He could dramatize—

> O world, O life, O time,
> On whose last steps I climb . . .

or—

> If I were lord of Tartary. . . .

It is true they do not become dramatic in any strict sense, but they are more than mere translations out of one form into another. Thus the lyric motive gains in volume as if magnified and multiplied by the voices of many instruments. "Pelléas et Mélisande," for example, might have grown out of that fragment of song about her long hair unbound which Mélisande sings; all that long tale of loving her lord's brother is little more than the blare and pomp of instruments. Such parts are easy to overact. A woman with a Burne-Jones face and a bird-like voice needs to do little more than speak her words clearly to play Mélisande, for example. A full-sized living actress breaking her fingers against a door in the part of Ygraine must be terrible to witness. The scenery also of these plays cannot but lose by material representation on the stage. A not too clear mental image is more appropriate. The terror of caves or castles imagined by one who has never known it, is what is necessary, not the real terror of dark, dripping limestone and lamp-darkened, still waters in the labyrinths of the earth's bowels. And so with the stairs, the walls, the corridors, the windows, the doors—these are mind-stuff, and it is arrogant to translate them with anything but a brush dipped in fog and melancholy. Nevertheless, they have been much admired when put on the stage, even when they have not been played behind a curtain of black gauze. " Pelléas et Mélisande " in particular makes a charming melancholy spectacle, except at the moments when Golaud, spying on the lovers or chasing them with uplifted sword, or torturing Mélisande's last minutes for a confession of adultery, interrupts it with an air of physical customary life. The lost Mélisande (an actress with a cooing voice) crying outstretched by the pool in the forest, the unhappy wife singing, and, like William Morris's Rapunzel, letting her marvellous long hair down from a window of the tower to her lover below —these things have the beauty of scenes from " Aucassin and Nicolete," with, and even without, the aid of music. Mr. J. W. Mackail says that there was "only one opinion as to the scenic effectiveness " of " Pelléas et Mélisande," when it was played in London in 1894 by M. Lugné-Poe and his company. Mr. Archer goes so far as to say: " If one were to rewrite this play (it could quite well be done), as a drama of common life, excluding symbolism altogether, one could probably retain at least half of the existing dialogue ; and, where it could be retained at all, it could not possibly be bettered." It has twice been given a musical form, in which it gains almost as much as it loses. " La Mort de Tinta-giles" also has been set to music.

Maeterlinck's own words on these plays—to be

found in an Introduction to the three volumes of
his "Théâtre"—are to be admired for their kindliness
and clear sight. He republished the plays with
little alteration, not because they were perfect but
because a poem is not to be bettered by a succession
of corrections. He could, he says, have suppressed
several things in " Princesse Maleine," including
most of " those surprising repetitions which give the
characters the appearance of rather deaf somnam-
bulists constantly torn out of a painful dream ";
he would thus have been spared some smiles, but
this lack of promptitude in hearing and replying
belongs to their psychology and their rather haggard
idea of the universe, and it cannot be altered without destroying its one quality : a certain harmony
of affright and gloom. The other plays, he says,
mix the Christian god with the classic idea of
fatality, in an impenetrable night of nature. There
is to be found in them an unknown which most
often takes the place of death—death indifferent,
inexorable, blind, working almost by chance, taking
by preference the youngest and least wretched. And
this, he says, is not without reason. For long yet—
unless a decisive discovery of science or a revelation
such as a communication with a planet older and
wiser than ours teaches us at last the origin and
aim of life—for long, or for ever, we shall be preca-
rious and fortuitous beings abandoned without
appreciable designs to all the breaths of an indifferent night. To paint this immense and useless
feebleness with some gesture of grace and tenderness, some words of sweetness, frail hope, pity and

love, is all that can humanly be done when life is transported to the verge of this great indifferent truth which freezes energy and the love of life. But this is not enough. We must rather seek to cross these boundaries, to destroy our ignorance, to use truths as admissible and more encouraging. The last three-quarters of a century have made impracticable certain majestic or terrible incertitudes for which poets used to be thought great and profound. The lyric poet, he continues, will perhaps not be troubled by this evolution of thought. The dramatist must be sincere; and even so Tolstoy and Ibsen have remained true to life without missing that sense of " the mystery which dominates and judges things "—a sense essential to fine poetry. He himself thought it honourable and wise to cast down death from the throne to which it certainly has no right: in " Aglavaine and Selysette " he wished to give part of the ancient power of death to love, wisdom, and happiness; but, he says, he was unable. Death would not obey, and he had to wait for a conqueror to be revealed. There is something naive and touching in this avowal of the strife between the philospher and the artist in one breast.

VII

PHILOSOPHIC STUDIES : RUYSBROECK, EMERSON, AND NOVALIS

MANY of the conversations in the early plays, and whole characters like the old man in "Intérieur" and Arkel in "Pelléas et Mélisande," might have taught us that Maeterlinck was not a dramatic artist pure and simple. Side by side with his work of creation he was reading, if not far and wide, yet much and deep. In 1891 he published his translation of "L'Ornement des Noces Spirituelles" of the Flemish mystic, Ruysbroeck. Maeterlinck warns literary idlers against this book, which is "a boundless desert, where they will die of thirst." It was translated for "a few Platonists," fearless of the judgment which most men will pronounce. They will think it the work of a deluded monk, of a pale solitary, a hermit, dizzy with fasting and worn with fever. In reply to such an opinion of the mystics, he himself avers that "they alone are the possessors of certainty," and this is exactly true, because the mystics alone have had a revelation unquestionable, if imperfect, which enables them to grasp the whole of things in

a manner impossible to mundane intelligence or
effort.   Equally true is Maeterlinck's forecast of
the ordinary reader's opinion of Ruysbroeck.   The
opening chapter, in particular, on the three comings
of Christ, on the two kinds of humility in Jesus
Christ, on the abdication of the will, on zeal and
diligence, etc., are of an aridity which compels the
question whether the words correspond to things
at all; no trace is left in them of the life of the
man in his hut at Grónendal, in the forest of
Soignes, at the beginning of the fourteenth century.
They make us think of a man fed exclusively on
books, whereas in fact he knew no Greek and
perhaps no Latin, was alone and poor.   And yet,
as Maeterlinck says, " He knows, though he is
unaware of it, the Platonism of Greece, the Sufism of
Persia, the Brahmanism of India, and the Buddhism
of Thibet."   He was one who knew the divine
splendour which blinds all created vision and
causes reason and all created light to cease ; and
knew that in this light, though the power of
observation and distinction is lost, a man's eyes
are truly opened in the stillness and emptiness of
the spirit where he has lost himself in the love of
God.   The pure satisfaction of the heart was not
only greater than any which earth could bestow,
but greater for the body as well as the soul—so
great that, in its intoxication, one man would
imagine that the whole world was partaking of it
and another that he was the first to taste.   He
thought that the spirit was more exalted and
nature more humbled in heavy suffering than in

great works.   Nor is it the only place where his
limitations are clear, when he says that God does
not will, nor counsel, nor effect in any man things
which are contrary to the teaching of Christ and of
the Church.   He was a Christian who happened to
be a mystic, not a mystic who happened to be a
Christian.   What is fundamental in his Christianity,
and what Maeterlinck quotes from his other books,
seems to show that his qualities were for the most
part of a local and temporary kind.   I shall quote
an example from a book interpreting the Jewish
sacrifices and the symbols of the ark of the
covenant partly for its own sake, but more because
it may reveal to us something of Maeterlinck.   He
is speaking of the offering of the poor :

" And they [the doves] shall keep near streams
and beside clear waters, so that if any bird flies
downwards to seize them or to do them any injury,
they may recognize him by his reflection in the
water and beware of him.   The clear water is
Holy Scripture, the lives of saints, and the
mercy of God.   We shall reflect ourselves therein
when we are tempted, and so none shall be
able to hurt us.   These doves have a loving
nature, and young doves are often born of them,
for wherever, to the glory of God and for our
own felicity, we think of sin with scorn and hatred,
and of virtue with love, we give birth to young
doves—that is to say, to new virtues."

Doubtless Maeterlinck, like many another, could
at one time envy the freedom from nature in this
and many other passages—a freedom so much

more easy and complete than any achieved by
him in " Serres Chaudes," as he must also have
envied him " a language which has the intrinsic
omnipotence of tongues which are almost
immemorial."   The Flemish dialect, he continues :

" The Flemish dialect possesses this omnipotence,
and it is possible that several of its words still
contain images dating from the glacial epochs.
Our author, then, had at his disposal one of the
very oldest modes of speech, in which words are
really lamps behind ideas, while with us ideas
must give light to words.   I am also disposed to
believe that every language thinks always more
than the man, even the man of genius, who
employs it, and who is only its heart for the time
being, and that this is the reason why an ignorant
monk like this mysterious Ruysbroeck was able, by
gathering up his scanty forces in prayers so many
centuries ago, to write works which hardly correspond to any scenes in the present day."

This last sentence contains a highly characteristic but perhaps not entirely original thought.
And as to Flemish, it may be noticed here that
a French critic has said that it is well for
Maeterlinck to be a Belgian : " For he knows the
language like a foreigner who is without a sense
of the tradition.   He has provincialisms, something slow and uneasy in his manner, awkward and
inexact.   Not finding the right word, he uses several
of the second best.   It is a style that trembles."
And thus he is helped in giving an impression
of mystery.

With this admiration for the primitive, and even primeval Ruysbroeck, should be contrasted his scorn for the excessively modern and purely literary. He knows that Ruysbroeck is obscure, he says, but believes—

"That a sincere and honest author is never obscure in the eternal sense of the word, because he always understands himself, in a way which is infinitely beyond anything that he says. It is only artificial ideas which spring up in real darkness and flourish solely in literary epochs and in the insincerity of self-conscious ages, when the thought of the writer is poorer than his expression."

He goes on, with the help of Carlyle's "Woe to us if we have nothing in us except that which we can express and show to others," and with the help of Plotinus, to write a most eloquent piece of prose full of images peculiarly his own, comparing, *e.g.*, some of Ruysbroeck's phrases with "transparent icicles on the colourless sea of silence." This introduction leaves us with a knowledge of Maeterlinck's interest in Ernest Hello, Plotinus, Porphyry, Novalis, Coleridge, Plato, Behmen, and Carlyle, and an admiration for his power of graceful and ingenious appreciation. It is the writing of one who perhaps could not write ill. But it is neither original nor profound, and it reveals chiefly a man of temperament. It reveals too the lover of "divine metaphysic," and in the numerous quotations it is not hard to see, not the source perhaps, but the impulse, of much

later writing. Take, for an example, the following
from another book by Ruysbroeck:

"But above all things, if we desire to enjoy
God, or to experience eternal life within us, we
must rise far above human reason, and enter into
God through faith; and there we shall remain
pure, at rest, and free from all similitudes, lifted by
love into the open nakedness of thought. For
when in love we die to all things, when in
ignorance and obscurity we die to all the notice
of the world, we are wrought and reformed by the
eternal Word, who is an image of the Father. And
in the repose of our spirit we receive the incomprehensible splendour which envelopes and penetrates
us, just as the air is penetrated by the brightness of the sun. And this splendour is merely
a boundless vision and a boundless beholding.
What we are, that we behold; and what we
behold, that we are; for our thought, our life, and
our essence are closely united with that truth which
is God, and are raised along with it. And that is
why, in this pure vision, we are one life and one
spirit with God; and this is what I call a contemplative life. . . .

If Maeterlinck had lived at Grönendal in the
fourteenth century he would have written thus.
Indeed, the hermit of Grönendal is to be divined
more simply from " L'Ornement des Noces
Spirituelles," than is the citizen of Ghent and
the hermit of Grasse from "Le Trésor des
Humbles."

In 1894 appeared I. Will's translation of seven of
Emerson's essays into French, accompanied by an

Introduction from Maeterlinck. These essays are
"Confidence," "Compensation," "Spiritual Laws,"
"The Poet," "Character," "The Over-Soul," and
"Fatality." The Introduction is a piece of Maeterlinck's work which is interesting because it shows
us how naively he submitted himself to Emerson's
influence : it is, in fact, little more than a very
gracious variation upon an idea in "Spiritual
Laws." "The child who meets me will not be
able," says Maeterlinck, "to tell his mother what
he has seen ; and yet, as soon as his eye has
taken me in, he knows all I am and have been
as well as my brother and three times as well
as myself. . . . He has known me, for a moment,
as exactly as God." Then, again, he speaks of
people in a room talking of the rain and the fine
weather ; but under this poor stuff their souls are
holding such converse as no human wisdom could
touch save at its peril ; and this is why they
have a kind of mysterious joy of their *ennui*,
without knowing that which within them is aware
of the laws of life, of death, and of love that pass
like incorruptible floods about the house. He is
going, he supposes, to see for the first time a
friend whose work he already knows. This man
comes in ; behold ! all the explanations which he
has given us for years crumble to dust at the
motion of the door as it opens upon him. He is not
what he thinks himself; he is different from his
thought. For we live only as one soul to another,
and we are gods who ignore one another, and
the strangest thing in man is the gravity and
8

wisdom that lies hid in him. Beyond our involuntary agitations we lead a marvellous existence, still and pure and unerring, and this is hinted unceasingly by the stretching of the hands, the opening of the eyes, the meeting of glances. All our organs are mystic instruments of a superior being, and we know not a man but always a soul. He was not the poor beggar on my steps that I saw, but something else : in our eyes two destinies saluted one another kindly, and, as he put out his hand, the little door of the house gave a view, though for but an instant, of the sea. So far Maeterlinck, and it is charming. But he himself quotes the passage from Emerson where he says that his 'accomplishments and his money avail nothing with his child ; what is in his soul alone counts. The disciple is careless, perhaps oblivious, of the fact that in his master's essay on " Spiritual Laws " the following passage occurs :

" A man passes for what he is worth. Very idle is all curiosity concerning other people's estimate of us, and idle is all fear of remaining unknown. If a man knows that he can do anything—that he can do it better than any one else—he has a pledge of the acknowledgment of that fact by all persons. The world is full of judgment-days, and into every assembly that a man enters, in every action he attempts, he is gauged and stamped. In every troop of boys that whoop and run in each yard and square, a new-comer is as well and accurately weighed in the balances, in the course of a few days, and stamped with his right number, as if he had undergone a formal trial of his strength, speed,

and temper. A stranger comes from a distant
school with better dress, with trinkets in his
pockets, with airs, and pretension. An old boy
sniffs thereat, and says to himself, ' It's of no use:
we shall find him out to-morrow.'

"Always as much virtue as there is, so much
appears; as much goodness as there is, so much
reverence it commands. All the devils respect
virtue. The high, the generous, the self-devoted
sect will always instruct and command mankind.
Never a sincere word was utterly lost. Never
magnanimity fell to the ground. Always the
heart of man greets and accepts it unexpectedly.
A man passes for what he is worth. What he is
engraves itself on his face, on his form, on his
fortunes, in letters of light, which all men may read
but himself. Concealment avails him nothing;
boasting nothing. There is confession in the
glances of our eyes, in our smiles, in salutations,
and the grasp of hands. His sin bedaubs him,
mars all his good impressions. Men know not why
they do not trust him. His vice glasses his eye,
demeans his cheek, pinches the nose, sets the mark
of the beast on the back of the head, and writes
' O fool! fool!' on the forehead of a king."

This leaves Maeterlinck with little for himself.
Emerson has exaggerated beyond the warrant of
experience; Maeterlinck exaggerates a little more,
giving the thought a turn of his own and a yet
greater unreality. And even so he cannot conceal,
though he disguise, his humble discipleship. Emerson has written : " I love and honour Epaminondas,
but I do not wish to be Epaminondas. I hold it
more just to love the world of this hour than the

world of his hour. . . . Besides, why should we be cowed by the name of Actæon? 'Tis a trick of the senses—no more." Then Maeterlinck, in this Introduction, writes: "There is no great life and no little life, and the action of Regulus or of Leonidas is unimportant when I compare it with a moment of my soul's secret life. Regulus and Leonidas replace Epaminondas." And he continues: "Emerson comes to affirm the equal and secret grandeur of our life. He has shown all the forces of heaven and earth busy in sustaining the threshold where two people are talking of the rain and the wind, and over the heads of two wayfarers greeting one another he has shown us a God smiling upon a God." Here he repeats himself, and varies a phrase in "The Over-Soul," where Emerson says "that somewhat higher in each of us overlooks this by-play, and Jove nods to Jove from behind each of us. Jove replaces God; nothing more. Emerson, at least, gives illustrative instances out of his experience or his reading; Maeterlinck's variations smack less of Ghent or Paris than his master's of Boston, and it is remarkable that, at the age of thirty, he should be incapable of asserting himself in the presence of another writer, and so uncritical as not to have observed or corrected correspondences at once clear and fundamental.

A year later, when Maeterlinck published, with an Introduction, his translation of "The Disciples at Saïs" and some of the fragments of Novalis, he gave a further proof of his naive submission to

the thought of Emerson. In " The Over-Soul "
Emerson had written :

" The soul is superior to its knowledge, wiser
than any of its works. The great poet makes us
feel our own wealth, and then we think less of
his compositions. His greatest communication to
our mind is to teach us to despise all he has done.
Shakespeare carries us to such a lofty strain of
intelligent activity as to suggest a wealth which
beggars his own ; and we then feel that the
splendid works which he has created, and which
in other hours we extol as a sort of self-existent
poetry, take no stronger hold of real nature than
the shadow of a passing traveller on the rock."

This passage Maeterlinck quotes in his introduction to the translations from Novalis, after he has
been urging that " all that does not go beyond
mere experimental and everyday wisdom does not
belong to us and is not worthy of our soul," and
has written as follows about " Othello " :

" We listen to the dialogue between the Moor
and Desdemona as a perfect thing, but without
being able to put aside matters more profound.
Whether Othello has been deceived or not by the
noble lady of Venice, he has another life. Even
at the moment of his most wretched suspicions and
most brutal anger, events a thousand times more
sublime must have been passing, in his soul and
about his body, which his ravings could not trouble ;
and behind the superficial disturbance of jealousy
another and impregnable existence maintained
itself which, so far, the genius of man has only
presented in passing.

"Does the sadness of the masterpieces spring from this? Poets could not write except on condition that they shut their eyes to the terror of the infinite, and enforced silence upon the too deep and thronging voices of their souls. If they had not done this, they must have lost heart. Nothing is sadder or more deceptive than a masterpiece, because nothing shows more clearly man's powerlessness to acknowledge his own grandeur and dignity. And if a voice had not taught us that the most beautiful things are nothing compared with what we are, nothing would have humiliated us more."

Maeterlinck soars up and away from his original in a beautiful manner, pointing out, for example, that if a being from another world came down and asked us for the supreme works of the human spirit, we should be unjust to offer "Othello," "King Lear," and "Hamlet." "No, we are not that!...we are invisible beings.... We should have nothing to say to the heavenly visitor, and nothing to show him, and our most perfect works would suddenly appear to us like those poor family treasures that seemed so precious to us at the bottom of a drawer, but appear so trifling when for a moment they are taken out from their darkness before an indifferent eye." No, if anything could touch this imaginary visitor it would be the spectacle of a man praying, with "thoughts that have no name and lips that cannot speak," or of those whose works "border close upon silence"; and he himself would not blush if the stranger surprised him reading Pascal, Emerson, or Hello—

" and perhaps he himself would thence have some idea of a fellow-being condemned to silence, or would know at least that we are not all satisfied with ourselves as inhabitants of the earth." It is as if Emerson had taken us to a favourable peak of earth from which to behold some miracle of cloudland, and Maeterlinck alone of the company had flown up to the clouds for a brief tour of inspection. It may be easy to exaggerate his indebtedness, but it is certainly apparent at many points. Here again, for example, he advances to a yet more dizzy height from Emerson's remark about the unconscious wisdom of a child in " Spiritual Laws."

" Put in the balance against the unconscious wisdom of that child passing yonder all the words of the great sages, and you will see that what Plato, Marcus Aurelius, Schopenhauer, and Pascal have revealed to us will not cause the great treasures of unconsciousness to rise up one hair's-breadth, for the silence of the child is a thousand times more wise than the speech of Marcus Aurelius."

He adds, it must always be remembered, that " if Marcus Aurelius had not written his twelve books of ' Meditations,' part of the un-known treasures of this child would not be the same." A very impressive variation upon the same theme is where he says that but for Plato, Swedenborg, or Plotinus, the soul of the peasant who has never heard of them would not be what it is to-day. He calls Novalis an ecstatic and melodious child with a sense of unity. There can be little doubt that Maeterlinck is curiously aware of the inexpressible mysteries of life, but he has scarcely begun to show that he is aware of them with his own spirit, and not only through Emerson's, as through a telescope. His examples are still like those of Emerson, and might have been modelled on them with a difference for the sake of a difference. It is in his simple sense of mystery that he shows himself, if at all. We see, for example, the writer of the early plays in a phrase like : " We are slaves, who cannot preserve the love of life except by increasing, without being dismayed, the pitiless load of their chains," or where he says that it is hard to question the soul and to recognize " its little, child-like voice " amid the vain clamours that encompass it. We see him in his description of the mother of Novalis as one of those sweet and pious mothers who are content to be silent and to hide all they know and divine under " a pitiful smile of humility "—*un pauvre sourire humilié*; yet he knows nothing of this woman, except that " it is the mothers that make men's souls." But for the rest, the writing is mainly dependent, if not imitative. If it has an airy, spiritual fervour it seems also to lack conviction. The " probably " in the following sentence betrays rather the caution of the intellect than the meek confidence of the spirit : "It is probably," he writes, " at the point where man seems to come to an end that he begins." But, having set up this

" probably," he advances with equanimity, saying
that the essential and steadfast parts of man belong
only to the invisible, and that on the faint peaks
where he dwells with the invisible are to be seen
perhaps the lights which alone upon earth are
beacons in the spiritual world.

Novalis does not so easily make a disciple as
Emerson. He is less emphatic and less didactic,
and no one is farther from being a professional
writer and moralist. But we feel the presence
of a kindred nature to Maeterlinck in his unearth-
liness, in the description of the child who was one
of the disciples at Saïs :

" Scarcely was he there but the Master wished
to resign the teaching into his hands. This child
had great dark eyes with blue depths ; his skin
shone like lilies, and his locks like lustrous cloud-
lets at eventide. His voice thrilled through our
hearts ; we would have gladly given him our
flowers, stones, feathers, all that we had. He
smiled with an infinite gravity ; we felt strangely
happy to be beside him. One day he will return,
said the Master, and live among us. Then the
lessons will cease. . . ."

" The silence of the child," as Maeterlinck says,
" is wiser than the speech of Marcus Aurelius."
Novalis had said that " the fresh gaze of a child is
less bounded than the presentiment of the most
pure of seers." But Novalis had none of the gift
of Emerson and Maeterlinck for multiplication.
Having said that " Philosophy is, properly speaking,

home-sickness, the desire to be at home in the world," he says no more ; having said that " If God became a man, He could also become stone, plant, animal, element, and perhaps in that way there is a liberation continually going on in nature," he says no more. He said : " Man began with instinct and will end with it," and Maeterlinck has multiplied the thought. Equally prophetic is he when he speaks of virtue disappearing and becoming innocence. He foresees poetry such as the symbolists tried to write when he speaks of

" Poems which are simply sonorous and full of impressive words, but without sense and cohesion, of which at most only pen-strokes are comprehensible, like fragments of the most diverse things. This true poetry might have, at most, a general allegoric sense and an indirect action like that of music. This is why nature is so purely poetical, like the call of a magician or physician, a nursery, a granary, a market, etc."

VIII

MAETERLINCK published three books in
1896. " Le Trésor des Humbles " marks a
beginning, and is largely prophetic, and " Aglavaine
et Selysette " points both to the future and to the
past of his work. " Douze Chansons " belongs
entirely to the past ; but it has now been enlarged
as " Quinze Chansons," and includes the virgin's
song from " Sœur Béatrice," the song about Orlamonde's five daughters from " Ardiane et Barbe
Bleue," and a song for Mélisande in place of " Mes
longs cheveux descendent." The poems in this
second volume are clearly connected in style with
the early plays, and especially with " Les Sept
Princesses." Most of them look like rudimentary
allegories, and depend for their power upon a
mysterious use of numbers and an appearance of
condensed significance, equally mysterious. Some
one chains a maiden in a grotto, where she forgets
the light ; a sign is made on the door, and the
key falls into the sea. She waits for the days of
the summer ; she waits more than seven years,
like the " seven long years by land and sea " of the

ballads; and each year some one passes by. She
waits for the winter days, and her hairs remember
the light—they find it, and glide between the
stones and light up the rocks. One evening, some
one passing by notices the light, but does not
understand and does not approach. He thinks it
a strange sign—a spring of gold—angel's work;
at any rate, he turns aside and goes away.

Another poem of four verses tells how three
little girls were killed to see what was in their
hearts:

> They have slain three little girls
> To see what's in their hearts.
>
> The first was full of happiness;
> And everywhere her blood flowed
> For three years hissed three serpents.
>
> The second was full of gentleness;
> And everywhere her blood flowed
> Three lambs for three years browsed.
>
> The third was full of misery;
> And everywhere her blood flowed
> Three archangels for three years kept watch.

If this were an old poem it would keep the
learned busy many years to no purpose; but, as
it was made up by Maeterlinck, its meaning need
not trouble learned or unlearned, while, apart from
a meaning, the images can only satisfy those who
have a love of mystery for its own sake as well as
a natural feeling for numbers. It is not likely
that Maeterlinck wished to teach that misery here
begets happiness hereafter. In another poem some

girls with bandaged eyes are seeking their destinies.
At midday they open the palace in the meadows,
and salute life, but do not go out. In another
there are three blind sisters with golden lamps,
who ascend the tower and wait seven days, when
the first says, " I am waiting for our lights " ; the
second, " The king is coming up "; the third and
most holy, " No, they are out." Another has the
refrain : " My child, I am afraid." Some one is
going away ; a lamp is lit ; at the first door the
flame trembled ; at the second spoke ; at the
third went out. Here again only our curiosity is
aroused, and that very imperfectly. " The seven
daughters of Orlamonde " is better :

> The seven daughters of Orlamonde,
>   When the fairy was dead,
> The seven daughters of Orlamonde
>   Sought the doors. . . .
>
> They lit their seven lamps,
>   Opened the towers,
> Opened four hundred rooms,
>   Without finding daylight. . . .
>
> Arrive at the sonorous grottos,
>   Then descend ;
> And in a closed door
>   Find a golden key. . . .
>
> See the ocean through the chinks,
>   Are afraid of dying,
> And knock at the closed door.—
>   Without daring to open it. . . .

The number "seven" and the name "Orlamonde,"

followed by the word "fairy," unless they evoke the word "bunkum," lull us in a way which the killing of the three little girls cannot do. The "seven lamps," the towers, the four hundred rooms, the sonorous grottos, the closed door, the golden key, the ocean seen through the chinks, the not daring to open it, are all significant in themselves; but they have little more value in this particular poem than in an inventory, and especially as there are so many of them. In one poem there are three sisters who want to die, and go out in search of death, and, seeking it from the forest in exchange for their three crowns, they receive twelve kisses, which reveal the future; from the sea they have three hundred kisses and a revelation of the past; from the city an indefinite number and a revelation of the present. Here the numbers twelve and three hundred are useless without a key. There are other poems with lighted lamps, lost keys, sunshine seen through chinks.

Maeterlinck could have made charades or plays of any or all of them, but in their present form they are like the rhymed outlines of plays. Many begin as if they belonged to something else, which the reader is supposed to know, but does not. One of the most musical and admired is the second in "Quinze Chansons":

> What shall I tell him
>   Should he return?
> Tell him my life was spent
>   Waiting for him. . . .

Should he still question
   Nor know who I am?
Speak to him sisterly,
   Lest he be sad. . . .

And if he should ask me
   Where you are gone?
Give him my golden ring
   And say not a word. . . .

And if he asks why
   I'm alone in the room?
The open door show him,
   The burnt-out lamp. . . .

And if he then asks
   About the last hour?
Say that I smiled,
   Lest he should weep. . . .

This is the haunted, whispering resignation of the early plays, though nothing survives in the translation except an obtrusively modest sentimental tale.

But for the most part these poems have too hard a finish. They are superficially precise, internally obscure or naught. The song in "Pelléas et Mélisande," which was originally a fragment of naive beauty, was changed into another of these. It used to say: "My long locks fall down to the foot of the tower; my locks hang ready for you all down the tower, all day long and all day long. . . . Saint Daniel and Saint Michael, Saint Michael and Saint Raphael. I was born on Sunday, a Sunday at noon." Perhaps this seemed to Maeterlinck too Elizabethan. He substituted for it the poem which Miss Alma Tadema thus renders :

> Thirty years I've sought, my sisters,
>   For his hiding-place ;
> Thirty years I've walked, my sisters,
>   But have found no trace. . . .
>
> Thirty years I've walked, my sisters,
>   And my feet are worn ;
> He was all about, my sisters,
>   Yet he was unborn. . . .
>
> Sad the hour grows, my sisters,
>   Bare my feet again ;
> For the evening dies, my sisters,
>   And my soul's in pain. . . .
>
> You are now sixteen, my sisters,
>   Time it is for you ;
> Take my staff away, my sisters,
>   Go and seek him too. . . .

The eighth poem is of one who had three golden crowns, and gave one to her parents, one to her lover, and one to her children. This is not the only one recalling a folk-song or ballad, such as " The Cruel Brother," with its—

> " Oh what would ye leave to your father dear ? "
>   *With a heigh-ho ! and a lily gay.*
> "The milk-white steed that brought me here,"
>   *As the primrose spreads so sweetly.*

But in these traditional things both the mysterious and the unintelligible gain by their age and the knowledge that something has been worn away by it. You cannot by a stroke of the pen emulate—

> This ae nighte, this ae nighte,
> *Everie night and alle,*
> Fire and sleet, and candle-lighte,
> *And Christe receive thy saule.*

One or two of these "Chansons" bring into the mind the ballad of "Bessie Bell and Mary Gray," and they perish in the comparison. But there are, besides the song which was left unsung by Shakespeare, "Mariana in the Moated Grange," other poems of known authorship with which they may or even must be compared. There are, *e.g.,* Tennyson's two poems on Mariana and his "Lady of Shalott"; and Coleridge's magic song in "Remorse":

> Hear, sweet spirit, hear the spell,
> Lest a blacker charm compel!
> So shall the midnight breezes swell
> With thy deep, long-lingering knell.
>
> And at evening evermore,
> In a chapel on the shore,
> Shall the chaunters sad and saintly,
> Yellow tapers burning faintly,
> Doleful masses chaunt for thee,
> *Miserere Domine!*
>
> Hark! the cadence dies away
> On the quiet moonlight sea:
> The boatmen rest their oars and say,
> *Miserere Domine!*

9

This is beyond anything in "Douze Chansons."
But in Poe may be found a poem which is perhaps
exactly equal to one of Maeterlinck's in subject,
method, and failure in effect. I refer to the
"Bridal Ballad," beginning "The ring is on my
hand." The abruptness, the subdued elliptical
style, the refrain, of these five verses, are so like
that they might be offered to a reader who
knew no French as an equivalent to one of the
"Douze Chansons." For that reason only I will
quote it:

> The ring is on my hand,
>   And the wreath is on my brow;
> Satin and jewels grand
> Are all at my command,
>   And I am happy now.
>
> And my lord he loves me well;
>   But, when first he breathed his vow,
> I felt my bosom swell—
> For the words rang as a knell,
> And the voice seemed *his* who fell
> In the battle down the dell,
>   And who is happy now.
>
> But he spoke to reassure me,
>   And he kissed my pallid brow,
> While a reverie came o'er me,
> And to the churchyard bore me,
> And I sighed to him before me,
> Thinking him dead D'Elormie,
>   "Oh, I am happy now!"
>
> And thus the words were spoken,
>   And thus the plighted vow,
> And, though my faith be broken,

And, though my heart be broken,
Here is a ring, as token
    That I am happy now!

Would God I could awaken!
    For I dream I know not how!
And my soul is sorely shaken
Lest an evil step be taken—
Lest the dead, who is forsaken
    May not be happy now.

If Maeterlinck has a manner even more full of mystery, it must be conceded that he is guiltless of the particular fatuity of "D'Elormie."

But the poet who has achieved effects most like those attempted by Maeterlinck is William Morris. His "Blue Closet" has the effect of an early play of Maeterlinck's, and more than that of any poem in "Douze Chansons":

Alice the Queen, and Louise the Queen,
Two damozels wearing purple and green,
Four lone ladies dwelling here
From day to day and year to year;
And there is none to let us go,
To break the locks of the doors below,
Or shovel away the heaped-up snow;
And when we die no man will know
That we are dead.

"Two Red Roses across the Moon" is another; and even this has a sense of life and locality which is not anywhere in "Douze Chansons." "The Sailing of the Sword," again, has a similar use of

the refrain and of conspicuous but indefinitely
significant distinctions, as in—

> Alicia wore a scarlet gown
>   *When the Sword went out to sea,*
> But Ursula's was russet brown :
>   For the mist we could not see
> The scarlet roofs of the good town,
>   *When the Sword went out to sea.*

This may be nothing more than jugglery, but at
least the length of the poem accumulates sufficient
colour and gesture to compose a picture. The
same is true of " Shameful Death," which is like
some of Maeterlinck's poems in its abrupt and
unexplained opening :

> There were four of us about that bed, . . .

and still more of " Near Avalon " :

> A ship with shields before the sun,
>   Six maidens round the mast,
> A red-gold crown on every one,
>   A green gown on the last.

Nevertheless, there is an essential difference
between the methods and aims of Morris and
Maeterlinck which partly invalidates the comparison. Morris depends upon life, though it
may be dreamed ; upon a mediæval background,
however artificial. His castle is not merely an
ideal black castle stifled among poplars in a

nameless island and a nameless age, but a particular one:

> Midways by a walled garden,
>   In the happy poplar land,
>   Did an ancient castle stand,
> With an old knight for a warden.
> Many scarlet bricks there were
>   In its walls.

Maeterlinck writes in colourless water and
depends upon nothing in time or space save words.
His one success is the ninth poem:

> She came towards the palace
> —The sun was hardly rising—
> She came towards the palace,
> The knights looked at one another,
> All the ladies were silent.
>
> She stopped before the door
> —The sun was hardly rising—
> She stopped before the door,
> They heard the queen walking,
> And her lord was questioning her.
>
> Where are you going, where are you going?
> —Take care, they can hardly see there—
> Where are you going, where are you going?
> Is some one expecting you below?
> But she made no answer.
>
> She went down towards the unknown
> —Take care, they can hardly see there—
> She went down towards the unknown,
> The unknown embraced the queen,
> They spoke no word to one another,
> And went away at once.

Her lord was weeping on the threshold
—Take care, they can hardly see there—
Her lord was weeping on the threshold,
They heard the queen walking,
They heard the leaves falling.

This, at least, could not have been pilloried like
"Quand l'amant sortit" and "On est venu dire"
in Tolstoy's "What is Art?" where they are unfairly
printed as one poem and condemned as unintelligible, with the fair comment: "Who went out?
Who came in?   Who is speaking?   Who died?"

IX

"AGLAVAINE ET SÉLYSETTE"

"AGLAVAINE ET SÉLYSETTE," the play which appeared in the year of "Le Trésor des Humbles," is Maeterlinck's first play of character. The scenery and the Arthurian names of some characters are the chief points in which it resembles its predecessors. Meleander and his wife Selysette are expecting the arrival of Aglavaine, widow of Selysette's brother, whom they have asked to come and live with them. He reads out her letter saying that, though she has only seen him once, three years ago, she feels as if she had known him from infancy. Meleander tells his wife that Aglavaine is beautiful as no other woman is, and that "nothing can live near her that is not true." Selysette, nevertheless, wants to go away. Meleander and Aglavaine have been writing to one another, but she has not seen the letters; yet Meleander thinks her happy. At sunset Aglavaine arrives and kisses them. Meligrane, Selysette's grandmother, awakening from a strange dream, will not take a kiss from her. Selysette promises to take her to an old tower on the shore,

of which her sister Yssaline has found the key.
She will love Selysette like a small sister. But
Selysette, overhearing Aglavaine and Meleander
confessing their love, runs away, and Aglavaine
sends her husband after her and cries. Alone
in the park Selysette reflects that her husband
pities her, and when he kisses her dare not look
at her except with a seeming prayer for forgiveness. She sees Aglavaine asleep near a well and
awakens her instead of pushing her in, so that
Aglavaine says she has loved against her will.

She tells Selysette that she and Meleander love
her. Selysette says that she loves her, but that
she is concealing her knowledge of things from her
husband and keeping back her tears. Aglavaine
says that she would go away if Meleander no longer
loved his wife. She speaks of going away. She must
not, and Selysette tells her she may kiss Meleander
even when his wife is not there. Meligrane
notices that Selysette grows thin, and thinks that
either she must die or Aglavaine must go away ;
and Aglavaine says she is right, and promises
never to kiss Meleander again, telling her moreover
that he loves Selysette better than Aglavaine.
Meleander tries to tell Selysette that he loves
them both. Selysette now goes often to her tower
to see a great strange bird. Meleander tells
Aglavaine that when she is there and Selysette
gone, he forgets his wife. A month passes, and
Selysette is often at her tower, not so unhappy
but more troubled. She is sorry to be happy, for
she has a secret and will never weep again. But

Aglavaine tells her she is going away, and had better never have come ; to which Selysette replies that if Aglavaine had never come she herself would never have been either happy or unhappy. Selysette wishes to go away or to die, for thus she would be yet more happy. Aglavaine has seen her up in the tower dislodging stones ; she throws away the new key, but Selysette finds the old one that was lost. And now Selysette is taking her sister Yssaline to catch the green bird. She kisses her grandmother good-bye ; she kisses Meleander so violently that his lip bleeds. After climbing the tower, she returns to kiss her grandmother again, and leaves her sobbing. She goes up to the top of the tower again with Yssaline, and, talking to her of things the child does not understand, she leans out and falls. They can learn from Yssaline only that Selysette had seemed less sad than usual. " Love," says Meleander, " is as cruel as hate." Aglavaine asks the dying woman to forgive her. All that Selysette will say is that she was leaning over the wall and she fell. . . .

Without the tower, this would have been a modern play of refined middle-class life. For the first time the characters have a perfectly recognizable foundation in common reality ; they are changed by Maeterlinck's handling, indeed, but they are not metamorphosed and reduced, like Maleine or Alladine, or seen as a spectacle in a dream, like the seven princesses or the people of " Intérieur." Aglavaine is at bottom a common type : the glib, confident woman " in sympathy with advanced thought," but sicklied over with the pale cast of Maeterlinck. Selysette is the pretty little, womanly, misunderstood wife, who turns out to be more golden at heart than Aglavaine, with her superior powers of speech. Meleander could be happy with either, but he cannot keep them separate. A little longer and he might have been freed by a virtuous conspiracy of the two. Selysette's decisive action solves the difficulty, and two persons will be happy where formerly three were unhappy. The characters explain themselves and one another. We see not only their acts and feelings, but what they think of these. It is full of sharp turns such as are not to be found in the earliest plays—turns that reveal the working of the spirit with exquisite truth, as when Meleander is reading aloud Aglavaine's beautiful letter, and Selysette will see that the sun is setting, and that her grandmother is asleep and is not happy. "Oh! I want to kiss her," she says, and Meleander goes on reading the beautiful letter. Selysette's quickness of instinct is a wonderful piece of nature. Meleander is thinking of nothing whatever but Aglavaine. Selysette's spirit is feeling about among a hundred things in darkness. She is easily interrupted by Yssaline coming in with the key to her tower, and then, in the same breath as she tells Yssaline her nurse is waiting she asks, "Is she beautiful?" Of course Meleander does not know whom she is speaking of. Then again, when he has told her that nothing can live near Aglavaine except what is true, Selysette repeats his words merely. He says: "Selysette?" She: "Meleander?" Then he goes on and forgets her big blank question, and proposes, with the optimism of the blind, that when Aglavaine comes they shall be even happier than they were before. There are times, indeed, when Selysette speaks not only the thoughts but the very words of real life, as when she is petulant with Meleander and says that when she does something that pleases him, it is because she has been trying to imitate Aglavaine, which is just after the speech where she expresses with such tragic lucidity and calm—as if she had learnt it by heart—the result of her deep brooding about Meleander and Aglavaine.

"'I have often said to myself that I am only a poor little creature who could never follow in your footsteps ; but you have both been so good to me that I did not realize this as soon as I should, and you have often wanted me to go with you, because I was sad. And when I was there, each of you seemed very light-hearted, but there was not the same happiness in your souls, and I was between you like a stranger shivering with cold. And yet it was not your fault, nor was it my fault either. I know full well that I cannot understand ; but I know also that this is a thing that has to be understood. . . .'"

To which Meleander replies with self-revelation as complete :

"'My dear, dear, good Selysette, what is it that you think you do not understand ? . . .'"

and proceeds to tell her that one soul is beautiful in one way, and another in a different way. It is all very modern and perhaps very English. In Muther's "History of Modern Painting," when he turns from the English to the Flemish, he says that "Belgian painting differs from English as a fat Flemish matron from an ethereal young lady." But in Fernand Knopff he finds a Belgian artist who, "standing in connection with Maeterlinck and the literary decadents, has introduced an intellectual and spiritualized and delicate trait into the fleshly and sensuous Flemish art." In Aglavaine and in Selysette we seem to see those "blind and blue-eyed girls" whom Knopff depicts as "thoughtfully looking before them, with their heads resting on the table; slender women sitting dreamily at the piano in the dusk, lost in a world of sound," or "beings with aristocratic movements and an ethereal delicacy, standing with a serious air in the melancholy landscape." Of their Belgian fleshliness they retain only so much as makes them extraordinarily inactive. None of these women can ever be angry or make a wild gesture, unless it is Queen Ann of Jutland. When Selysette kills herself she does not leap from the tower, but gently lets herself slide out into the air—an act impossible to any but the most inactive body, if not to that.

Aglavaine is perhaps Maeterlinck's own mouthpiece, and she talks out of a book when she deliberately and in so many words proposes that her lover's wife should strive towards "the love

that disdains the pettiness of love." Meleander
replies to her with words more closely connected
with experience, but still too much like an extract
from one of Maeterlinck's essays. He says that
it is futile and exhausting to struggle to make
their love like that of brother and sister, and says
that it is by "the kiss" that all is transformed,
that the eyes of a woman who loves see more
clearly than the sister's. When Selysette asks what
would happen if Meleander loved Aglavaine more
than his wife, she replies that he will love the
same thing in both of them, and that he could not
love one without the other. In fact, when first
she came among them she was "wiser than one
had need to be," wiser, that is to say, with a too
purely reasonable and expressible wisdom. It is
significant that she altered her mind and came
to see something in foolish human goodness which
can do without such wisdom, and to believe that
in the less conscious Selysette there was something
beyond herself; she sees that life will not conform to her plans. Under Selysette's undesigned
tutelage she learns some of the "feeble, tortuous
wisdom" of ordinary woman, and is going to tell
her that she no longer loves Meleander or is
loved by him, and will therefore leave them, just
as Astolaine, to save Palomides, tells her father
that she loves him no more. Meeting Selysette—
"little Selysette"—she is powerless and almost
stupid beside the penetrating natural creature.
In the end she confesses herself blinder than any
wretched girl. Nor does she ever reach a point

equal to that where Selysette talks to Yssaline
before she falls from the tower, for she is as
Philosophy compared with Life. Yssaline does
not understand her sister, who teaches the child
to tell the others that she was not sad before the
end. She tells her that she cannot understand
her words now, but that a day will come when she
can, and then she will never forget this scene, and
will weep over it ; and therefore she asks forgiveness ; but the child turns to see the flocks of birds
coming back to the tower. This is the Selysette
who taught her that it would be better to be in
error all a lifetime than make one weep who is
in error.

This last dialogue between Selysette and
Yssaline is a perfect specimen of Maeterlinck's
tragic irony :

Yssaline. On ne voit presque plus le soleil, petite
sœur. . . .

Sélysette. Attends, attends encore, ma petite
Yssaline, car autre chose approche à mesure qu'il
s'éloigne, et j'y vois bien plus clair à mesure qu'elle
s'approche . . . Je ne sais plus si j'ai bien fait de te
mener sur cette tour ; et cependant, il fallait bien
que quelqu'un vint ici, car il en est qui voudront
tout savoir, et qui seront heureux pourvu qu'ils ne
sachent pas. . . . À présent, petite sœur, tout ce
que je te dis, tu ne le saisis pas. . . . Oui, mais un
jour viendra où tu saisiras tout, et où tu verras
tout ce que tu ne vois pas pendant que tu le
vois. . . . Alors tu seras triste et tu ne pourras
oublier ce que tes pauvres yeux apercevront tantôt.
. . . Et cependant ne faut-il pas que tu voies sans

comprendre, afin que d'autres aussi ne comprennent pas ? . . . Mais tu ne pourras pas t'empêcher de pleurer lorsque tu seras grande, et cela pèsera peut-être sur ta vie. . . . Et c'est pourquoi, je te demande de ma pardonner aujourd'hui sans comprendre, ce que tu souffriras plus tard en comprenant trop bien. . . .

Yss. Les troupeaux rentrent, petite sœur. . . .

Sél. Et demain les troupeaux rentreront aussi, Yssaline.

Yss. Oui, petite sœur. . . .

Sél. Et demain les oiseaux chanteront aussi. . . .

Yss. Oui, petite sœur. . . .

Sél. Et demain les fleurs fleuriront aussi. . . .

Yss. Oui, oui, petite sœur. . . .

Sél. Pourquoi faut-il que ce soit la plus jeune. . . .

Yss. Il n'y a plus qu'une petite ligne rouge, petite sœur. . . .

Sél. Tu as raison ; il est temps. . . . C'est toi-même qui m'y pousses ; et les étoiles aussi s'impatientent déjà. . . . Adieu, mon Yssaline, je suis très, très heureuse.

Yss. Moi aussi, petite sœur, hâte-toi, les étoiles vont venir. . . .

Sél. Sois sans crainte, Yssaline, elles ne me verront plus. . . . Lève-toi, assieds-toi dans ce coin, et laisse-moi serrer les bouts de mon écharpe autour de ta poitrine, car le vent est bien froid. . . .

Maeterlinck himself, apart from his characteristic handling, is prominent in the book. He makes Aglavaine's letter say what Arkël said in " Pelléas et Mélisande," but with a difference : that they can make their lives marvellous so that even if sorrow comes to them it will first have become

beautiful ; and he makes her say that she is "glad
to have suffered," and wait for the silence to speak,
and tell her lover that their souls speak before the
words are uttered, and reply to Selysette—when she
has asked if Meleander said that his love for her
was deeper than he had known—that if he had
said so she would not have been sure that it was
true. He puts into her mouth the speech about
that deeper truth which is out of reach of words,
however beautiful. But the obsession of God or
Fate is absent from the play. Aglavaine, it is
true, speaks of the "simplicity of things" against
which it is vain to strive, but this is something
very different from the hidden queen of "La Mort
de Tintagiles," though it is terrible. Not until the
last moment is it certain that Selysette will decide
to die ; we feel at least that she had a purpose
and felt a choice, though up in the tower she
asked why it was that the younger of the two
"had" to go. She is always "little" Selysette,
but perhaps "little" has become with Maeterlinck
one of those terrible *mots propres* which cannot
be avoided, expressing him in spite of himself :
Selysette herself half laughs at it.

The castle is not terrible in this play ; it is old,
but not dark, and the old grandmother Meligrane
is not grim, in spite of her inexorable wisdom and
her refusal to kiss Aglavaine. The sun shines here,
and not until it set could Selysette throw herself
down. Nor is the tower, with a long corridor
according to custom, wholly sinister, even though
Meleander would like the key to be lost for ever.

He was giddy during his only ascent. Selysette and Yssaline alone have climbed it often. It is surrounded on three sides by the sea, and was once a lighthouse. Now it is ruined and haunted by seabirds and doves, who recognize Selysette and will not be driven away. Nevertheless, this tower is not a natural part of the dwelling-house of this pale wife. Ibsen would have put her in a modern house—a doll's house. Selysette is a Nora who would certainly not have killed herself had she lived at Bedford Park or Hampstead, instead of a castle by the sea with a gull-haunted tower. A romantic suicide instead of " the dull sound of a door shutting in the lock " was the price to be paid for this last indulgence of his taste for castles and towers. It was a princely expenditure. Maeterlinck presents a tower to Selysette where another dramatist would either have made her build one, as Solness did at Lysanger, or have contented her with a castle in Spain. But although the characters are modern the play is no more a modern play than it is an Arthurian romance. Modernity is only so much colour for the painter ; he dips his brush in our pale blood to help make a picture of an old castle ; it is colour just as the names—Aglavaine, Meligrane—are colour ; nor is the philosophy in it any more than colour. What survives in the mind from this play is not the solution of a problem of one man and two women by suicide, nor yet an Arthurian family going to and fro in a castle. It is the tower that survives—a high, crumbling tower amid wings that sway and circle, and over the top-

10

most edge, where it is broken, a beautiful girl,
pale and very quiet, leaning out in a dream to
reach a strange pale-green bird that has come
newly to the tower.   On the top of the tower, in
solitude, away from the castle and high above it,
looking out towards the sea, she seeks a solution
which she could not find down in the world.   She
returns out of this backwater into the main
stream of eternity in order to be happier than
before, with more than a half-belief that Meleander
and Aglavaine will remain in it for as long as
possible.

Mr. J. W. Mackail tells us of some one who
read "Aglavaine et Sélysette" and declared himself "sick of that tower."   But it is a mistake to
confuse it with the tower of " La Princesse Maleine,"
" Alladine et Palomides," etc.   Not only has it no
dungeons and Plutonian waters, but it is not in
any sense a tower of dream.   It is an extraordinary
tower sprung up during the night at the edge of
some suburb or watering-place.   It should thus
be painted, casting its shadow upon " Lyndhurst "
and " Bella Vista."   Nor is the invention to be
blamed.   The music of the place is doubled by
it, and it has perhaps been among the influences
that produced the first verse of the lyric chorus
sung upon the entrance of Deirdre in Mr. W. B.
Yeats's choice play of " Deirdre " :

> "Why is it?" Queen Edane said,
> "If I do but climb the stair
> To the tower overhead,
> When the winds are calling there,

Or the gannets calling out
In waste places of the sky,
There's so much to think about
That I cry—that I cry?"

Take away the tower from "Aglavaine et Sélysette," and we might have had an Ibsenitish play
of inferior reality.   As it is, we have something as
perfect and as rare as anything of Ibsen's.

X

FIRST ESSAYS : " LE TRÉSOR DES HUMBLES " ;
" LA SAGESSE ET LA DESTINÉE "

" LE TRÉSOR DES HUMBLES," the first
in a long series of books of essays, marks
no obvious departure from the period of the early
plays which it closes. Arkel, the old man in
" Intérieur," and Aglavaine had already talked in
the language of " Le Trésor des Humbles." The
essays on Ruysbroeck, Emerson, and Novalis dis-
closed the nature of Maeterlinck's reading and
thinking. That on Emerson showed us, like the
plays, how he loved the idea of silence so much
that the words of the people in his plays often
seem no more than swallows flying about a deep
and still lake, whose surface they ruffle seldom and
but for a moment. " Le Trésor des Humbles "
opens with a quotation from Carlyle upon silence
and secrecy, saying that " silence is the element in
which great things fashion themselves together,"
and that " speech is too often . . . the act of quite
stifling and suspending thought, so that there is
none to conceal. . . . Speech is of Time, silence is
of Eternity." As in the Introduction to the trans-

M. AND MADAME MAETERLINCK

lations from Emerson these words by another suffice to set him travelling up and on in his airy path, beginning with the words: "It is idle to think that, by means of words, any real communication can ever pass from one man to another." In this book, again, he introduces a variation upon "The silence of a child is wiser than the speech of Marcus Aurelius"; for he asks now what difference there is between words of his and words of a child who complains of cold. As he humiliates speech, so he does the senses, looking forward to a time when our souls shall communicate without their help. Even now, he argues, we know very much without them, and instead of saying, as in the essay on Emerson, that a man's soul is something different from his words or from his own presentation of himself, he imagines the soul stripped of her veils, so that the most secret thoughts only remain, and he sees the soul of a prostitute "with the transparent smile of the child in her eyes," or a murderer surrounded by an air of purity, a philosopher by "unendurable gloom." It may be, he thinks, the supreme aim of life to set free these yet inexplicable powers, such is that invisible goodness which is denied to no man. Life has deepened in recent times, and has gained in depth and spiritual gravity what it has lost in external attractiveness; the pomp and the picturesqueness of life survive chiefly in books and on the stage, but are as nothing compared with the reality of silent trees or an old man in an arm-chair beside a lamp in solitude. Now that the big and the violent have no authority the child emerges into significance, and with the child the woman ; and women, he says, are more naturally in harmony with the mysteries of life ; " they are nearer to God " ; and he speaks of " those profound moments " when a man's head lies on the breast of a woman—profound moments when, perhaps, the hero learns " to know the strength and steadfastness of his star." In intellect they may be inferior, but in the higher regions all are equal. Of such a world as this which is seen or foreseen by Maeterlinck, women like Aglavaine and Maleine are fit inhabitants, and in it Maleine would have no need to die by the cord nor Aglavaine to cause the death of Selysette. Women he calls the " veiled sisters " of the great unseen things, and the phrase is only one of many which belong to the world of the plays. These silent, divining women, looking so insignificant, are like the characters of those plays. Still more like them are those silent and mysterious beings who are destined to an early death and are dimly aware of it, timid yet grave and steadfast. Their resignation seems beautiful to him, and in " The Star " he speaks of " the meek, resigned smile " of the soul as being its deepest expression. In " The Invisible Goodness " he compares men with sleep-walkers or the blind, and recalls " Les Aveugles " when he says that we never see or touch each other in this life. The predestined are those on whom death has set a visible doom, such as Arkël saw on Mélisande. But they are not essentially exceptional in Maeterlinck's opinion, for death he calls the guide and the goal of life.

Everywhere is to be seen his belief, and a tender fervour in advocating it, that the mere fact of living is wonderful, so wonderful that our distinctions between the important and the unimportant fade away. Only external things make these distinctions, and of external things he takes no account. What lies beneath is what is valuable and significant, and at present we know little or nothing of this, except that it is unfathomable in all men. Hence at present an equality of mystery and greatness in all. What is known is uninteresting, and he says, with Whitman :

What is known I strip away,
I launch all men and women forward with me into the unknown.

Maeterlinck also says "All." Arkël called Mélisande a poor little mysterious being, "like everybody else," and Maeterlinck allows no differences of good and bad, great and small, young and old. The prostitute and the murderer may have white, lovely souls, while the philosopher and the martyr may spread gloom wherever they go. In Ford's play of "'Tis Pity She's a Whore," which Maeterlinck translated, Giovanni says to his incestuous sister Annabella before he stabs her :

Since we must part,
Go thou, white in thy soul, to fill a throne
Of innocence and sanctity in heaven.

This is the note of Maeterlinck, but Giovanni

confidently expects, not an inner and heavenly
sanction only, but that of intelligent posterity:

> If ever after times should hear
> Of our fast-knit affections, though perhaps
> The laws of conscience and of civil use
> May justly blame us, yet when they but know
> Our loves, that love will wipe away that rigour
> Which would in other incests be abhorred.

What lover says to lover in the ecstasy of tragedy
Maeterlinck says quietly to all the world. But for
his soft and shadowy voice, his words are those of
Walt Whitman in the " Salut au Monde":

> Each of us inevitable,
> Each of us limitless—each of us with his or her right
> upon the earth,
> Each of us allow'd the eternal purports of the earth,
> Each of us here as divinely as any is here.

Only Maeterlinck has scarcely an equivalent for
Whitman's praise of the body, when he says
that the skin, the hair, the bones, the marrow . . .
" are not the parts and poems of the body only,
but of the soul, O I say now these are the soul."
To Whitman all that is, all visible things, are so
glorious and strange that though he would have
life better, yet he cannot think of making it so
except through love of what it already is. Whitman sees that men are divine, and Maeterlinck has
intimations that they are: at the bottom of all
our acts, he says in his Introduction to Camille
Mauclair's " Jules Laforgue " (1896), there is " a
kind of childish and divine smile . . . which might

be named the soul's smile." He is shy and gentle
with all his asseveration, having neither bulk nor
weight, but speaking like a disembodied spirit.
Just as his plays show "the reaction of the
imagination against" what Mr. Symons unjustly
calls "the wholly prose theatre of Ibsen, into which
life comes nakedly, cruelly, subtly, but without
distinction, without poetry," so in these essays we
meet "children and spirits" rather than the men
and women of life or of Ibsen's plays. There are
places where he speaks so airily—like the legendary
bird of Paradise that had no feet, and could never
alight on earth or tree—that he might seem to be
only building up in fancy from some such words as
those of Novalis: "Blame nothing human, for all
is good, though all may not be good in every
place, or at all times, or for all men." Did he ever,
in writing this book, remember some other words
which he had translated a few years before, those
of Ruysbroeck's seventy-sixth chapter? The
mystic is writing of those egoists who attain a
natural idle calm which they mistake for the
heavenly calm of saints. They think themselves
contemplative, and, thanks to their natural calm,
believe themselves free and in direct union with
God, and therefore raised above the practice of the
Church and the commandments of God, the law,
and virtuous works. Therefore, too, they can do
all that their bodily natures desire, for they have
reached innocence, and there is no law for them ;
and if nature is tempted to some pleasure and a
refusal might darken or disturb the calm of the

spirit, they satisfy nature according to the desire, lest the calm of the spirit should be disturbed.

Probably Maeterlinck did not remember these words, or his book might have been hesitating as well as shy. But hesitating it never is. For his foundations are built upon truths within the experience of all, and he builds all the more audaciously because most men ignore these foundations altogether. Every one has come to the edge of a mystery, as of a deep sea for which no experience or thinking has prepared him ; every one has used powers of intuition and unconscious hidden activity for which he has no name. We have assurances and consolations inexplicable, the very reason for living is hidden from many. Very widely distributed is the kindliness felt for a scoundrel who is generous, the contempt for the man who is perfect according to some obvious rule or law. Tolerance and a sense of mystery are the foundations of " Le Trésor des Humbles." It brings those who are open to slender and vague voices out of the darkness some of the new assurances and consolations that are needed, or confirms the old. It plays the same part as Browning's " Rabbi Ben Ezra " in laying stress upon—

> All the world's coarse thumb
> And finger failed to plumb,
> So passed in making up the main account ;
> All instincts immature,
> All purposes unsure,
> That weighed not as his work, yet swelled the man's amount :

Though hardly to be packed
Into a narrow act,
Fancies that broke through language and escaped,
All I could never be,
All men ignored in me,
This I was worth to God, whose wheel the pitcher
shaped.

It makes for a reconsideration of old standards, for
charity, for subtle distinctions, modifications, reser-
vations, for an extending or a breaking down of
boundaries, for a broadening of the horizon of
common life. It can reveal the value of judgments
which have escaped explanation and even notice
because they were not purely or even mainly
rational, and were yet right. It can increase
reverence where it does not touch understanding.
It undermines our more massive and pompous
follies. It teaches not by information or by law,
but by making men more profoundly aware of
themselves and of the world. To read it is like an
experience of the uncomfortable silence that
descends by chance upon a circle of talkers. Most
are glad when the silence breaks up and talk
returns; but the silence is not to be forgotten. The
book points to mysteries under the surface of life
which are as impressive as the corridors, vaults,
and dark waters which are their symbols in the
plays.

But "La Sagesse et la Destinée" must be considered along with "Le Trésor des Humbles" if a
fair view is to be had of Maeterlinck's early writing
upon life and conduct. It is a book written without

rigorous method, " composed," as he tells us himself,
" of oft-interrupted thoughts, that entwine themselves with more or less system around two or three
subjects." It is not meant to convince or prove,
and Maeterlinck takes the opportunity to say that
books are less important than it has been claimed,
telling us of a friend who said that it was well
to love and admire the word " Equanimity," which
Antoninus Pius, when on his death-bed, gave
as watchword to the captain of the guard, but
better to spend the time given us by fortune to
admire it " in favour of the first little useful, living
deed " offered by the same fortune. And later in
the book he says that truest morality bids us to
cling to daily duties and acts of brotherly kindness.

The book was published in 1898, two years after
" Le Trésor," and already Maeterlinck is farther away
from the world of his early plays. He sees around
him not only men who are oppressed by men and
events, but others with " some kind of inner force,
which has its will not only with men, but even with
the events that surround them." That is to say,
Jesus Christ and Marcus Aurelius are not open to
misfortunes of the same complexion as Hamlet and
Œdipus. There is, he says now, " no inner fatality,
and much that now seems fatal is avoidable and is
even human and natural." As to resignation, he
now sees that it may come to the pettiest ; what is
good is " the thoughts and the feelings in whose
name we embrace resignation." Wisdom, he says,
is deeper than our consciousness, and it contains love
which is not in reason ; and again, that wisdom lies

above all in "those ideas that are not yet clear." The sage suffers, but his wisdom helps him to convert the suffering and make the manner of his accepting it harmless. He compares the "magnificent sorrow" of a great man with the puny joy of another ; this also is part of the wisdom which is armed against destiny. And now he asks when men will give the place of importance to life instead of to death, and count the joy as well as the sorrow in computing a man's destiny. Happiness, he says, can be taught and learnt. He calls renunciation a virtue that is often a parasite, and it does not produce wisdom ; in fact, wisdom grows faster in happiness than in misfortune, while the horizon of sorrow differs little from that of happiness when surveyed from the height of a lofty thought. Sacrifice, he says, should not be the means, but the sign of ennoblement ; for self-sacrifice is easier than the fulfilment of our spiritual destiny. Not only sacrifices, but other acts, are higher when done consciously than when instinctive. Like Richard Jefferies and many others he says that the knowledge that he is alone is a source of strength to man, and he asks, "Where shall the virtue of man find more everlasting foundation than in the seeming injustice of God ? " The vastness of nature is still something of an obsession to him. We should act as if for eternity, and yet know that whatever we do is insignificant. Something in us makes us prefer tears in an infinite world to perpetual happiness in a petty one. Justice is man's idea, and our instinct tells us that " he who is morally right must be happier than he who is wrong." There is no waste of goodness. Even an unwise act may help a wise man ; and again he insists that a man's reaches and attempts are more important than his achievements. He has no doubt of the essential happiness of Emily Brontë, because her life was intense. Yet he does not applaud mere loftiness of desire or dream which is characteristic of the weak and absorbs them entirely. A healthy vice is better than a morbid virtue. Whereas he seemed in " Le Trésor " to encourage an indolent and amiable confusion of mind he now asks scornfully whether we think that anything will come in answer to mere vague desires, and his open- ing words allow us to see that he is conscious of the intangibility of the happiness, justice, and love of which he speaks, compared with the reality of the sorrow and injustice of life. The most dangerous thought is that which mistrusts reality, he writes—perhaps in correction of conclusions drawn from " Le Trésor des Humbles." To the same cause perhaps may be attributed the statement that a man's thought will not change his place in the world, but his actions will, thought being " solitary, wandering, fugitive," while each deed is effected by ideas and desires with a " foothold in reality." And again he contrasts thought which may be deceptive with the sincerity of human feeling.

Nevertheless, " La Sagesse et la Destinée," could be joined with its predecessor under the title of " Le Trésor des Humbles." Both together offer a store of encouragement and consolation for humble hearts. In the new book the same tolerance prevails. The deeper down we go into life, the more inevitable is it that the eye must watch and approve and love "every soul in existence," if for no other reason than that it has "the mysterious gift of existence," and that it must be clear that falsehood and weakness and vice are superficial, and wickedness is only "goodness bereft of its guide," and treachery is loyalty astray, and hatred is love digging its own grave. Balzac, he points out, can make the emotion of a simple heart stir us as much as the passion of a king. And when, almost in the spirit of his early plays, he puts man beside "the vastness of nature" and sees his littleness, he comes to think that the extraordinary things in the life of saints, famous lovers, or generals, are illusions in comparison with the wisdom of an unambitious, healthy, honest man who does not desire to be anything but a man. He adds that everything beautiful, noble, or profound which is possible to human life may be found in "the simplest, most ordinary life."

Theoretical toleration and a large but indefinite sense of mystery are in the air. The tyranny of the too rigid and pretentious standards of conventional Christianity is being broken down. It has not been replaced, and, in the meantime, there is toleration—and myriads of intolerances. The predominance of the middle class has helped also to produce a widespread craving for anything that will vividly contrast with the life of this class. Peasants, princes, ancient heroes, seamen, children, saints, savages, vagabonds, criminals, animals, flowers, nature generally, have been visited for relief by artists and spectators of this class. Even the maniac has found his praiser—not merely his pitiful chronicler, like Herrick, or Cowper, or Wordsworth. Ernest Dowson has a poem "To One in Bedlam," and sees in his melancholy something "germane to the stars" and enviable. "O lamentable brother!" he exclaims:

O lamentable brother! if those pity thee,
Am I not fain of all thy fine eyes promise me;
Half a fool's kingdom, far from men who sow and reap
All their days, vanity? Better than mortal flowers
Thy moon-kissed roses seem: better than love or sleep,
The star-crowned solitude of thine oblivious hours!

Here is the contrast between the freedom of madness and the entrammelled life of those who sow and reap vanity. "Anywhere out of the world," as Baudelaire cries, and, following modestly behind, a multitude is willing to see in dreaming, in childhood, in what is untouched by routine, law, and custom an escape from what is clear, limited, and fixed. Another modern poet, Francis Thompson, writes of a maid in love, almost in the words of Maeterlinck, as:

Feeling the infinite must be
Best said by triviality. . . .
With daintiest babble shows her sense
That full speech were full impotence;
And while she feels the heavens lie bare—
She only talks about her hair.

It is this common truth of experience that Maeter-

linck wishes to draw from its retreat in our unconsciousness and make it serve not only as a
memorial but as a prophecy, not only as an isolated
fact but as a rule. Mostly town-dwellers, living
sheltered lives and pursuing occupations that do
not satisfy them, the people whom he addresses
have much leisure and much solitude, and the
characteristic occupation of the less active is reading. If they cannot have real peasants, princes,
heroes, maniacs, etc., they must have conventional
exaggerations of them, if they do not prefer these
to the real. And along with these tastes have
gone many attempts to preserve or to ameliorate
the condition of the peasants, children, etc. To
this middle class, and to the humble or more hesitating members of it, Maeterlinck makes a sweet
and insinuating appeal. No writer is more tolerant,
more mysterious than he, and none is more easy,
if as easy, to read. The writing is graceful, and
as decorative as is compatible with extreme fluency.
It can be read for the pure unintellectual pleasure
of reading. Nothing in the thought or style can
shock, amuse, or astonish—not because the books
contain nothing shocking, amusing, or astonishing,
but because the grave air of the whole enchants or
hypnotizes. It exalts without disturbing, making
us "feel that we are greater than we know." We
do not envy Maleine and Mélisande and Alladine
and Ygraine the majesty of woe which was given
to them by the corridors and impassable doors of
their castles, and the dungeons and caverns below
them, and the surrounding forests, and the sea and

11

the seabirds. The meanest of us has a yet more majestic stage for his joys and sorrows in the breadth of eternity and the complication of unintelligible laws. Take, for example, the following passage from the essay called "L'Étoile":

"Les paysans écossais ont un mot qui pourrait s'appliquer à toutes les existences. Dans leurs légendes ils appellent *Fey* l'état d'un homme qu'une sorte d'irrésistible impulsion intérieure entraîne, malgré tous ses efforts, malgré tous les conseils et les secours, vers une inévitable catastrophe. C'est ainsi que Jacques Ier, le Jacques de Catherine Douglas, était *Fey* en allant, malgré les présages terribles de la terre, de l'enfer et du ciel, passer les fêtes de Noël dans le sombre château de Perth, où l'attendait son assassin, le traître Robert Graeme. Qui de nous, s'il se rappelle les circonstances du malheur le plus décisif de sa vie, ne s'est senti possédé de la sorte? Il est bien entendu que je ne parle ici que de malheurs actifs, de ceux qu'il eût été possible d'éviter ; car il est des malheurs passifs, comme la mort d'un être adoré, qui nous rencontrent simplement et sur lesquels nos mouvements ne sauraient avoir aucune influence. Souvenez-vous du jour fatal de votre vie. Qui de nous n'a été prévenu ; et bien qu'il nous semble aujourd'hui que toute la destinée eût pu être changée par un pas qu'on n'aurait point fait, une porte qu'on n'aurait pasouverte une main qu'on n'aurait pas levée, qui de nous n'a lutté vainément sans force et sans espoir sur la crête des parois de l'abîme, contre une force invisible et qui paraissait sans puissance ?

"La souffle de cette porte que j'ai ouverte, un soir, devait éteindre à jamais mon bonheur, comme il aurait éteint une lampe débile ; et maintenant,

lorsque j'y songe, je ne puis pas me dire que je
ne savais pas. . . . Et cependent, rien d'important
ne m'avait amené sur le seuil. Je pouvais m'en
aller en haussant les épaules, aucune raison humaine ne pouvait me forcer à frapper au vantail.
. . . Aucune raison humaine ; rien que la destinée."

Such a passage at once belittles and aggrandizes
the common mortality of us all by colouring with
the temperament of one man experiences that, as a
rule, go for little and are forgotten.

When we read these things we can say of him
what he said of Emerson, that he vindicated the
grandeur of life, and has made a pathway of light
for the workman leaving his workshop ; that he
has given a meaning which is almost sufficient to
this life, which had lost its traditional horizon, and
perhaps has shown us that it is so strange, profound, and mighty that there is no need of any
aim but itself. He does not know more of it than
the others ; but he makes affirmations with more
courage and has confidence in the mystery. He
does not stand alone. If a man has understood
and accepted Wordsworth's—

> Come forth into the light of things,
>   Let Nature be your teacher.
>
> She has a world of ready wealth,
>   Our minds and hearts to bless—
> Spontaneous wisdom breathed by health,
>   Truth breathed by cheerfulness.
>
> One impulse from a vernal wood
>   May teach you more of man,
> Of moral evil and of good,
>   Than all the sages can—

—if a man has understood this Maeterlinck offers no difficulties and few novelties. Maeterlinck's early essays are entirely without the modern feeling for Nature ; but what has Wordsworth left him to say about the wisdom of a child—that "best philosopher"?—

> Mighty Prophet ! Seer blest !
> On whom those truths do rest,
> Which we are toiling all our lives to find.

More than a century earlier Thomas Traherne was praising and lamenting "the learned and the happy ignorance" of childhood, wishing to return again to infancy to improve his manhood. "How wise was I in infancy!" he cries. He desires simplicity, and is weary not only of adult worldliness, but of "all that since the Fall mine eyes on earth can find"; and "a quiet, silent person" seems to him one who may "possess all that is great or good in blessedness," for—

> The Inward Work is the Supreme ; for all
> The other were occasion'd by the Fall.

Except where his thought is confused by superficial religious forms he is much like the author of "Le Trésor des Humbles." Like him, and like Rousseau, he "sees in man's eating of the fruit of the tree of knowledge the cause of his fall from Nature, much as the theologian sees in the same event the cause of his fall from God"—in the words of Mr. Irving Babbitt's "New Laokoon." To the passages quoted from Wordsworth should be added a phrase or two from Blake's "Everlasting Gospel," such as—

> Thou art a man. God is no more.
> Thy own humanity learn to adore.

Or these words on the life of Jesus:

> He left his father's trade to roam,
> A wandering vagrant without home,
> And thus he others' labours stole,
> That he might live above control.
> The publicans and harlots he
> Selected for his company,
> And from the adulteress turned away
> God's righteous law that lost its play.

Or these, from "Auguries of Innocence":

> A skylark wounded on the wing
> Doth make a cherub cease to sing. . . .
>
> A truth that's told with bad intent
> Beats all the lies you can invent. . . .
>
> He who mocks the infant's faith
> Shall be mocked in age and death.

If these things had been understood there would have been no need for Maeterlinck to write or us to read. Seventeen hundred years ago an old Epicurean of Cappadocia inscribed upon a wall these words of a faith which doubtless included all that has been learnt—apart from books—ever since:

"There is nothing to fear in God. There is nothing to feel in death. That which man desires can be attained. That which man dreads can be endured." (Professor Gilbert Murray, *Hibbert Journal*, October 1910.)

Wherever we turn we can see the thoughts of Maeterlinck. At the beginning of De Quincey's essay, "On the Knocking at the Gate in 'Macbeth,'" for example, is a remark upon the feebleness of the understanding, which is as forcible as anything in Maeterlinck. "Here," says De Quincey, "I pause for one moment, to exhort the reader never to pay any attention to his understanding when it stands in opposition to any other faculty of his mind. The mere understanding, however useful and indispensable, is the meanest faculty in the human mind, and the most to be distrusted. . . ." Nor could a reader have been surprised to find in the essay "On Women" the very words of the man in Browning's "Cristina":

> Doubt you if, in some such moment,
>   As she fixed me, she felt clearly,
> Ages past the soul existed,
>   Here an age 'tis resting merely,
> And hence fleets again for ages,
>   While the true end, sole and single,
> It stops here for is, this love-way,
>   With some other soul to mingle.

Browning, in particular, gives many instances of seeming magical intuition. In "A Blot in the 'Scutcheon," for example, one who has just rashly killed another in a duel is told that, if he had but

listened to his enemy's explanation, all would have
been well; but he exclaims:

> Why, as he lay there,
> The moon on his flushed cheek, I gathered all
> The story ere he told it: I saw through
> The troubled surface of his crime and yours
> A depth of purity immovable;
> Had I but glanced, where all seemed turbidest,
> Had gleamed some inlet to the calm beneath;
> I would not glance: my punishment's at hand.

But even if a hundred men should wear out
their eyesight and find sources or precedents for
every thought in Maeterlinck, they would not thus
lower his position. The combination of them is
his own, and he can reach ears that are closed
to Blake. The new, the unique thing in his books
is in fact Maeterlinck. He is the advocate, and
the preacher. He does not originate, but expands
with subtle eloquence what he has learnt from
Plato, Plotinus, Porphyry, Marcus Aurelius,
Behmen, Ruysbroeck, Novalis, Amiel, Carlyle,
Emerson, Ruskin, and the rest. He addresses,
not philosophers or scholars, but the humble, the
magazine readers, the general public, and he is
neither technical nor obscure. As a rule the
mystics have not been easy to understand, because
they speak with tongues which the rest have to
learn with much labour; not being artists their
language owes its depth, not to tradition, but
apparently to immediate inspiration, and it is
turbid from transit out of the heavens. Maeterlinck is perfectly clear. Though warm, he is not

disturbed. He can draw upon all the resources of eloquence. It is worth while noticing how often he uses words of a certain colour to produce his own effect. Look, for example, at the essay on " The Predestined," how well weighted with pathos it is by the " few mothers " of the opening sentence, by the words "sad," " gentle," " piteous," " strange," " grave," " mysterious," " timid," " beseeching," etc. The following sentences from " Les Avertis " are a good example of the means taken to make the " predestined " children effective ; and they are not unfairly chosen as a specimen of Maeterlinck's early style :

" Au collège nous les discernions obscurément. Ils semblaient se chercher et se fuir à la fois comme ceux qui ont la même infirmité. On les voyait à l'écart sous les arbres du jardin. Ils avaient la même gravité sous un sourire plus interrompu et plus immatériel que le nôtre, et je ne sais quel air d'avoir peur de trahir un secret. Presque toujours ils se taisaient lorsque ceux qui devaient vivre s'approchaient de leur groupe. . . . Parlaient-ils déjà de l'événement, ou bien savaient-ils que l'événement parlait à travers eux et malgré eux, et l'entouraient-ils ainsi afin de le cacher aux yeux indifférents ? "

It is not easy to say whether this indicates a peculiar experience of the writer's, or rather a peculiar method of remembering events, or of transfiguring memory, or adorning it ; but I incline to think that the difference from the ordinary is one of style and not of experience. The "*presque* toujours" is an exceedingly impressive modification, and yet not convincing. It is the artist of "Alladine et Palomides" who draws the picture of some of those predestined beings "lingering" a little longer than the rest, looking at men with an "eager" smile, and then "towards their twentieth year" slipping away with "muffled" footsteps from among men; who makes it "evening," "a sudden evening," when we dare not look at these persons, because it is as if they were "on life's further shore," and now we feel that it is time for saying something deeper than common, saying something that is "piteously struggling" and "craving" to be spoken. The sentimentality of the chapter is perfectly un-restrained. Then observe the "veiled queens," as he calls our intuitions, in "Mystic Morality," thus recalling the queens who steered the death-barge of Arthur. Superlatives abound; words of terror, mystery, and darkness are continually used; words, above all, of tenderness, sorrow, resignation—as when he speaks of lovers recognizing one another, and speaking "tearfully" like a girl who has found a lost sister; or women in their "little" homes, one bending forward, another "sobbing"; or the soul smiling a "meek, resigned smile"; or turning the past into nothing but a few "saddened smiles," and thus mastering the future; or learning how to "weep in the silence of humblest kindliness." When he wishes to describe the "timidity of the divine" in man, he says that upon it rests "the tender meekness of the little

ailing girl for whom her mother will not send
when strangers come to the house." In "La
Sagesse et la Destinée" this eloquence is less
obvious, but essentially the same, and we smile
when he pleads that we diminish things if they are
expressed in words, for in the same chapter he
asks whether, if we become pure, we shall conceal
our petty motives from *the angels* before us, and
then, in the next sentence, whether there is not
much in us that will need the pity of *the gods
on the mountain.* The eloquence which gave
modern Selysette her tower gives each of Maeterlinck's ideas at least a rag of royal purple. Once,
in "La Sagesse et la Destinée," he is so carried
away by his description of a stream as an image
of the man who is oppressed by fate that he
beholds it staggering—struggling—and *climbing*
as well as falling. And no better proof of the
power of this eloquence could be given than its
effect upon the admirable translator, Mr. Alfred
Sutro. In the thirty-sixth and thirty-seventh
sections of his translation of "La Sagesse et la
Destinée," for example, may be felt the rhythm of
numerous dimly veiled hexameters and pentameters, often several in succession. What makes
hexameters and pentameters in Mr. Sutro's prose
probably produces a corresponding effect in those
readers who are not also writers.

But Maeterlinck's store of eloquence is richer
yet. He has his clear and sweet style, his senti-
mentally coloured words, his infectious rhythms,
and he has the vague, often in alliance with

exaggeration, as in " Le Réveil de l'Âme," where he speaks of spiritual phenomena manifesting themselves in the workaday lives of the humblest —" mysterious, direct workings, that bring soul nearer to soul," and where he asserts that " all " that men in other generations have learned of the heart, soul, and spirit has been handed down to us. Phrases abound like that where he speaks of words in poetry revealing, " I know not what intangible and unceasing striving of the soul towards its own beauty and truth," of "the thousands of mysteries" surrounding us, of "the inexplicable within ourselves." He tells us that if we look at the sky instead of at the wall before the embrace of love, the embrace will "not be the same." In one place he tells us that we must not despise ourselves if we are saddened by another's happiness, because farther on the road we shall find what will not sadden us, and, if we do not, "it matters little : something there was that was not sad." When in "Wisdom and Destiny" he bids us live ready to welcome a great revelation, he tells us that we must crave for it, desire it as "lofty," "perfect," "vast," "en-nobling," "beautiful," "glorious," "ample" ; and that, whether it accords with our hopes or not, it will add to us what is "nobler" and "loftier." He alludes often to "beauty," "justice," "love," and feelings that are "noblest" and "loftiest." His defence is in one place that he can only be understood by those having "the same point of sensibility as himself," and in another that the best in us lies in "those ideas that are not yet clear."

Maeterlinck has another advantage, perhaps the greatest of all, in his extraordinary experience. Mr. Sutro has told us, in the Introduction to his translation of " La Sagesse et la Destinée," that Maeterlinck used often to watch the quiet and monotonous life of the Flemish peasants near his home, and that he often peeped into one cottage where lived seven brothers and a sister, "all old, toothless, worn," who worked together and in the evening sat together silent or talking with repetitions like those of " Les Aveugles." In " The Predestined " he speaks of the mystery that almost finds expression in the presence of one of these strange beings, but not quite. He tells us that he has often seen such things happen, and once before his brother died, though he characteristically tells us nothing definite. In the same chapter he tells us how he has noticed presentiments and strange signs in the faces of men who were to die even by accident. A page later he reveals that he has known many destined to die by the same death, and that at school he and others were "vaguely conscious" of them; yet further they were observed to frequent certain places together and he knew their looks perfectly. Still more remarkable is the experience, mentioned in "Mystic Morality," of standing before the corpse of his bitterest enemy, or several of his bitterest enemies perhaps. He would perhaps wish us to be impressed by the breath of air from an opening door which was to destroy his happiness for ever; but he can only say that, when thinking of it now, he cannot persuade himself that he was not at the moment aware of what was to happen.

There is a touch of the incredibly romantic—or is it only immaturity?—about these personal references, and it is to those which are simpler that we turn when we feel the lack of roots in Maeterlinck. They are not to be found in the essay on women, nor easily perhaps in any part of " Le Trésor." In " La Sagesse et la Destinée " they are commoner. It is Maeterlinck we see in the writer who insists on the humbleness of man's place on earth, who can give no reasons for a rule except out of his feelings, and who says that a sage might well answer the question, whether it would be good or not for the Jews to vanish or to preponderate, with the words: " In what comes to pass will be happiness." Significant is his comment upon the death of Emily Brontë, unmarried in her twenty-ninth year, that it is " sad to die a virgin," because it is every one's duty to " offer to his destiny all that can be offered to the destiny of man." Another curious passage is one that begins " If God there be ". . . . As a pendant to this should be taken the sentences where he says that the tranquillity and calmness of any man's soul are due to human virtues, and that Fénélon's, for example, were due rather to his loyalty to Madame Guyon and his love for the Dauphin than to the promise of his religion—which reminds us of the Christian Wordsworth calling this earth the place

where we have our happiness "or not at all."
Other readers may find other passages of this
boldly revealing kind, but most would perhaps
agree that they are few for such a book. They
are not enough to add to the weight of the ideas
and the eloquence that also of a human personality.
The tenderness and pity, the placidity compounded
of gentle resignation and hope, the sense of terror
and vastness, and also of the beauty of life, are not
intense enough to define a personality as well as a
type. But I am not sure; the wistful optimism
is perhaps peculiar to Maeterlinck, and his frequently vague intangibility as well. These qualities, at least, have done most to recommend him to
men, these and the ideas, common in themselves,
which in him attain a noticeable combination.
Above all, he preaches the mystery and greatness
of life on earth, of everything in this life and of
every one. He would make the depth of this
mystery and the height of this greatness so universal that the old crude judgments of men should
appal us. Though he sometimes lets slip a phrase
about a common or petty soul, his writing suggests
that there is no such thing, and that all men are
equal except in appearances, and that all men are
different. " Divine," which used to be the most
honouring of compliments, he would either apply
to all men or substitute for it, with implied increase
of honour, the epithet "human." Not that he
wishes or thinks it possible to destroy all distinctions, but that for the time being this
fundamental equality in spirit seems to him to

be the one thing needful to mention after its obscurity and ignominy of ages. He condemns no man ; he would have us condemn no man. Nor is it only every man and every woman and every child that he exalts, but every action. The subtlety of our actions and the lost profundity of their sources weigh upon him like " the silence of those infinite spaces " upon Pascal, and behind each one of them he is aware of infinity and eternity. These spaces terrify him still ; the enormity of Nature and the might of chance terrify him without over-whelming, and though they make men pigmies in aspect yet they dignify them still more. For the creator and ruler of such beings, the various bene-volent, insolent, or indifferent powers that have been called God seem to him inadequate, and he uses the word sparingly and either without con-viction or simply in connection with persons who used it when they were alive.

Like the poets and like the religious writers of old, he makes men familiar with the idea that life is not what it seems and is never so little, and his quiet tones are all the more startling after the bullying roars of Carlyle and Ruskin. He is kindly, and never dogmatic ; he proposes nothing difficult ; he will inflict no painful searching of heart, and to such as expect physic to be nasty he is disappointing. It must be hard to be a true and full mystic after having read Plato, Plotinus, Ruysbroeck, Behmen, Novalis, and the rest ; but only a mystic could rightly judge the reality of Maeterlinck's mysticism, and he would not judge at all. He must be left to mystic Life itself to be judged. In the meantime I can only say that I find in these two books a certain appearance of facility and unreality, as of one whose power of expression exceeded his thought and experience but not his reading ; and the voice might be that of one coming out of a library, not a wilderness.

XI

"SŒUR BÉATRICE" and "Ardiane et Barbe Bleue" followed "Aglavaine et Sélysette" after an interval of five years. "Sœur Béatrice" is founded upon an old story which John Davidson used in his "Ballad of a Nun," and it might have been written as a parable of pardon to illustrate the "mystic morality" of "Le Trésor des Humbles."

Sister Beatrice is about to elope from the convent with Bellidor, and is praying before the Virgin's image. She hears the horses of her lover—he comes in with costly garments and jewels, and while she has swooned, protesting against his wild embraces, he takes off her veil and mantle. She revives, but he dresses her in the costly dress while she still prays to the Virgin. She would have sounded the matin-bell, only the nuns are heard approaching; then she throws her nun's things before the image, calling for pity; but when Bellidor again embraces her she returns his kiss for the first time, and they go out. As the sun shines into the corridor, the Virgin stirs and comes to life and puts on the dress of Beatrice. Impersonating Beatrice, she makes miraculous gifts to the poor who come to the convent, but the nuns, all save one, think that she has robbed the image, so that she is condemned to be scourged. Instead of the scourging there is another miracle of "flames and strange splendours" and "living garlands." Abbess and priest kneel and confess that they have sinned, "For sister Beatrice is holy." The Virgin assumes the likeness and duties of Beatrice. Twenty-five years later, while the last strokes of the matin-bell are heard, the aged Sister Beatrice enters, worn out and in rags, and falls at the feet of the statue, though she has forgotten how to pray. Her mantle and veil, lying where she left them, she puts on. The nuns enter and see nun Beatrice and the restored image. They fall on their knees. She talks, as if in dream, of her children and their death in want. She sees that the nuns do not look angry. Presently the Abbess kisses her hands, and she snatches them away ; and another kisses her feet, that "used to run to sin." She wanders again, telling how Bellidor ceased to love her after three months, and how she became a prostitute, and how she killed her last child. The Abbess tries to stop her mouth in vain, and tells her she is most holy. They believe that Beatrice has never left them, and that this is only part of the terrible strife about "great saints." She cannot understand, but supposes that an angel has taught them to know and to pardon all. She sinks back exhausted, and the nuns fall on their knees around the bed.

"Sœur Béatrice" is a graceful dramatic entertainment which could probably hold many different audiences. It has three or four scenes of a significance so large and distinct that words are almost unnecessary, and nothing too mysterious or too surprising mars the brilliance of the melodrama. It has, in fact, an outline very much like that which any play upon this subject by a modern writer would have, and it might be performed without revealing its authorship. But while it proves that Maeterlinck can rival men of alien talents on their own ground, it is also saturated with his own doctrine. In "La Morale Mystique" he had written :

"Il semble que notre morale se transforme et qu'elle s'avance à petits pas vers des contrées plus hautes qu'on ne voit pas encore. Et c'est pourquoi le moment est peut-être venu de se poser quelques questions nouvelles. Qu'arriverait-il, par exemple, si notre âme devenait visible tout à coup et qu'elle dût s'avancer au milieu de ses sœurs assemblées, dépouillée de ses voiles, mais chargée des ses pensées les plus secrètes et traînant à sa suite les actes les plus mystérieux de sa vie que rien ne pouvait exprimer ? De quoi rougirait-elle ? Que voudrait-elle cacher ? Irait-elle, comme une femme pudique, jeter le long manteau de ses cheveux sur les péchés sans nombre de la chair ? Elle les a ignorés, et ces péchés ne l'ont jamais atteinte. Ils ont été commis à mille lieues de son trône ; et l'âme du Sodomite même passerait au milieu de la foule

sans se douter de rien, et portant dans ses yeux
le sourire transparent de l'enfant. Elle n'est pas
intervenue, elle poursuivait sa vie du côté des
lumières, et c'est de cette vie seule qu'elle se
souviendra. . . . Elle n'aura point honte de ce
qu'elle n'a pas fait ; et elle peut rester pure au
centre d'un grand meurtre. Souvent, elle transforme
en clartés intérieures tout le mal auquel il
faut bien qu'elle assiste. Tout dépend d'un principe
invisible et de là naît sans doute l'inexplicable
indulgence des dieux."

What Maeterlinck writes in " Le Trésor des
Humbles" the Virgin sings in " Sœur Béatrice."
She sings this song, to be found also in " Quinze
Chansons " :

> A toute âme qui pleure,
> A tout péché qui passe,
> J'ouvre au sein des étoiles
> Mes mains pleines de grâces.
>
> Il n'est péché qui vive
> Quand l'amour a parlé,
> Il n'est âme qui meure
> Quand l'amour a pleuré.
>
> Et si l'amour s'égare
> Aux sentiers d'ici-bas,
> Ses larmes me retrouvent
> Et ne s'égarent pas.

This is the core and essence of the play. Love
pardons all. In the first act, when Beatrice is
tempted to go away, she appeals to the Virgin to
hear her as " Only a girl who does not understand," as one who knows nothing, while Our Lady
knows all. When the peasant girl reports that

Beatrice is said to have been seen riding on the prince's horse, the Virgin says

> Only God saw her not, and nothing heard,

and again to the crowd of poor :

> God does not see the ill
> Done without hatred.

The Virgin impersonates the lost nun, and gathers credit for her name under the disguise. But Bellidor boldly anticipated this. While Beatrice was kneeling to the Virgin he asked : " Is it not she that asks, and you that pardon ? " and he sees the Virgin and Beatrice as two sisters.

Hating the gross code by which men and women are appraised for actions and their obvious consequences, Maeterlinck is inclined to say that actions are not to be considered for or against, or if they are it must be contrariwise. He cannot leave the beautiful mediæval tale to preach its own gospel, but seems almost to raise it from a tremendous and warning exception into a controvertible moral and a barren law. He discards mere pity for the sinner, and gives glory. She is sainted by her sister nuns, though it is impossible not to dwell on the fact that they praise her in ignorance of her life, and also under the belief that the Virgin's acts have really been hers. She has been a prostitute, and she has neglected or killed her children, but she has suffered, and the Virgin protects her against the customary judgments of her fellow creatures. Unless the Virgin again intervenes, the next sufferer will meet with these judgments exactly as if nothing had happened. It is a miracle, isolated and unavailing.

" Ardiane et Barbe Bleue" is a version of the story of Blue Beard. The scene is a hall in the castle of Blue Beard, and a crowd outside is shouting out because a sixth wife has come to the tyrant. Ardiane and a nurse enter, and the nurse tells her that Blue Beard has killed five women, but she thinks that they are not dead. She has six silver keys and one of gold, and this alone, being forbidden, she keeps. But the nurse picks up the six, and one by one they open the six lesser doors of the hall. Out of the first pour amethysts, from the second sapphires, from the third pearls, from the fourth emeralds, from the fifth rubies, from the sixth diamonds, and with these Ardiane decks herself. She opens the great door with the golden key, and hears the song of—

> Orlamonde's five daughters,
>   When the faery died,
> Orlamonde's five daughters
>   Sought to win outside,

and Blue Beard emerges and accuses her at once of opening the forbidden doors, like her sisters. He tries to drag her away, and at her cry the crowd bursts in to save her, but she puts them back, saying that he has done her no harm. In the next act Ardiane, with her nurse, is descending the steps of a dark, subterranean hall. She finds five captive women in rags, dazzled by her light.

They have never sought for escape. Ardiane's lamp goes out, and, as she feels along to the bolts and bars, the others are terrified because they think that the sea is without and will burst in. She breaks a pane in an old window, and then other panes, flooding the hall thus with intolerable light, in which gradually they can see the sky, the green world, the village, the people. Ardiane goes out, and they follow into the light and wind. Again in the third act the women are in the hall of jewels, and Ardiane helps them to adorn themselves. Blue Beard is away, but no escape has been found. At last the crying of the crowd announces his return. The uproar grows; he is deserted by his negroes and struck down, and the women are in terror lest he should be killed. The peasants bring him in bound and wish to kill him, but Ardiane sends them away. The women kneel about him. Ardiane cuts his bonds and then bids him good-bye, going away, but leaving the others behind with Blue Beard.

Here again the spectacles are noble and distinct, and the play is a series of tableaux with optional words. The scenery may recall the halls and vaults of the early plays, but it has only a superficial resemblance, except when Ardiane is breaking an entrance for the light like the sisters of Palomides. Four of the characters bear the old names—Ygraine, Mélisande, Sélysette, Alladine; but the atmosphere is purely that of the theatre. The magic is stage magic; the mystery is contrived. The vaults and the hall with the many doors really seem to emphasize the difference between this play and the early ones. In them there was a natural mystery of darkness, space, and obscurity, the mystery of a yet dim and half-understood dawn world. In " Ardiane et Barbe Bleue " all is theatrical : it begins and ends in a theatre, and has no existence save as a number of picturesque and uncertainly symbolic scenes. It provides opportunities for impressive and subtle staging, and its words are worthy. Ardiane's speech when she sees the cataract of diamonds is a brilliant piece of the eloquence of Maeterlinck, the descriptive essayist :

" O mes clairs diamants ! Je ne vous cherchais pas, mais je vous salue sur ma route ! Immortelle rosée de lumière ! Ruisselez sur mes mains, illuminez mes bras, éblouissez ma chair ! Vous êtes purs, infatigables et ne mourrez jamais, et ce qui s'agite en vos feux, comme un peuple d'esprit qui sème des étoiles, c'est la passion de la clarté qui a tout pénétré, ne se repose pas, et n'a plus rien à vaincre qu'elle-même ! . . . Pleuvez, pleuvez encore, entrailles de l'été, exploits de la lumière et conscience innombrable des flammes ! Vous blesserez mes yeux sans lasser mes regards."

As the pictures, so some of the words, are symbolic. Such is Ardiane's reply to Blue Beard when he has told her that, by opening the door, she has lost the happiness he had willed for her :

The happiness I would lives not in darkness.

But it no more depends upon its value as an allegory than "Pilgrim's Progress." It is an old tale reconstructed in Maeterlinck's manner, which is to multiply symbols. It is more material and plainly sensuous than any of the works which preceded it. It says all that it means and suggests nothing. It has something of the air of a piece of bravado, and in its kind—its hard, gorgeous, pictorial kind—it is triumphant. It is only fair to recall here that, in the Introduction to his three volumes of plays, Maeterlinck spoke of both "Sœur Béatrice" and "Ardiane et Barbe Bleue" with genial disparagement. He said that they belonged to a class of composition that was useful because it gave musicians a theme for lyric development. They aimed at nothing more than this, and moral or philosophic second intentions were not to be looked for in them.

The later "Joyzelle," acted and published in 1903, is a play of the same class, except that the story is unfamiliar. The characters are Merlin, Lancéor his son, Joyzelle, and Arielle, who is Merlin's invisible genius. The scene is Merlin's island. Merlin and Lancéor are strangers to one another, according to some compact, and Merlin is not permitted to save his son, though the old man knows already that if the youth's love—which he can foresee rapidly approaching—is perfect, he must die soon. The father and Arielle believe that Joyzelle will bring him this perfect love; but, except by difficult proofs, they cannot certainly know. Then they see the two lovers meet for the first time.

They are strangers on the island; Joyzelle betrothed to one whom she does not love, and
Lancéor promised to one whom he cannot refuse,
because—as he believes—of his father's dying
wishes. Joyzelle scorns in both cases the bonds
not of love's making. She fears that the king of
the island, who saved her life, is in love with her—
a strange old man who is always thinking of a
lost son. He enters—it is Merlin. He asks Joyzelle if she knows Lancéor, and she answers "Yes,"
and that, though they have but just met, it is
enough. He tells her that her happiness is his
own, but he condemns Lancéor to keep within
certain limits upon the island; if he meets Joyzelle,
he is lost. Lancéor promises to fly from her " if
her life is at stake "; but Joyzelle will make no
promise. In a neglected garden they meet again.
Joyzelle cannot persuade Lancéor to go away and
avoid the doom. They embrace, and Joyzelle says
that she used to embrace him in her dreams, and
together they enjoy the present and recall the
enjoyment of the past dreams. When they look
round they see the garden transfigured by flowers
and birds' songs, which will betray their meeting
to Merlin. At the coming of Merlin Lancéor hides
in a thicket and is mortally wounded. His father
alone can restore him, and he does so : left alone
with him, he embraces him, and bids him have no
fear, because all this is for his happiness. Still,
Lancéor knows nothing of their relationship.
Merlin is powerless to forbid Arielle's plan to
transform herself into a fair woman to tempt

Lancéor, which she successfully performs. The two are found embracing by Joyzelle. Lancéor begins by denying all, and ends by driving away Joyzelle. In the third act Lancéor appears worn, like Beatrice. He confesses to Joyzelle that he did kiss Arielle, but that his soul was not a prey to the hostile power which overcame him. But Joyzelle had seen his soul, and, having her great gift of love, she knew that it was not Lancéor that was lying. In another scene Arielle kisses the sleeping Joyzelle, and finds her constant even in dreams. She advises Merlin to find his happiness in Joyzelle, because otherwise he must fall under the fatal enchantments of Viviane. Merlin tries to corrupt Joyzelle by telling her that her lover is again in another woman's arms, but she does not even turn her eyes to deny this ; she denies because " he is herself." In the fourth act Lancéor is lying lifeless, and Joyzelle is trying to restore him. She will say that she no longer loves him if only Merlin will save his life. She even promises to give herself to Merlin, which is the condition he lays down. Merlin, restoring Lancéor, begs to be forgiven for the torture he has been compelled by " destiny " to inflict. She does not reveal the condition to her awakened lover. In the last act Lancéor has learnt that Merlin is his father. Merlin has explained himself as an instrument of fate. Lancéor is happy until he learns that Joyzelle's most dangerous proof is yet to come. Arielle tries to persuade Merlin against this proof, but in vain. Joyzelle comes to his bed, and, finding him asleep, raises her dagger. The blow is turned aside by Arielle, and Merlin rises and embraces her, saying that she has triumphed. Lancéor enters, and both embrace their tormentor, who himself goes to meet less kindly evils.

This play is made entirely out of the philosophy of the essays, and, unlike "Béatrice" or "Barbe Bleué," has nothing in it which is common property. It is even like the early plays in so far as destiny is a prominent character, but much unlike because destiny is not a hidden, dark, and inhuman power, but personified in the form of a fatherly and in the end benign old man. As in "Barbe Bleué," the characters seem to be actors and actresses, and the play is altogether theatrical. Compared with the early plays, it has great warmth of feeling and brightness of colouring, but it is even less real. Mélisande and Alladine were the creations of a poet who was turning philosopher; Joyzelle is the creation of a philosopher who is a dazzling rhetorician. Like the early plays, this one has a deserted palace, with marble staircases, a prison tower, etc.; but they are cheerful and sunny (if with a theatrical sunlight) instead of gloomy and astonishing. Not so easily as "Barbe Bleue," it might be played without words, so large and obviously significant are the combinations of the characters into scenes. Nine-tenths of it would thus, however, be lost, for nine-tenths of it are given to the questions of the power of love and man's control over the future. As in "Béatrice," it is a woman's love that is glorified; but here love helps her to endure the suffering which leads to the perfection of her love, and love, not suffering, triumphs. All is forgiven to Béatrice because she has once loved; Joyzelle forgives everything because she has loved. Joyzelle is willing to suffer anything, and to say anything, extreme truth or extreme falsehood, and her love never wavers or changes or knows fear. Even in her sleep she is not to be tempted, while Lancéor gives way at once to Arielle. Nevertheless, Merlin calls it a " noble and beautiful " love which is thus " reduced to nothing in the arms of a phantom." So great is Joyzelle's love that Merlin admits she has something in her which he has not known before, and it can change the future. She begs Lancéor to tell the truth because she thinks that, when confessed with a kiss, a fault is a truth " more beautiful than innocence " ; if he confess, " all will again become pure as it was." She knows the truth about her lover when he kissed another, and she knows because she loves. Sorrows matter nothing when they lead to love, says Merlin. Nothing matters ; yet she refuses to say anything but " No " in answer to Merlin's persuasions that she should look and catch Lancéor at his infidelity. When Lancéor lies lifeless she feels that " it must be possible to give life to those whom we love better than ourselves." Fate itself, in the person of Merlin, blushes to have to tempt such a one, and when she has consented to surrender her body to Merlin to save her lover she wishes at once to tell him. And when she has raised the dagger to strike the sleeping seducer —even though she strikes a vain blow—Merlin pronounces that "she has conquered fate by listening to love." There is but one qualification. When Joyzelle asks whether it is ordained that love should strike and kill what is in its way, Merlin admits ignorance and diffidence: "Let us not make laws with a few scraps picked up in the darkness that surrounds our thoughts."

Lancéor is nothing but a creature that sins, is wretched, and is pardoned. The reason of his pardon is that, in sinning, he was obeying he knows not what; but it was not his soul that sinned; in fact, while he was sinning "he himself" tries hard to resist, but he heard his own voice and saw his own body betraying him, all but his soul being in the hands of a mysterious "hostile force." This is an illustration of "Mystic Morality," but the doctrine is not strengthened by a figure so unlike a human being.

Merlin, like Shelley's Jupiter, is the helpless tool of some higher power which he does not understand, and not only helpless but regretful. Lancéor sins, but explains that it was not really himself. Merlin tortures the lovers, but in the name of their destiny which demands it, and he asks to be forgiven, and even says, like his son, "It is not I that speak." He resembles the ragged philosopher who chalks up on his barrel-organ: "Out of work through no fault of my own." He has thought about this superior power of which he is the instrument and it seems to him that it demands that happiness should be accompanied by tears. Whatever it is, he earns the pity of the lovers: "He was," says Lancéor, "obliged to make us suffer." It may strike us as an excess of fancy and humanitarianism to be sorry for the fate which afflicts us because there is a power governing that fate as it governs us; but it is no more than the logic of the fatalism coupled with tenderness that are so characteristic of Maeterlinck. And furthermore, the natures of these persons, all bodiless and invisible as Arielle—the Prospero, Ferdinand, Miranda and Ariel of an island off the moon—should ensure a toleration in the reader as sublime as Joyzelle's. We should not be less astonished had Blake written a play to illustrate the words:

> A tear is an intellectual thing,
> And a sigh is the sword of an angel king,
> And the bitter groan of a martyr's woe
> Is an arrow from the Almighty's bow.

XII

"LA VIE DES ABEILLES," published in 1901, was destined to great popularity in the country of "The Complete Angler," "Selborne," "Rural Rides," "Climbing Plants," "The Amateur Poacher," and "A Shepherd's Life." It is founded on learning, experience, and love; it is a monument of eloquence and of rural felicity. We have books which are all these things; but we have nothing to be compared with "La vie des Abeilles." It would be difficult, indeed, to point to books in any literature where practice and speculation are wrought up with such elaborate and unpausing art into a whole of equal size and delicacy. If it were possible to have "Red Deer" composed by Sir Thomas Browne in the mood of "Urn Burial" we should have a companion to "La Vie des Abeilles."

It is not a monograph, the author tells us, and he has even reserved his more technical notes for another book—which has yet to appear. He does not offer to instruct a man in bee-keeping, but to repeat most of what is known of bees in a livelier manner than the text-books, and to add his own comments and conjectures. He will not, he says, adorn the truth by false invention. Nevertheless, the book is essentially an adornment of the known truth about hive-bees. It is a piece of sustained eloquence, which has for its subject-matter what the writer has seen and read of the swarm, the foundation of the bee city, the young queens, the nuptial flight, the massacre of the males, the progress of the race of bees. It depends not upon discovery, but upon a presentation of facts and opinions. Like the " Georgics," it will be read and loved most by those who know little of natural history. Its accuracy is but a small part at most of its merit, though without it the book could not have entered into favour with pedants and a pedant-led multitude. It is addressed, not to men of science, but to amateurs and readers of picturesque books ; and in " La Fondation de la Cité " he apologizes for too many details to those who "may never have followed a flight of bees, or who may have regarded them only with passing interest"; though this may be the irony of politeness.

Though he desires not to be too didactic, it can hardly be denied that the book is aimed deliberately and consciously throughout at a public. It is not, that is to say, a masterpiece that has grown up naively in darkness and solitude ; and the author is never lost in his subject, but remains, with all his eloquence, steadfastly outside. Take, for example, a charming passage in the first part, " Au Seuil de la Ruche," wherein he recalls the first apiary where he learned to love bees :

> " C'était, voilà des années, dans un gros village de cette Flandre Zélandaise, si nette et si gracieuse, qui, plus que la Zélande même, miroir concave de la Hollande, a concentré le goût des couleurs vives, et caresse des yeux, comme de jolis et graves jouets, ses pignons, ses tours et ses chariots enluminés, ses armoires et ses horloges qui reluisent au fond des corridors, ses petits arbres alignés le long des quais et des canaux, dans l'attente, semble-t-il, d'une cérémonie bienfaisante et naïve, ses barques et ses coches d'eau aux poupes ouvragées ; ses portes et ses fenêtres pareilles à des fleurs, ses écluses irréprochables, ses pont-levis minutieux et versicolores, ses maisonnettes vernissées comme des poteries harmonieuses et éclatantes d'où sortent des femmes en forme de sonnettes et parées d'or et d'argent pour aller traire les vaches en des près entourés de barrières blanches, ou étendre le linge sur le tapis découpé en ovales et en losanges et méticuleusement vert, de pelouses fleuries.

> " Une sorte de vieux sage, assez semblable au vieillard de Virgile :

> > " ' Homme égalant les rois, homme approchant des dieux,
> >   Et comme ces derniers satisfait et tranquille,'

aurait dit La Fontaine, s'était retiré là, où la vie semblerait plus étroite qu'ailleurs, s'il était possible de rétrécir réellement la vie. Il y avait élevé son refuge, non dégoûté—car le sage ne connaît point les grands dégoûts—mais un peu las d'interroger les hommes qui répondent moins simplement que les animaux et les plantes aux seules questions intéressantes que l'on puisse poser à la nature et aux lois véritables. Tout son bonheur, de même que celui du philosophe scythe, consistait aux beautés d'un jardin, et parmi ces beautés la mieux aimée et la plus visitée était un rucher, composé de douze cloches de paille qu'il avait peintes, les unes de rose vif, les autres de jaune clair, la plupart d'un bleu tendre, car il avait observé, bien avant les expériences de Sir John Lubbock, que le bleu est la couleur préférée des abeilles. Il avait installé ce rucher contre le mur blanchi de la maison, dans l'angle que formait une de ces savoureuses et fraîches cuisines hollandaises aux dressoirs de faïence où étincelaient les étains et les cuivres, qui, par la porte ouverte, se reflétaient dans un canal paisible. Et l'eau, chargée d'images familières, sous un rideau de peuplier, guidait les regards jusqu'au repos d'un horizon de moulins et de près.

" En ce lieu, comme partout où on les pose, les ruches avaient donné aux fleurs, au silence, à la douceur de l'air, aux rayons du soleil, une signification nouvelle."

It reminds us of Virgil, ot Statius, of Cowley, of George Borrow, but perhaps of Cowley above all, and of Borrow least. The old man who gave Borrow an excess of mead in his gratitude is alive, in a manner beyond and outside of Maeterlinck's art. The sentiment is rather that of Cowley's essay on gardens, though Maeterlinck's is the Flemish land-scape, as precise as an interior, and the sage who " ne connaît point les grands dégoûts." Only, as in Cowley's prose, we feel the presence of literature in the passage rather than of life : it might be pure invention. But this is an exceptional passage.

In many places the description is as faithful as it is minute and elaborate, and his method is probably the only one that could combine calm exactness with picturesqueness. For he has set himself the task of depicting, for the first time, things which few have seen or will ever see. He has no tradition behind him, except that which says that the bee is wonderful for industry and intelligence, and that the comb is a miracle. Moreover, his own feeling, enthusiastic though it be, is scientific rather than human, and could not be otherwise. The mere scale of the hive adds yet again to his handicap. Yet it is certain that he often shows himself successful as well as faithful, minute and elaborate. As an example, I will give the page where the swarm issues from the hive :

"On dirait que toutes les portes de la ville s'ouvrent en même temps d'une poussée subite et insensée, et la foule noire s'en évade ou plutôt en jaillit, selon le nombre des ouvertures, en un double, triple, ou quadruple jet direct, tendu, vibrant, et ininterrompu qui fuse et s'évase aussitôt dans l'espace en un réseau sonore tissu de cent mille ailes exaspérées et transparentes. Pendant quelques minutes, le réseau flotte ainsi au-dessus du ruche dans un prodigieux murmure de soieries diaphanes que mille et mille doigts électrisés déchireraient et recoudraient sans cesse. Il ondule, il hésite, il palpite comme un voile d'allégresse que des mains invisibles soutiendraient dans le ciel où l'on dirait qu'elles le ploient et le déploient depuis les fleurs jusqu'à l'azur, en attendant une arrivée ou un départ auguste. Enfin, l'un des pans se

rabat, un autre se relève, les quatre coins pleins
de soleil du radieux manteau qui chante, se
rejoignent, et, pareil à l'une de ces nappes intelli-
gentes qui pour accomplir un souhait traversent
l'horizon dans les contes de fées, il se dirige tout
entier et déjà replié, afin de recouvrir la présence
sacrée de l'avenir, vers le tilleul, le poirier, ou le
saule, où la reine vient de se fixer comme un clou
d'or auquel il accroche une à une ses ondes
musicales, et autour duquel il enroule son étoffe
de perles tout illuminée d'ailes."

Here he possesses the advantage of relating a
matter not quite unfamiliar and not without a
prestige of its own. Where he is describing what
is usually hidden, what is also silent and still, he
has need of humanizing comparisons and of his
own eloquence. These are successful in such
places as the following, where the hive is described after a swarm has departed :

"Mais si le présent paraît morne, tout ce que
l'œil rencontre est peuplé d'espérances. Nous
sommes dans un de ces châteaux des légendes
allemandes où les murs sont formés de milliers de
fioles qui contiennent les âmes des hommes qui
vont naître. Nous sommes dans le séjour de la
vie qui précède la vie. Il y a là, de toutes parts en
suspens dans les berceaux bien clos, dans la
superposition infinie des merveilleux alvéoles à six
pans, des myriades de nymphes, plus blanches que
le lait, qui, les bras repliés et la tête inclinée sur la
poitrine, attendent l'heure du réveil. A les voir
dans leurs sépultures uniformes, innombrables et
presque transparentes, on dirait des gnomes chenus

qui méditent, ou des légions de vierges déformées par les plis du suaire, et ensevelies en des prismes hexagones multipliés jusqu'au délire par un géomètre inflexible."

In the whole, and especially in "jusqu'au délire," we are reminded of the castles of the early plays ; and there is a promise of the scene of the unborn in "L'Oiseau Bleu." Human comparisons abound of necessity. The queen-bee gnawing the lid of her cell to escape is a "princess" reducing "the walls of her tower" but thwarted from without by an "enchanted obstacle." The accepted queen and the unborn others are "the wandering queen and the virgins in prison." To make the cry of the queens more impressive, it is contrasted with night and the hushing of noises and even "the silence of the stars." The hairy humble-bee forcing its way into a flower is compared with "a cave-bear that might have forced its way into the silken, pearl-bestrewn tent of a Byzantine princess." Such comparisons are characteristic. When the dawn is being swallowed up in full day it is "like a maiden caught in the arms of a heavy warrior"— "a naked maiden," says the original. This is from the book devoted to the nuptial flight of the queen bee. It is a celebrated piece, but it is necessary to quote part of it—where the queen emerges from the hive not long after dawn :

"Elle part comme un trait au zénith de l'azur. Elle gagne ainsi des hauteurs et une zone lumineuse que les autres abeilles n'affrontent à

aucune époque de leur vie. Au loin, autour des
fleurs où flotte leur paresse, les mâles ont aperçu
l'apparition et respiré le parfum magnétique qui se
répand de proche en proche jusqu'aux ruchers voisins.
Aussitôt les hordes se rassemblent et plongent à sa
suite dans la mer d'allégresse dont les bornes lim-
pides se déplacent.   Elle, ivre de ses ailes, et
obéissant à la magnifique loi de l'espèce qui choisit
pour elle son amant et veut que le plus fort l'atteigne
seul dans la solitude de l'éther, elle monte toujours,
et l'air bleu du matin s'engouffre pour la première
fois dans ses stigmates abdominaux et chante comme
le sang du ciel dans les mille radicelles reliées aux
deux sacs trachéens qui occupent la moitié de son
corps et se nourrissent de l'espace.   Elle monte toujours. Il faut qu'elle atteigne une région déserte que
ne hantent plus les oiseaux qui pourraient troubler
le mystère.   Elle s'élève encore, et déjà la troupe
inégale diminue et s'égrène sous elle.   Les faibles,
les infirmes, les vieillards, les mal venus, les mal
nourris des cités inactives ou misérables, renoncent
à la poursuite et disparaissent dans le vide.   Il ne
reste plus en suspens, dans l'opale infinie, qu'un
petit groupe infatigable.   Elle demande un dernier
effort à ses ailes, et voici que l'élu des forces incom-
préhensibles la rejoint, la saisit, la pénètre et, qu'em-
portée d'un double élan, la spirale ascendante de
leur vol enlacé tourbillonne une seconde dans le
délire hostile de l'amour."

Here the endeavour to recommend a small
matter by exaggeration is fatal. I do not mean
that the nuptial flight of a bee is insignificant, but
that it is small in scale when compared with the
acts of men or with the depths of the air in which
it takes place. I believe that it would be possible

to convey something of the grandeur of the
miniature event without altogether destroying the
scale : a naturalist like Mr. W. H. Hudson—if
there were one like him—would not fail were he
to attempt it, and he would leave us no thoughts
but of the immortal little insect and the wild air.
Does Maeterlinck give us a thought or a vision
of the bee and the summer air ? If he does, its
effect is faint in the mind when compared with
that of the eloquence simply as eloquence. It
brings before me, not so much the bee, as the poet
admiring the bee. But this, if true, is not to
condemn the passage or the book. "Comus"
does not give one direct fragrance of the earth,
yet is it the loveliest pastoral verse. "La Vie
des Abeilles" has not the same excuse as "Comus."
It begins and ends upon an every-day plane, and
its backbone is instruction or description of
natural facts, and the perfect book of this kind
would be one without obvious art. Maeterlinck's
is not such a book : let us remember here, again,
that it is an adornment, a gorgeous apparelling, of
the truth ; and, having done so, it is not permissible
to object to the eloquent description of the nuptial
flight except on the ground that it exceeds the
limits of its own kind. This, I think, it does.
The epithets "tragic" and "prodigious," applied
to these nuptials, are more applicable to the
description itself. When he speaks of the queen
descending from the "azure heights" trailing, "like
an oriflamme, the unfolded entrails of her lover,"
I see a magnifying glass and an exuberant voca-

ABBEY OF SAINT WANDRILLE: THE REFECTORY

bulary which is exposed still more by the quiet tone of the succeeding sentences relating how he has often watched the return of the queen and never noticed any unusual emotion. Nor can Maeterlinck's eloquence cease, but must revive again and again, to exclaim, for example :

" Voilà de prodigieuses noces, les plus féeriques que nous puissions rêver, azurées et tragiques, emportées par l'élan du désir au-dessus de la vie, foudroyantes et impérissables, uniques et éblouissantes, solitaires et infinies. Voilà d'admirables ivresses où la mort, survenue dans ce qu'il y a de plus limpide et de plus beau autour de cette sphère : l'espace virginal et sans bornes, fixe dans la transparence auguste du grand ciel la seconde du bonheur, purifie dans la lumière immaculée ce que l'amour a toujours d'un peu misérable, rend inoubliable le baiser, et se contentant cette fois d'une dîme indulgente, de ses mains devenues maternelles, prend elle-même le soin d'introduire et d'unir pour un long avenir inséparable, dans un seul et même corps, deux petites vies fragiles."

In a passage which follows this Maeterlinck shows that he is well aware of what he has done. " Profound truth," he says, has not the poetry of the above passage, but it has another which in the end we may equally understand and love. His excuse for rejoicing in regions " loftier than the truth "—which he admits to be impossible— is that the truths we perceive are but small and fragmentary : therefore " should any motive whatever cause an object to reveal itself to us in a more beautiful light than to others, let that motive be first of all dear to us." To admit and dwell upon the physical fact of these nuptials, and upon this alone, would, he thinks, be to content ourselves with less truth than if we saw only what is vulgarly called the " poetry " of this " lyrical " act. This passage is excellent criticism, and it would excuse " poetry " far more extravagant than anything in " La Vie des Abeilles." What it does not excuse is writing which gives an impression of words instead of things, of methods instead of results, and such writing is common in the lyrical descriptions of " Le Vol Nuptial."

This fault may spring from an inability to keep the eyes loyally upon a physical object, and a willingness to turn aside too soon, to think and feel " about it and about." Maeterlinck can describe still or inanimate things, forests, great waters, caves, castles, precious stones, but of living things he sees chiefly the soul, and his bodies are misty things, like the Arielle in " Joyzelle." And what pleases him chiefly in the bee is its intelligence—its possessing somewhat of that power which, as he says, transfigures necessity and organizes life. He compares it often with man, excusing it when some deliberate human experiment deceives it by asking if man would be more successful if a corresponding higher power set out to deceive him ; again, when zeal in collecting for the hive leads the bee into disaster, he pronounces that such disinterested " follies " in men are called by another name; and in his conclusion he estimates the achievement of the bee as above that of man, and says that if a visitor from another world were to ask for the "most perfect creation of the logic of life" on earth we should be bound to show a honeycomb. This is a vain extravagance of comparison, but certainly the bee has led Maeterlinck to some admirable and some characteristic thought. For example, he shows how rash it is to condemn the bees from our exterior observation by supposing an onlooker from another world watching us. Such a one, he points out, with irony like that of the author of "Erewhon," would conclude, from the fact that those who performed the heaviest toil dwelt in the worst hovels, that labour was a punishable offence upon the earth, and that, in spite of their offence and its punishment, they remained inoffensive and content to have the leavings of the rest of mankind who are evidently "the guardians, if not the saviours of the race." This thought was evidently strong in Maeterlinck's mind when he wrote the book, for he repeats it with very little variation at the end: he imagines an outside observer—a bee—watching us and seeing the earth "insufficiently and painfully" cultivated by two or three tenths of the human race; seven-tenths labouring to make the life of the idle remaining tenth "more complex and more inexplicable." Such an observer might conclude that our reason and moral sense were different from his and obeyed incomprehensible principles. Himself looking upon man as he has done upon the bee, Maeterlinck sees in us creatures made to produce thought, reason, spirit, or the power we know by these and many other names: he sees it is our first duty to do everything necessary to develop this power, and concludes the book with praise of this power as containing within itself the solution of all:

"Nourrissons-la de nos sentiments, de nos passions, de tout ce qui se voit, se sent, s'entend, se touche, et de sa propre essence qui est l'idée qu'elle tire des découvertes, des expériences, des observations qu'elle rapporte de tout ce qu'elle visite. Il arrive alors un moment où tout se tourne si naturellement à bien pour un esprit qui s'est soumis à la bonne volonté du devoir réellement humain, que le soupçon même que les efforts où il s'évertue sont peut-être sans but, rend encore plus claire, plus pure, plus désintéressée, plus indépendante et plus noble l'ardeur de sa recherche."

Curious is this power of seeing mankind on so small a scale as if it were no more than a fœtus; it is the writing of a god and not of a man. And yet he is no more than a man gifted with an extremity of consciousness, who sees "the extraordinary fluid we call life" animating us and the rest of the world, producing "the very thoughts that judge it, and the feeble voice that attempts to tell its story." He sees men as part of Nature, yet with that in them which seems to make their best achievements something apart from Nature and in spite of it, though he admits the possibility that our development may have no other purpose than to "amuse the darkness." This does not alarm him. The destiny of man, to develop the power known as reason or spirit, gives him such pride that nothing terrible can turn him aside— not the malice or stupidity of Nature. All that we have achieved we have done for ourselves, he says almost in the words of Richard Jefferies ; we are alone and we advance. Everywhere he sees a morality utterly different from our own, yet Nature seems to him less terrible than it was, and the names " Nature," "life," " death," " spirit of the race," etc., are less menacing than were " God," " Providence," " reward," etc. Nature is less terrible, and, though still foreign, she is not to be thought of as merely hostile or indifferent. Out of her chaos a greater wisdom may come. With his ear towards her great voices, some human things sound weak and untrue. All knowledge, everything that is a gain to this distinguishing power of man, is good, and he pictures a sage at once probing deep in the immorality of life yet himself living by "the most humanly beautiful truth," and this also is " as profoundly natural " as everything else ; and herein he returns by the way he came and falls spent, like many another, upon the infinite.

But if " La Vie des Abeilles " is even more remarkable as a chapter in the spiritual auto-biography of a characteristic man of the age than as a history of the bee, its ,vivacity and accuracy as history must not be forgotten. This age has complained again and again that science is a dead and death-dealing thing : books that are mortuaries and ossuaries have wearied us. "La Vie des Abeilles" is one of the replies to this complaint. Only time can pronounce whether it has triumphed by life or by the galvanism of consummate and even unconscious artifice, but at least it is a temporary classic. Dealing with what used to be called "the wonders of creation," it is written to glorify not so much the creator as the creature. Its prejudices are slight or transparent, yet it is dominated by the note of an intensely personal artist. It can inform and delight at once, or it can inform without delighting or delight without informing, according to the reader's taste : that is to say, it is not obviously a work of instruction or of diversion. In spite of the author, it is, however, a treatise in disguise—in the harmless disguise of the author's personality. It aims, probably in all unconsciousness, at showing that a modern naturalist can be as marvellous and readable as an ancient one, and with a fidelity equalling his infidelity. It is never dull or obscure ; it is, in fact, always lively and brilliant, and it is hard to believe that Maeterlinck will consent to be less so, if he ever writes the "more technical work" of which he speaks. It is without contemporary rival in its own kind whether among books on the bee or among natural histories in general, for no other writer of comparable power has concentrated himself upon one subject in the same imaginative spirit. It would be hard to overpraise it except by saying, as Maeterlinck refuses to say of Buchnër's essay, that it "smells of the bee." It smells of *belles lettres*, and while it is one of the most delicate in this class, it is also honourable among books of science and deserving of as much imitation as honour.

XIII

"LE TEMPLE ENSEVELI"

IN 1902, a year after "La Vie des Abeilles" and
four years after "La Sagesse et la Destinée,"
appeared "Le Temple Enseveli." Like "Le Trésor
des Humbles" it is divided into distinct but related
chapters, having, as titles, "La Justice," "L'Évolution du Mystère," "La Règne de la Matière," "Le
Passé," "La Chance," "L'Avenir." Of these "Le
Passé" and "La Chance" were written in 1901,
and the others appeared in *The Fortnightly
Review* in 1899 and 1900, while only one chapter
of "La Vie des Abeilles" had been separately published. Maeterlinck's popularity was increasing;
he must have begun to feel that a public lay
delighted and expectant about the waters that
flowed, full of tranquillity and refreshment, from
his fountain-pen. Whether for this reason, or
because he was gaining in maturity, his manner
was changing. "Le Temple Enseveli" begins
with the words "Je parle pour ceux qui ne croient
pas à l'existence d'un juge unique." He speaks
with a certain confidence, if not authority. His
style has less silence as well as fewer dots than it

had in "Le Trésor," and probably few strangers to Maeterlinck's development could see in "Trois petits Drames pour Marionnettes" and "Le Temple Enseveli" the work of one and the same man, if it had not been that "L'Évolution du Mystère" contains some criticism of the early plays. The early essays were addressed more to the unconsciousness than to the reason, and they demonstrated nothing. They were likely to stir and encourage those who were not afraid or ashamed of mist and uncertainty: they were certain to be treated as sacramental by coteries and to be brusquely ridiculed by the "no nonsense" school. "Le Temple Enseveli" is different. It addresses everybody and not merely kindred souls, and it does not avoid the intelligence. It says everything, and there is no undertone of silence. It is a work of pure intelligence: intuition and pretence of intuition are absent, and if that bevy of predestined school-fellows was mentioned in it we should expect to hear that 50 per cent. were still living and that the others were not to be traced.

The manner alone has changed. Maeterlinck's mind is occupied or obsessed by the same thoughts, but his curiosity and desire to investigate have increased. If he speaks with more firmness and confidence it is not because he knows more, but because he is older and less pathetic and less easily disturbed. His self-consciousness is the same. At the end of the chapter on the young queens in "La Vie des Abeilles" he reminds us, with a

14

touch of his earlier mystery, that we who judge this " extraordinary fluid " of life are ourselves animated by it, like the friendly and indifferent and hostile forms round about us ; and now again in " La Justice " he comes to an unanswerable question, saying that we ourselves " form part of the mystery we seek to solve." Man, now as a part of Nature, and now as distinct from Nature, is his never-forgotten subject.

His way of thinking is in the main and in many details like that of Richard Jefferies in " The Story of my Heart." In the ninth chapter of that book and onwards Jefferies asseverates that " in human affairs everything happens by chance ; that is, in defiance of human ideas, and without any direction of an intelligence." This gives him ground for hope, because " if the present condition of things were ordered by a superior power, there would be no possibility of improving it for the better in spite of that power," and so, " acknowledging that no such direction exists, all things become plastic to our will." Nothing, he says, has been done for us in the past ; nothing will be done. Man has made the good, and he is responsible for the evil ; he can prevent disease, misery, and perhaps death ; but he has idled and malingered. We must now deliberately begin " to roll back the tide of death, and to set our faces steadily to the future of life," and he exhorts every one " to do their utmost to think outside and beyond our present circle of ideas." And he does not believe in the reason alone.

"Often," he says, "I have argued with myself
that such and such a course was the right one to
follow, while in the intervals of thinking about it
an undercurrent of unconscious impulse has desired
me to do the reverse or to remain inactive, and
sometimes it has happened that the supersensuous
reasoning has been correct, and the most faultless
argument wrong. I presume this supersensuous
reasoning, proceeding independently in the mind,
arises from perceptions too delicate for analysis."

These things are the stuff also of Maeterlinck's
thought. He is more careful and subtle ; Jefferies
is more forcible and passionate, writing "as a dying
man to dying men."

Maeterlinck is not quite able to decide which is
more important, that man is part of Nature, or that
man has separated and fenced himself against
Nature. As in "Monna Vanna" he makes Marco
say that "Life is right," so in "La Justice" he says
that "the lake is right" and not the "curious
incident" of the fountain which man causes it to
feed. He feels that what we call justice is ours
and ours alone, saying that our bodies were made
for the earth, as our minds were made for justice,
and that this human justice is opposed to instincts
planted in us by nature. But he knows also that
this justice is equally "natural." He looks on
benevolently at Nature's cruelty and injustice, not
knowing whether she be "just or unjust" from a
universal point of view, and therefore not condemning her ; but we are not to imitate her—our
only safety is in human justice. The individual

man is opposed to Nature, to his own natural instincts, and also at many points to his own species, which is like "the great unerring lake" of the comparison just mentioned. He is not disturbed even by "the probable futility" of mankind in the history of the solar system. Sadly but eloquently he writes:

"Laissons la force regner dans l'univers et l'équité dans notre cœur. Si la race est irrésistiblement et, je pense, justement injuste, si la foule même paraît avoir des droits que n'a pas l'homme isolé, et commet parfois de grands crimes inévitables et salutaires, le devoir de chaque individu dans la race, le devoir de tout homme dans la foule, est de demeurer juste au centre de toute la conscience qu'il parvient à réunir et à maintenir en lui-même. Nous n'aurons qualité pour abandonner ce devoir que lorsque nous saurons toutes les raisons de la grande injustice apparente; et celles qu'on nous donne: la conservation de l'espèce, la reproduction et la sélection des plus forts, des plus habiles et des 'mieux adaptés,' ne sont pas suffisantes à déterminer un changement si effroyable. Certes, chacun de nous doit tâcher d'être le plus fort, le plus habile, et de s'adapter le mieux possible aux nécessités de la vie qu'il ne peut transformer; mais à considérer les qualités qui le font vaincre, manifestant sa puissance morale et son intelligence, et le rendent réellement heureux, le plus habile, le plus fort, et le 'mieux adapté,' c'est jusqu'ici le plus humain, le plus honnête et le plus juste."

Like Jefferies, he is struck by the fact that a just man drowns as easily as an unjust; like

Jefferies, he inclines not to call poverty an irre-
mediable ill, and asks if it is not we men who
condemn "three-fourths of mankind" to misery.
But even as to storms and the like, he believes
that he has found a human power of foreknowing
them : he asserts in "La Chance" that most ships,
trains, mines, and factories, when destroyed,
contain fewer persons than is usual with them
on days of no danger. Not that he believes the
mind of man constructed to forecast the future,
for he says himself that, when attempting to do so,
it can rarely produce anything "very salutary or
very enduring." Maeterlinck sees two very different facts, and, instead of harmonizing them,
he draws attractive, but perhaps incompatible,
conclusions from both. In the same way he bids
us in one place to labour to improve our standing
in this indifferent universe ; and in another seeks
to discover an unlucky race :

"Ils prennent infailliblement le train qui déraill-
lera, passent à l'heure voulue sous la tour qui
s'écroule, entrent dans la maison où déjà le feu
couve, traversent la forêt que l'éclair va percer,
portent ce qu'ils possèdent au banquier qui va fuir,
font le pas et le geste qu'il ne fallait point faire,
aiment la seule femme qu'ils eussent dû éviter.
Au rebours, s'il s'agit de bonheur, lorsque accourent
les autres, attirés par la voix profonde des forces
bienveillantes, ils passent sans l'entendre, et jamais
prévenus, livrés aux seuls conseils de leur intelligence, le vieux guide, très sage mais à peu près
aveugle, qui ne connaît que les petits sentiers au

pied de la montagne, ils s'égarent dans un monde
que la raison humaine n'a pas encore compris."

These men, he says with characteristic refinement, have a right to complain against destiny,
because they have not been given the instinct
which could have preserved them ; but, he adds,
" the universe is not hostile to them. Calamities
do not pursue them ; it is they who go towards
calamity." For he assumes that these people are
guided solely by intellect, and not by instinct.
But this is a matter of opinion, and cases might
be brought forward to show that many who perish
in accidents were never in one before in the
course of lives which may have been long, or
fortunate, or both ; and that, of those who avoid
fatal or great accidents, many have met countless
little ones or have been wretched without a single
definable misfortune except that of birth. But
Maeterlinck still allows some power to what he
calls chance, and to the superiority of intellect
to instinct or unconsciousness upon occasion.
Like Jefferies, he believes that this unconsciousness
may be developed. He suggests that " the history
of our fortune is the history of our unconscious
being," and that this belief is more encouraging
than the old one that the stars, for example, were
interested in our lives. It would thus be a " proud
consolation " in the direst misfortunes, he thinks,
to know that they come from within and that
they were " perhaps only recording the necessary
form of our own personality." If only, he seems

to believe, if only we could be certain that an event was necessary we should not suffer by it ; but at present this is far from being universally true. His conclusion to this very cunning essay on luck reminds us altogether of Jefferies in its appeal to men to follow all paths leading "from our consciousness to our unconsciousness," because the secret of life lies hidden at the end of those paths.

This same power of man to control events is the chief subject of the essay on the past. He touches no questionable matter, but is content to point out that our past, or its practical value and effect, depends upon what we are and is inevitably changed by this; and what now produces this change without our voluntary co-operation or conscious knowledge can at last, he trusts, be counted among the faculties to be commanded and not obeyed by man. If a man controls his past to-day he does not know how it is done, while very many are controlled by it in such a way that it is above all their other gods. Maeterlinck says that we should consult the past only when we are strong ; we should choose from it and forbid the rest "never to cross our threshold" except under command. A characteristic winged passage follows about the past :

"Comme tout ce qui ne vit en somme qu'aux dépens de notre force spirituelle, il prendra tôt l'habitude d'obéir. Peut-être essayera-t-il d'abord de résister. Il aura recours aux ruses, aux prières. Il voudra nous tenter et nous attendrir. Il nous fera voir des espoirs déçus, des joies qui ne reviendront plus, des reproches mérités, des affections brisées, de l'amour qui est mort, de la haine qui expire, de la foi gaspillée, de la beauté perdue, tout ce qui fut un jour le merveilleux ressort de notre ardeur à vivre, et tout ce que ses ruines recèlent maintenant de tristesses qui nous rappellent, et de bonheurs défunts. Mais nous passerons outre, sans retourner la tête, écartant de la main la foule des souvenirs, comme le sage Ulysse, dans la nuit Cimmérienne, à l'aide de son épée, écartait du sang noir qui devait les faire revivre et leur rendre un instant la parole, toutes les ombres des morts—même celle de sa mère— qu'il n'avait pas mission d'interroger. Nous irons droit à telle joie, à tel regret, à tel remords dont le conseil est nécessaire ; nous irons poser des questions très précises à telle injustice, soit que nous voulions réparer celle-ci s'il est encore possible de le faire ; soit que nous venions demander au spectacle de telle autre que nous avons commise et dont les victimes ne sont plus, la force indispensable pour nous élever au-dessus des injustices que nous nous sentons encore capables de commettre aujourd'hui."

The lover of images who wrote that is Maeterlinck, and no other. Too rarely, for a book whose chief argument should be the convinced spirit of a man, do we feel such certainty. As in " Joyzelle," he utters a caution against hasty conclusions, though in another place he bids us accept the hypothesis most encouraging to "our existence in this life." The metaphysician is admirable, but what of the man ? He speaks out at times in strong but general terms. For example, in " La

Justice" he mentions three among perplexing cases
where the spirit of a race has demanded something
offensive to the individual sense of human justice :
the war of the United States with Spain ; the case
of Dreyfus ; and the war of Great Britain in the
Transvaal. The case of Dreyfus he calls that of
" an innocent man sacrificed to the preponderating
interests of his country " : the Boer war is
" iniquitous." Again, in somewhat remote terms,
he asks whether there may not be something in the
social conditions of to-day as disconcerting to
posterity as the injustice to women revealed in
" The Arabian Nights " ; and a little later he
alludes to the sense of injustice towards those who
are very poor, which must chill the aspirations
of the comfortable class to a better life, when even
the leisure which sets it free " to think more
fraternally of the injustice others endure " is a fruit
of this great " anonymous injustice." Thereupon
Maeterlinck holds up, as a proof of development in
the individual sense of justice, the calmness with
which Marcus Aurelius acknowledged and passed
by the enormous " anonymous injustice " of his
own day. It was, he believes, a calmness beyond
the reach of men with anything like the same
sensitiveness in our day. He quotes the following
passage from the Fourth Book of the " Meditations "
of Marcus Aurelius, with the comment that we are
now concerned with other matters than this perfect
ease and tranquillity :

" They seek for themselves private retiring

places, as country villages, the sea-shore, mountains ; yea, thou thyself art wont to long much after such places. But all this, thou must know, proceeds from simplicity in the highest degree. At what time soever thou wilt, it is in thy power to retire into thyself, and to be at rest, and free from all businesses. A man cannot any whither retire better than to his own soul ; he especially who is beforehand provided of such things within, which whensoever he doth withdraw himself to look in, may presently afford unto him perfect ease and tranquillity."

But there is proof that acquaintance with the great "anonymous injustice" need not destroy the tranquillity of self-culture in a sensitive mind. A book of uncommon consistency and many beauties, written with a still more uncommon curious seeking after felicity, Mr. Robert de la Condamine's "The Upper Garden," contains the following passage :

" Am I, by serving others, the lepers, decadents who choke the hospitals and swoon in the streets, am I, by ministering to those who are only worthy of annihilation, so to reduce my soul until it is purged of all its own responsibilities and fit at length for the ultimate pure nothing, the characterless ether ? Rather will I suffer for the welfare of my spirit's pleasure than be drugged by the disease of others. Rather will I develop my soul and reject all those things that will not do it honour by the increase of sensation and the fullness of material for its possession ; and, if

I fail, I choose to be destroyed through the fault of too great an attempt, and, having risen for a moment to overpowering pinnacles, rather will I travail with a purpose that is too divine than I will squander my powers, however weak and ridiculous they may be, upon needs of which I and all others are ignorant. Rather than debase my personality before the multitude of the blind and the dumb and the diseased, I will develop what spirit I can muster and be lost. Though I may deal with it but weakly, rather will I be wrapped and shrouded in the doom which my power shall earn for itself than I will spend my care on the personalities of all these others who are strangers veiled in mists that yield to no explorer, that are impossible of penetration."

This may be too deliberate and emphatic to be quite sincere in its extremity. It is in the nature of a challenge or a retort. Behind its distemper lies a desire as definite and accessible as the emperor's ; only, the writer has had to exert his will in order to be indifferent to the mass of life which he shuts out from his " upper garden." Other examples might be given, and I am not sure that later men will regard with any great awe, if with credulity, the voice of concern and pity descending out of almost divinely remote altitudes in the writings of Maeterlinck himself. Even so he writes of bees ; even so, perhaps, would his imagined observer from another world regard us. He speaks in one excellent passage in " L'Evolution du Mystère " of ideas, such as those relating to evolution, natural selection, etc., which have not yet "turned into feelings" except in the minds of a few men like John Davidson ; and also of ideas which are "purely ideas." His own ideas are often too remote from feelings. Seldom can he move us by a phrase like : "And truly there goes a great deal of providence to produce a man's life unto threescore." His tone is a shade too noble. For example, he speaks of the crime of the slavery and degradation of women in "The Arabian Nights" as "infinitely more revolting, infinitely more monstrous" than any poverty :

". . . l'esclavage, et surtout l'asservissement de la femme qui, si haute qu'elle soit, et dans le moment même où elle parle aux hommes de bonté et de justice, et leur ouvre les yeux sur leur devoirs les plus touchants et les plus généreux, ne voit pas l'abîme où elle se trouve et ne se dit pas qu'elle n'est qu'un simple instrument de plaisir, qu'on achète, qu'on revend, ou qu'on donne à n'importe quel maître répugnant et barbare, dans un moment d'ivresse, d'ostentation ou de reconnaissance."

Nearly always, when writing of women, he uses this noble tone. But it is an insignificant trick of temper, or perchance a genuine, human accent, which sounds in a very different phrase in "La Chance"—"the chance-governed heart of women." He is speaking of a good but unfortunate man, who had many virtues and a pleasing appearance ; yet, in spite of a loving disposition he was sacrificed by "the chance-governed heart" of women to men far less worthy of being loved. This man is referred to by Maeterlinck as a friend, and it may well be that his warmth has betrayed him into a touch of nature in this phrase, and in another where he speaks of "the paltry snares" prepared for his friend by "malicious fortune" at every step. He is a little less noble, and perhaps a little more natural, in a few other places. "La Règne de la Matière," for example, reveals that he sees a definite though a small reason for hope in the peasant who prefers a book in the orchard on Sunday to the beershop, in the citizen who prefers "a reposeful afternoon" to the racecourse, in the workman who takes a country walk or watches the sunset from the walls of the city instead of singing "obscene or ridiculous" songs in the street. In the same essay he declares calmly in favour of a vegetarian diet and of abstention from alcohol on the ground that they mean a physical and moral improvement ; but I should conclude that he had himself not given up meat or alcohol. These things are not to be despised, but they do not make up the personality which could unite and illumine the great subtlety of "La Justice" and the great wisdom of "L'Évolution du Mystère." The essays are invaluable as contemporary opinion, and the style makes them irresistible ; but they lack foundation. When Maeterlinck was a young man he wrote with the intensity and narrowness incident to youth ; he was a hundred things which could not have been guessed from his writings. He has lost the narrowness and most of the in-

tensity, but I cannot feel that he has yet, in " Le
Temple Enseveli," reached a steadfast, whole,
and mature expression. He is many things, but
he is not yet one. A man, not a writer, of
this type would probably be called deficient in
character.

XIV

"MONNA VANNA" was published, like "Le Temple Enseveli," in 1902, and acted in the same year. It is the first of Maeterlinck's plays to have a precise date--the end of the fifteenth century. Prinzivalle, a mercenary of Florence, is besieging Pisa. He is a dreamer, a Platonist, a lover of beauty. In his childhood he met Monna Vanna, and his love has endured. She, though he touched her heart, has all but forgotten him, and is sleepily happy as the wife of Guido Colonna, a Pisan noble. Prinzivalle is willing to feed the starving Pisans if Monna Vanna, clad only in a mantle, is sent out to his tent at night. He wishes, it might be supposed, to learn whether she is one—for he knows her to be pure in life—who is well enough versed in spiritual love not to regard the body separately, or whether she has become the slave of social circumstances. That a virtuous woman becomes less virtuous by having only a mantle on, is a point that should trouble even a prude or a rake in the proving. Let that pass. Monna Vanna, who has no cause for suspecting Prinzivalle's identity, consents to go. Guido, a high-minded, possibly pure-living man, assumes that her honour is to be sacrificed, although he is told that Prinzivalle loves her. He raves; asks whether no other man's wife will do; declares that "our love has been a mere lie," and that he has "to bear it all"; and in vain orders that she shall be taken to a dungeon, as if she were his property; *i.e.* according to the spirit of the play, which need surprise no reader of "Le Trésor des Humbles," he does not love her utterly.

Prinzivalle loves Monna Vanna with a love to which Joffroy Rudel's was a pleasant whim. He does not lay a finger on her. Slowly she re-members, as he recalls how they first met in a Venetian garden in June. She bethinks her of the spiritual grossness of her marriage, but not until after long argument. Guido has made her "at least as happy as one can be when one has re-nounced the vague and extravagant dreams which seem beyond human life." Very slowly, Prinzi-valle's words disturb the early love, where it lies beneath the thin but heavy veil of married bliss. . . . In the dawn, with one kiss upon his brow, she takes him back to Pisa, to save him from his enemies.

The Pisans, starving no longer, greet Vanna deliriously. But Guido shows no joy; all night he has been planning revenge; he wants to hear from her the sickening tale which he has been telling himself. He pushes her rudely back when she would tell the crowd her story. Hearing that her companion is Prinzivalle, he rejoices. He believes that Vanna has delivered the enemy into his hands. "There is a justice after all": she is "greater than Lucrece or Judith." She explains. At first he thinks that she is mad, then that she loves Prinzivalle; and on the latter thought he orders his enemy to a dungeon, and will see him tortured. Whereupon Vanna lies, for Prinzivalle's sake, and begs that she shall be allowed to torture him, all to herself. Guido believes and consents, and her last words are to him, as he grants her the key of the dungeon:

"'Yes, it has been a bad dream . . . but the beautiful one will begin. The beautiful one will begin.'"

She will escape with Prinzivalle.

The mere outline of this play, like that of "Sœur Béatrice" or "Barbe Bleue," does not reveal much of Maeterlinck: it might have been the work of many other very different dramatists. Nor are the characters at once or obviously exceptional. Guido and his father, Marco Colonna, remain without surprises for us throughout the play. Guido is an ordinary possessive husband, but in a high place, and in an extraordinary position which tests him, and finds him wanting, whatever standard is applied. Marco is more remarkable, but quite credible as an old man of the Renaissance. He is sent to Prinzivalle to attempt to make terms, and he comes back to say that the condition of relief is the surrender of Monna Vanna; but he is in no

15

haste to tell it to Guido, because he has met the Platonist Ficino in the enemy's camp, and has found Prinzivalle a sensitive humanist who loves not war, and he is confident of attuning his son to the same key. Monna Vanna at first is not surprising. When her husband hears that she accepts the painful condition, he thinks that she means to kill Prinzivalle, and then, when she explains that this would mean that the city would not be relieved, he supposes at once that she loves the enemy, and asks, " Since when ? " But no one except Guido would find it impossible to believe that she is surrendering herself only to save the people. Guido threatens to kill her. She only says that he will do it if love commands ; to which he replies, repeating her words contemptuously because she has spoken of love which she does not know. He insults her in his pride and misery. She wants to look into his eyes—as Ablamore did with Astolaine—his eyes, which he has turned away whilst repulsing her. Apparently she sees there the truth—that this man's love is only a frantic, tyrannous affection for a beautiful thing entirely subject to his will and body, that he is one to whom her purity is but a sensual delight.

In the first scene of the second act Prinzivalle is expecting the sign which is to announce that Monna Vanna is coming. He says to his secretary that it is a strange thing that a man will risk his destiny, his reason, and his heart, for a thing as frail as the love of a woman. He is about to have

a happiness which he has been expecting since he
was a child. Evidently this happiness cannot be
the mere physical union with Monna Vanna, against
her will: that could not be "the only happiness
which he has dreamed of since he had dreams. . . ."
Monna Vanna comes in. He asks her if she is
naked under the mantle, and she answers "Yes,"
and also prepares to divest herself, but is checked
by a movement from Prinzivalle. This bold stroke
may be right because it is bold, since a cold
inventor could not have dared so much. Prinzivalle,
however, genuinely surprises us when he points to
his bed and begins to be eloquent about a warrior's
bed, where she will lie upon the skins of aurochs
and rams that are unfamiliar with a thing so sweet
and precious as a woman's body. This speech
suggests rather Maeterlinck's than Prinzivalle's
thoughts upon the occasion. But a moment later
he is on his knees, calling her Vanna as he had
been used to do when he was twelve and she eight.
Vanna's memory slowly and sadly awakens—she
remembers that he went away and never came
back. She reproaches him, that he never found
her out though he loved her; she even says that it
is never too late for one who has found a love
that can fill a life. She, if she had loved so, would
have told destiny—she speaks like Joyzelle—to
move out of her path. Nevertheless, she has
accepted the love that has fallen to her; she loves
Guido with a love less strange than Prinzivalle's,
but more equable, faithful, and sure. He asks her
if she has trembled or hesitated since accepting

this condition and since seeing him : she has not.
He confesses that he had no clear intention when
expecting her, and that a word or gesture would
have inflamed his hate ; but, on seeing her, he
knew at once that this was impossible—and she
also knew no fear, and had even felt that she knew
him though she could not remember how.   They
are talking together, as Vanna says, as though
they were alone on a desert island, and they are in
a solitude magically wrought by memory and first
love.   But she thinks of her husband and his
suffering.   She does not return alone, because
Prinzivalle is warned to fly from treachery.   She
will save him by taking him to Pisa and standing
surety for him.   She is happy at the sight and
sound of Pisa rejoicing, and she gives him " the
only kiss she can give him," upon the brow.

While Pisa is expecting the return of its saviour,
Marco is reasoning with Guido in the accents of
Arkèl, of Aglavaine, ot Merlin, of Maeterlinck
himself.   He urges Guido to make no sudden,
" irrevocable decision," telling him that a man who
wishes to be just can only choose among several
acts of varying injustice, and that for us, " the
playthings of irresistible forces," there is " goodness,
justice, and wisdom " in the mere lapse of time.
But Guido's one aim is to destroy the supposed
ravisher of his wife, and he curses his father.   The
old man, remembering his own youth, accepts this
benignly, asking only to be allowed to wait and
see Vanna throw herself into her husband's arms.
He greets her, and she, throwing herself into his

arms, tells him she is happy. She wishes to tell the crowd, as well as Guido, what has happened ; but he, who has repelled her approach, bids them all go. He forgives Vanna, and applauds her as greater than Lucrece or Judith when he thinks that she has brought in Prinzivalle with treachery, and he anticipates revenge. He tries now to kiss her, but she thrusts him back in order to explain the truth ; for she can now speak not truth only but " the profoundest truth, the truth one speaks only once, that brings life or death in its train." She explains that Prinzivalle loves her, and has therefore spared her. Guido will not believe that he has spared her. At last he thinks that he understands—she loves Prinzivalle ; but still he does not believe her. He offers to let them go away free if she will confess what he is convinced of and is gloating over in the stupefaction of rage and despair. She only repeats that she has spoken the truth, that Prinzivalle did not touch her. This condemns Prinzivalle in the eyes of Guido, whose rage culminates either because she persists in the supposed lie notwithstanding his generosity, or because he now believes her and sees in this mystic chastity something silently condemning himself. Only her simulated revulsion and confession at the last moment gives her the key of her lover's dungeon that she may torture him, as Guido thinks—but in fact that he may escape with her out of the evil dream into a beautiful one. Marco understands, and his judgment is Maeterlinck's : " It is life that is right." In the version of the play prepared for the music of Henry Février a fourth act is added, showing Prinzivalle and Vanna escaping at dawn and disappearing to-gether with all the world and all their life before them.

Marco's judgment that "Life is right" is more terrible than "Necessity is stern," and it is also pedantic. It is Maeterlinck's formula for surrender to the mystery and strength of the infinite. It in no way affects the quality of this brilliant play. Great gifts, including that of good fortune, were needed to make "Monna Vanna" so vivid, moving, and pictorial upon the surface, and at the same time so essentially spiritual. He has done this without any of his old paraphernalia : no towers, vaults, or impassable doors. Even the scene in the tent might have been used by another dramatist with little difference. That Prinzivalle should fall in love with Vanna is easily credible ; but that he—though a man of "dissolute habits" appar-ently—had loved her since early childhood, that she should remember this childish mutual affection, that she should gradually recover it, and at last lose her time-honoured love for her husband under its spreading triumph—this perhaps only Maeter-linck would ask us to believe. And we believe it as we read a scene like this :

V. Vous me connaissez donc ? . . . Qui êtes-vous ? . . .
P. Vous n'avez jamais vu celui qui vous regarde, comme on regarderait, dans un monde de

fées, la source de sa joie et de son existence . . .
comme je n'espérais pas vous regarder un jour ? . . .

V. Non. . . . Du moins je ne crois pas. . . .

P. Oui, vous ne saviez pas . . . et j'étais sûr,
hélas ! que vous ne saviez plus. . . . Or vous
aviez huit ans, et moi j'en avais douze, quand je
vous rencontrai pour la première fois. . . .

V. Où cela ? . . .

P. A Venise, un dimanche de juin. Mon père,
le vieil orfèvre, apportait un collier de perles à
votre mère.—Elle admirait les perles. . . . J'errais
dans le jardin. . . . Alors, je vous trouvai sous un
bosquet de myrtes, près d'un bassin de marbre. . . .
Une mince bague d'or était tombée dans l'eau. . . .
Vous pleuriez près du bord. . . . J'entrai dans le
bassin.—Je faillis me noyer ; mais je saisis la bague
et vous la mis au doigt. . . . Vous m'avez em-
brassé et vous étiez heureuse. . . .

V. C'était un enfant blond nommé Gianello.
Tu es Gianello ? . . .

P. Oui.

V. Qui vous eût reconnu ? . . . Et puis votre
visage est caché par ces linges. . . . Je ne vois que
vos yeux. . . .

P. (écartant un peu les bandages). Me recon-
naissez-vous, lorsque je les écarte ? . . .

V. Oui . . . Peut-être. . . . Il me semble. . . .
Car vous avez encore un sourire d'enfant. . . .
Mais vous êtes blessé et vous saignez aussi. . . .

P. Oh ! pour moi ce n'est rien. . . . Mais pour
vous, c'est injuste. . . .

V. Mais le sang perce tout. . . . Laissez-moi
rattacher ce bandage. . . . Il était mal noué. . . .
(Elle rajuste les linges). J'ai soigné bien souvent
des blessés dans cette guerre. . . . Oui, oui, je me
rappelle. . . . Je revois le jardin avec ses grena-

diers, ses lauriers et ses roses. . . . Nous y avons
joué plus d'une après-midi, quand le sable était
chaud et couvert de soleil.

P. Douze fois, j'ai compté. . . . Je dirais tous
nos jeux et toutes vos paroles. . . .

V. Puis un jour j'attendis, car je vous aimais
bien. Vous étiez grave et doux comme une petite
fille, et vous me regardiez comme une jeune reine.
Vous n'êtes pas revenu. . . .

The phrase, " Vous n'êtes pas revenu," recalls
the " Nous ne nous verrons plus " of " Alladine et
Palomides " ; the whole scene, the fountain and
the lost ring and the girl weeping, recalls " Pelléas
et Mélisande," but with a difference. In the earlier
play the scene had an unreal, vaguely significant
beauty ; in the later one, memory makes the
beauty natural and the significance is genuinely
that of moments not known as priceless until they
are past. In the earlier play he invented the
episode out of an inexperienced love of beauty ;
in the later he seems to have discovered it in life.
Yet it would be possible to see in his first use of
it a beauty as of intuitive divination which is wanting in the second.

From this point there is nothing difficult to
accept, save the moral speeches of Marco, and
these are worthy of a place in Maeterlinck's essays
or on the lips of a formal chorus rather than of a
character in the play. One of the best of critics,
Edouard Schuré, has, in a brief note on " Monna
Vanna," regretted that the escape should be due
to a lie. Maeterlinck's " Life is right " is a con-

venient reply, but there is no need of it. The
critic would not blame Vanna for a lie in her
position, but presumably blames the dramatist for
allowing the best to depend upon the lie. There
is no need to argue in favour of white lies, especially when they are conceived in the utmost
passion of a pure mind ; they are judged white by
those who come after, not by those who profit, and,
it may be, suffer by them. To avoid the lie I
should fear to see the heart's blood of Prinzivalle
and Vanna, and perhaps Guido himself. After
placing his characters in Italy of the fifteenth
century he was bound to provide a conspicuous
and decisive conclusion : a melancholy shutting of
the door would not have been audible among
princes and warriors. If there is a weakness, it is
that Vanna should see a beautiful dream beginning,
and that the dramatist should encourage a feeling
of cheerfulness, when it is certain that, so long as
the revengeful Guido lives, the evil dream will
remain with the lovers. This cheerfulness is less
fitting for two lovers in the fifteenth century than
to-day. In that age two such dream-lovers would
have had little chance of eluding the vengeance of
Guido. . . . But this incongruity is slight, and even
questionable, and is no high price for the triumphant combination of a noble presence and a
delicate spirit in the play. The need for this
combination, which might have to be condemned
by the most austere criticism, is to be sought in
Maeterlinck's character. He is fond of saying that
an old man reading by a lamp may be more tragic

than the " tragic loading of this bed," but his personal taste demands something more—stupendous castles, subterranean vaults, weird forests, strange islands, and now the opulent colour and movement and *morale* of Renaissance life. Whatever the surroundings, they have usually been not so much irrelevant as contrastful, and it is so in "Monna Vanna" also. Two children continue their dream while a city starves and is relieved, and a prince violently laments the loss of his lawful wife.

Like " Sœur Béatrice" and " Joyzelle " this play is an illustration of " La Morale Mystique," and like them, though in a less degree, it has the weakness of using characters belonging to no place or time, unless it be our own ; and, if it be our own, then the picturesque setting is a needless and even unfair distraction. As an artist appealing to audiences of theatres, Maeterlinck has advanced in this play, and has shown himself capable of holding an ordinary stage, whilst remaining faithful in the main to his proper ideals. At the same time he has practically relinquished the aim apparent in his earlier plays of making for these ideals a dramatic scheme peculiarly his own, and, at least by its independence of the world of to-day and yesterday, fit for the exhibition of characters dwelling in the world of his imagination and of the future.

XV

" LE DOUBLE JARDIN " was published in 1904, and it is still farther than its pre-decessor from " Le Trésor des Humbles " and " La Sagesse et la Destinée." The subject and method of the five long essays in " Le Temple Enseveli " gave the book a kind of unity, but " Le Double Jardin " has none. There are sixteen essays, and English translations of most, if not all, had already been published in a dozen different magazines and newspapers. The subjects are a bulldog, Monte Carlo, duelling, the appendicitis of Edward the Seventh, universal suffrage, the modern drama, Rome (for which fortune-telling is substituted in the English edition), a ride in a motor-car, the coming of spring, the bee's temper, field flowers and garden flowers, sincerity, a lady, and the present day. These prove him by far the most brilliant of essayists in this generation, never tedious or banal, always adroit, ingenious, cheerful, impressive, and picturesque.

Naturally enough, these being the subjects and the public that of the magazines, Maeterlinck now reveals more and more of his own tastes and interests. The essay in praise of duelling, for example, reveals him as a man of refinement, who sees vulgarity in the movements of boxing and something repugnant in its effects. "Le Drame Moderne" reveals him as an optimist looking forward to a time when men will have one duty— to do "the least possible harm and love others as we love ourselves." The essay on fortune-telling, or foretelling of the future, reveals him going to test the power of clairvoyants, seers, and mediums. "En Automobile" reveals him as an enthusiastic motorist willing to talk about his motor-car to the public as a "dreadful hippogriff." "Les Sources des Printemps" reveals him as a luxurious lover of nature who finds the cosmopolitan life of the Riviera "somewhat hateful." "Le Mort d'un Petit Chien" reveals him as a genial lover of dogs, who says that in a few days they get into their heads a conception of the universe, while a man takes "thirty or forty" years; who then asks whether, in the eyes of an all-knowing God, the dog's conception would not have the same weight and value as man's. Everywhere, in fact, he appears as a genial man with no extraordinary tastes, who differs from other men chiefly by his subtle refinements of thought and his exuberance and grace of style. From the beginning, however remote, he was never disturbing or exacting; now he is almost uniformly sunny and encouraging, as when he says that "in those problems in which all life's enigmas converge, the crowd which is wrong is almost always justified as against the wise man who is right." He condemns no man. While in one place he seems to look forward to a time when men will be a little lower than the angels, in another he bids us remember that we are "beings of prey and strife," and must be careful not to destroy "the qualities of primitive man, for it was not without reason that Nature placed them there." He could probably be all things to all men and to all editors. I should like to see him writing upon bantams for *The Feathered World*; it would be the most beautiful chapter ever written upon bantams, just as "Éloge de l'Épée" is the most beautiful upon duelling, unless we except Mr. Joseph Conrad's story of "A Point of Honour," which is undoubtedly more instructive. A friend of mine who admires Maeterlinck, but had had too much of "La Sagesse et la Destinée," once dreamed that he was a child again and was corrected at the luncheon-table for his ill-behaviour ; whereto he replied, with a consciousness of being unanswerable : "L'avare seul sait se distraire, et il communique au monde extérieur la cause de sa joie." He communicated it to me as an exquisitely Maeterlinckian product of his unconsciousness, and I feel sure that, if he lives long enough, Maeterlinck will achieve this same apology for the poor avaricious man. He finds what is admirable everywhere, and what is mysterious. The terminology of motoring, for example, he pauses to admire :

" Admirons en passant la terminologie spontanée

et bizarre, mais non pas sotte, qui est comme la langue de la force nouvelle. *L'avance à l'allumage* (qui correspond dans un autre ordre de phénomènes à *l'avance à l'admission* des locomotives), est un terme très juste, et il serait fort difficile d'exprimer plus simplement et plus sensiblement ce qu'il avait à dire. . . . D'où sortent-ils, ces mots qui naissent tout à coup, au moment nécessaire, pour fixer dans la vie les êtres ignorés hier? On ne le sait jamais. Ils s'évadent des ateliers, des usines, des boutiques; ils sont les derniers échos de cette voix commune et anonyme qui a donné un nom aux arbres et aux fruits, au pain et au vin, à la vie et à la mort; et quand les savants les regardent et les interrogent, le plus souvent il est heureusement trop tard pour qui'ils y changent rien."

Again, in his essay on sincerity, he asserts, in his quiet way, that "every man has the right to be what he is"; and, as to faults, he is not as sure as Joyzelle that the greatest fault becomes, by confession, a truth more beautiful than innocence, but he is sure that it is "younger, more vivid, more visible, more active, and more loving." His tender sense of the mystery of life reaches one of its highest points in this same essay:

"Il n'est pas indispensable qu'on se corrige des fautes avouées; car il y a des fautes nécessaires à notre existence et à notre caractère. Beaucoup de nos défauts sont les racines mêmes de nos qualités. Mais la connaissance et l'aveu de ces fautes et de ces défauts précipite chimiquement le venin qui n'est plus au fond du cœur qu'un sel inerte dont on peut étudier à loisir les cristaux innocents."

The simile is characteristically impressive, but the experience of some might lead them to think that it is inaccurately used to describe the effect of admitting faults, if it were not, however, adroitly qualified by the remark that this effect depends on the maker and the receiver of the admission. His is a possible view of sincerity, and with his customary skill he carries it rapidly out of the thick air of experience into the crystal inane, and a section of morals for angels or marionettes is the charming result. Reading this, it is hard to avoid an imperious impatience that Maeterlinck should so seldom attempt in fiction or drama to show us these morals at work, and that, when he does, he should so encumber them with secrecy and external mystery. In "Le Temple Enseveli," and now again in "Le Double Jardin," he repeats what he says in "Le Trésor des Humbles," that the modern stage has no need of the old violence and magnificence. "It is in a small room," he says, "round a table, close to the fire, that the joys and sorrows of mankind are decided." His own use of a silent, small room in "L'Intruse" and "Intérieur" is perfectly justified, but these plays are hidden away by the castles in the moon of the early plays, the marvels of "Barbe Bleue" and "Joyzelle," and the brilliant Renaissance setting of "Monna Vanna." He returns again to the question in "Les Rameaux d'Olivier." There he says that we are now emerging from a great religious period, and that the "gloomy and threatening" background of human life is disappearing. With good reason he believes that, nevertheless, the justice, the goodness, and "the quality of the general conscience" have increased. But he asks to what religion this improvement can be attributed. He thinks it due in part to increased knowledge, by means of which "the universe is beginning to penetrate into the conception which we form of it." Before this age of science he thinks that men were merely "prosing," with logic or imagination as their instrument, instead of knowledge and inquiry. True, we now have no fixed morality, no defined consolation, promise, or hope. The sense of our littleness has grown, and the power which enables us to perceive it has also grown. But then, if the importance of the individual is diminishing, that of humanity has increased, and the feeling of the greatness of humanity "is fashioning our morality" and preparing great changes. We are, perhaps, to have that sense of race which in the honey-bee swallows up egoism. Furthermore, Maeterlinck sees many new reasons for hope. The greatest dangers to man upon the earth "seem past"; he even hints that we shall have the respite of a few centuries, necessary for learning how to avoid collision with a stray star. We may even learn to understand gravitation. In short, we have grounds for magnificent expectations:

"Car nous sommes dans l'état magnifique où Michel-Ange a peint, sur ce prodigieux plafond de la chapelle Sixtine, les prophètes et les justes

de l'Ancien Testament : nous vivons dans l'attente ;
et peut-être dans les derniers moments de l'attente.
L'attente, en effet, a des degrés qui vont d'une sorte
de résignation vague et qui n'espère pas encore au
tressaillement que suscitent les mouvements les
plus proches de l'objet attendu. Il semble que
nous entendions ces mouvements : bruit de pas
surhumains, porte énorme qui s'ouvre, souffle qui
nous caresse ou lumière qui vient, on ne sait ; mais
l'attente à ce point est un instant de vie ardent et
merveilleux, la plus belle période du bonheur, sa
jeunesse, son enfance."

This magnificent expectation is clad in suitable
magnificence by Maeterlinck, but the matter of it
is fit rather to give a sad pride than either consolation or tranquillity. This is not a new subject,
and we are justly exacting in our criticism of who-
ever handles it. It used to be said that science was
destroying poetry and religion—as if science could
destroy anything that was still worth having! Poetry
itself has continued to be indifferent to the asser-
tion, and to offer refutation only by its triumphant
existence. Mr. Charles M. Doughty, Mr. Yeats,
Mr. W. H. Davies, Mr. Walter de la Mare—to name
only the first poets that come into my mind—do
so refute it. As to religion, an interesting book
has lately been written—"The Ascending Effort,"
by Mr. George Bourne—upon a text from a speech
by Sir Francis Galton upon Eugenics, where he
said that "if the principles he was advocating were
to become effective, they 'must be introduced into
the national conscience, like a new religion.'" Mr.

Bourne is not particularly concerned with Eugenics, but with the whole problem of art and science, of the vitalizing of science, of the broadening of art, and of the relations between the two. The word "religion" used by Sir Francis Galton does not, he thinks, stand for any one doctrine, but for "a certain activity of the vital energies," which is the same sort of activity in all religions:

"In partial manifestation, and under various names, the vital activity required is already familiar to us. We recognize it in reverence, faithfulness, sympathy, admiration: forms which lend themselves to treatment, and by known methods. And although it may be difficult to specialize our efforts so that enthusiasm shall flow in one particular direction, still, as enthusiasm is a form of vital force, the task is one for which we cannot pretend to lack the means. The means are summed up in the one word Art. The energies of the race may always be warmed by art."

Mr. Bourne's argument that "the intoxicating power of art" is what is needed to give effect to the doctrines of science is impressively supported by the reasoning and restrained emotion of a man whom we learn to trust, though when he says that "Art must adapt itself to the new philosophy" we can only reply that there are no "musts" in the future, but an infinite "may." This book has probably been the life-work of an artist without the slightest tinge of professionalism, and seems to be the meeting-place of all or many of the forces in a keen, sober, and mature life. It has a force of personality behind it stronger than that behind Maeterlinck's eloquence, but in neither forecast is there force enough to atone altogether for the lack of any showing how the thing will or may be done.

John Davidson's later work, his crude and furious pamphlets in verse, showed how a brave poet could fail and could cease to be a poet in attempting to do with his one mind what no one mind had ever done before—to face contemporary life and science and invent a new cosmogony better suited to its needs. His King Mammon told his wife, in phrases that might have been Maeterlinck's :

> Nothing is greater anywhere than us :
> We form the matter of the farthest star,
> The matter of the earth, the sea, the sky.

Addressing his soldiers, this King longs to be on top of Everest, and heard of all men :

> The parasites that in our bodies burrow ;
> The lily and the rose, whose passionate breath
> Perfumes our love-thoughts with the scent of love ;
> The tawny brutes whose anguished roar appals
> The desert and the jungle—they that suck
> The steaming blood and tear the shuddering flesh
> Of timid, browsing beasts . . .
> The woodland and the mountain and the sea ;
> The myriad suns that pave the Milky Way . . .
> All these—all that, is us, is you and me,
> The conscience of the infinite universe.
> No supernatural thought must cloud your minds.

Nor is such a roaring hot Utopia more encouraging than the frigid quiet of Vernon Lee's book on "Gospels of Anarchy": "I propose nothing, because I do not know. All I feel sure of is, that if people want a change sufficiently, strongly, and persistently, that change will work out its means in one way or another"; though even she is willing to believe that "the more we let nature work for us, the more we employ our instincts and tendencies, instead of thwarting them, the less will be the waste and the greater the achievement." Maeterlinck says materially little more than this, but he communicates a sense of the mystery and greatness of man and of human life which does some, perhaps, of the very work which he is powerless to define.

On the whole he is confident, and might be called an optimist if the word retained any value. He is confident about the future of the world and of man. He believes in universal suffrage, and is sure that "the harmonious use of liberty is acquired only by a long misuse of its benefits." Speaking on this subject, he varies a favourite phrase by saying that the natural appetite of a democracy, like that of every living thing, knows what is "indispensable to the mystery of life." He believes that the crannies are widening in the wall between reason, that knows "scarcely anything," and instinct "which knows all, but cannot make use of the knowledge." In the portrait of a lady he shows that he can still write of women with enthusiasm while averting his face, and he

speaks of one who has for ornament all the
passions and weaknesses of woman, asking how
she could be beautiful if she did not know mirrors.
It is worth noticing that something of the early
Maeterlinck survives. For example, he writes of
the fears of his dog in the solitude of night just as
he used to write of men :

" On se sent très petit et très faible en présence
du mystère. On sait que l'ombre est peuplée
d'ennemis qui se glissent et attendent. On suspecte
les arbres, le vent qui passe et les rayons de la lune.
On voudrait se cacher et se faire oublier en
retenant son souffle."

And to make the dog's friendliness more impressive he emphasizes the solitude of man upon
this planet in something like his old manner. It
can be seen in the chapter on field-flowers, where
he speaks of the pale earliest spring blossoms as
" anæmic captives " and as " convalescent patients,"
out of the " prisons " under the earth. The very
early Maeterlinck may perhaps be at the bottom
of a phrase which speaks of birds, precious stones,
and woman together as " ornaments of our planet,"
teaching man that things may be at once useless
and beautiful—phrases such as now and then
suggest a man rather different from the noble and
exalted prose-writer of most of these essays. And
in a passage already quoted, where he speaks of
the great expectations of humanity and the images
of superhuman footsteps sounding, of a great
door opening and light appearing to imprisoned

men, we are reminded of the light coming to
Maleine in her tower or to Alladine and Palomides
in their dungeon. Instead of ghastly, concealed
queens and sunless castles he now sees life as
threatened by the morality of nature, " horrible "
and " monstrous," which would destroy men if
they practised it entirely. When it suits him he
will write as if he had never scorned the false
old mysteries with which poets yet chill our
blood ; will speak, for instance, of Edward the
Seventh, lying ill of appendicitis, as an " illustrious "
victim of " a whim " of fate " hovering between
the crown and death." The whole essay is a
tissue of gaudy and almost tawdry eloquence : the
king, who had not been crowned though he was
king in every sense, is described as about to
attain " the sole object, the essential moment " of
his life ; and it is surmised that this " royal tragedy "
proves the impotence of man's love, prayers, and
" finest moral forces " against the will of nature.
These tones remind me of one whom I had never
thought to connect in any way with Maeterlinck.
Preaching upon the occasion of the sudden death
of the Duke of Albany in 1884, and taking as his
text, " For what is life ? It is even a vapour, that
appeareth for a little time, and then vanisheth
away," the late C. H. Spurgeon began his sermon :

" When a prince dies they toll the great bell
of the cathedral that all the city may hear it, and
that for miles round the tidings may be spread.
Swift messengers of the press bear the news

through the length and breadth of the land, and all men's ears are made to tingle. A *royal* death is a national warning. A death in any one of our families is a loud call to our household, a call which I trust we hear ; but a death in the royal family has a voice to the whole nation. It will be heard, it must be heard. In this great city the crowds who care not to come to the house of God, will nevertheless hear of this lamented death, and think of it, and speak of it each man to his fellow. Death is an orator whose solemn periods demand attention, especially when he preaches from the steps of the throne."

There are many differences between these two orators, but they agree alike in their theatrical use of the two panoplied phantoms, Royalty and Death. It was in this same spirit that, in " Le Temple Enseveli," Maeterlinck spoke of an event which seemed to begin a series of pitiful events as " no less tragic than that of Thyestes," and of his destiny hovering "like an enormous vulture" over the victim. He is easily carried away by these things into a thrilling but ultimately absurd eloquence. Nowhere is he more completely carried away than in the essay in praise of duelling as a method of securing justice such as no judge or magistrate can enforce. Nobody claims that any-thing more than a stiff and indelicate kind of justice is to be had from the law, nor denies that a sword or other deadly weapon seems, upon some occasions and for the moment, to some tempera-ments and in some countries, to be likely to give to one party as full a satisfaction as possible.

Maeterlinck himself has already pointed out incidentally some of its injustices—for example, to our "unlucky" friend who was a good swordsman. But Maeterlinck likes the beauty of the sword— he contrasts it with the vulgarity of the fist— and he composes a eulogy. The sword decides, "from the point of view of inexplicable life," whether a man is wrong or right. He admits that it might be better, in most cases decided by duelling, for the law to intervene, and yet he thinks the present state of things good " for those capable of defending themselves," because hereby initiative and personal character are preserved. This man, who is so sensible of the mystery and subtlety of life and the unintelligible gloom of nature, now for the sake of argument asserts that most of the wrongs done in the world are due to " the certainty of impunity" and to the superabundance of " good-natured souls " in the world. But this inconsistency is hardly to be noticed in a piece of reckless and occasional advocacy, composed perhaps in a genial hour for a society to promote duelling. The sword, he points out, enables the little man to confront and obtain justice from the enormous man. All that is necessary is to reach a general average of skill. The passage following is too brilliant not to quote it for those who have not great imagination or the good fortune to dream in the manner of Maeterlinck, like my friend :

"Cette moyenne atteinte, nous pouvons confier notre vie à la pointe de la frêle mais redoutable lame. Elle est la magicienne qui établit aussitôt des rapports nouveaux entre deux forces que nul n'aurait songé à comparer. Elle permet au nain qui à raison de tenir tête au colosse qui a tort. Elle conduit gracieusement sur des sommets plus clairs l'énorme violence aux cornes de taureau ; et voici que la bête primitive est obligée de s'arrêter devant une puissance qui n'a plus rien de commun avec les vertus basses, informes et tyranniques de la terre, je veux dire : le poids, la masse, la quantité, la cohésion stupide de la matière. Entre elle et le poing il y a l'épaisseur d'un univers, un océan de siècles et presque la distance de l'animal à l'homme. Elle est fer et esprit, acier et intelligence. Elle asservit le muscle à la pensée, et contraint la pensée à respecter le muscle qui la sert. Elle est idéale et positive, chimérique et pleine de bons sens. Elle est éblouissante et nette comme l'éclair, insinuante, insaisissable et multiforme, comme un rayon de lune ou de soleil. Elle est fidèle et capricieuse, noblement rusée, loyalement perfide. Elle fleurit d'un sourire la rancune et la haine. Elle transfigure la brutalité. Grâce à elle, comme par un féerique pont suspendu sur l'abîme de ténèbres, la raison, le courage, l'assurance du bon droit, la patience, le mépris du danger, le sacrifice à l'amour, à l'idée—tout un monde moral, entre en maître dans le chaos originel, le dompte et l'organise. Elle est, par excellence, l'arme de l'homme ; celle qui, toutes les autres éprouvées et elle-même inconnue, devrait être inventée, parce qu'elle sert le mieux les facultés les plus diverses, les plus purement humaines, et qu'elle est l'instrument le plus direct, le plus maniable et le plus loyal de son intelligence, de sa force et de sa justice défensives,"

Maeterlinck concludes that the swords force the destinies of the two duellists to judge them. What he means is that, if a man dies by his opponent's sword, his death was inevitable : he may not have been wrong in the matter which was being decided, but on the whole he must have been in the wrong because his unconsciousness has not found a way of saving him. "Life," as he has said elsewhere, "life is right."

The essay on chrysanthemums is of a like eloquence. He loves the chrysanthemum and takes a "brother's interest" in it because of its singular submissiveness to the perverse multiplication of forms. He concludes by saying that "perhaps," "if" plants are to reveal "one of the worlds that we are awaiting," the chrysanthemum will do it as the dog will "probably" reveal another. But for this passage the essay would be an entirely brilliant specimen of the studied rhapsodies of description which he began in "La Vie des Abeilles." For the most part these descriptions are sensuous, and devoted to the very surfaces of beautiful or sublime objects ; but they owe part of their quality to a highly characteristic, quite unmistakable use of the pathetic fallacy. Every one will recognize Maeterlinck in the comparison of the rare pink of chrysanthemums with that on the lips and brows of a "veiled and afflicted virgin praying on a tomb." The chapters on field-flowers and old-fashioned garden flowers are perfect examples of this descriptive work. As in all his writings, the soft, sensuous grace is unmitigated except by astonishing brilliancy. Though so fine, and probably studied, these essays are very simple, being no more than a chain of beautiful details, wrought with no pattern, but gaining such unity as they have from a lively, æsthetic impetus and from the slightest and most picturesque of reflections. The essay on field-flowers is hardly more than a number of old, pretty names and a still greater number of adjectives almost as pretty. At the end of one chain of names he writes :

" On récite un poème de grâce et de lumière en les énumérant. On leur a réservé les sons les plus aimables, les plus purs, les plus clairs et toute l'allégresse musicale de la langue. On dirait les *dramatis personæ*, les coryphées et les figurantes d'une immense féerie, plus belle, plus imprévue et plus surnaturelle que celles qui se déroulent dans l'îsle de Prospéro, à la cour de Thésée ou dans la forêt des Ardennes. Et les jolies actrices de la comédie muette et infinie : déesses, anges, démones, princesses et sorcières, vierges et courtisanes, reines et pastourelles, portent aux plis de leurs noms le magique reflet d'innombrables aurores, d'innombrables printemps contemplés par des hommes oubliés, comme elles y portent aussi le souvenir de milliers d'émotions profondes ou légères qu'éprouvèrent devant elles des générations disparues sans laisser d'autre trace."

He is as courtly as Herrick, and as dainty and lacking in wildness. Whether he writes of garden or field he never suggests anything but the delicacy of the *hortus inclusus* and the conservatory. For, in spite of his feeling for the majesty of mysterious Nature, he could never write, like Mr. W. H. Hudson, of the "mysterious, unheard-of retributions that revengeful deity Nature" may meditate against those who have spoiled "her ancient, beautiful order." He likes flowers, above all, for their long human associations. He bids us consider how much we should lose in expressing happiness if we had not flowers to help us :

"Une des cimes bénies de notre âme serait presque muette si les fleurs, depuis des siècles, n'avaient alimenté de leur beauté la langue que nous parlons et les pensées qui tentent de fixer les heures les plus précieuses de la vie. Tout le vocabulaire, toutes les impressions de l'amour sont imprégnés de leur haleine, nourris de leur sourire. Quand nous aimons, les souvenirs de toutes les fleurs que nous avons vues et respirées, accourent peupler de leurs délices reconnues la conscience d'un sentiment dont le bonheur, sans elles, n'aurait plus de forme que l'horizon de la mer ou du ciel. Elles ont accumulé en nous, depuis notre enfance, et dès avant celle-ci, dans l'âme de nos pères, un immense trésor, le plus proche de nos joies, où nous allons puiser, chaque fois que nous voulons nous rendre plus sensibles les minutes clémentes de la vie. Elles ont créé et répandu dans notre monde sentimental l'atmosphère odorante où se complait l'amour."

In none of his work so much as in these de-scriptions can his Flemish brightness, precision, and domesticity be seen. We have nothing in our literature that can be more nearly compared with them than the " Frondes Agrestes" and "Love's Meinie " of Ruskin ; but Maeterlinck's essays have a gaiety and simple sensuousness which these have not.

XVI

THREE years after "Le Double Jardin," in 1907, "L'Intelligence des Fleurs" was published. In the English translation, entitled "Life and Flowers," the essay on Rome, which was excluded from "The Double Garden," now appears. In addition there are essays on the various instruments for measuring time, on immortality, war, social duty, "L'Inquiétude de notre Morale," the psychology of accident, boxing, "King Lear," the intelligence of flowers, and on scents and their manufacture. The volume resembles its predecessor in variety of subject and uniformity of tone. On any page may be found a phrase which suggests the whole book. For example, I might take, as the keynote, two sentences at the opening of "L'Inquiétude de notre Morale." In one he speaks of the "great truth," that it is the duty of those who have to reduce themselves to the condition of those who have not ; in the other he says that this is an "absolute impossibility." Well may he speak in this essay of examining the question like "the unbiased denizen" of another planet.

But he is not solely this. As in all the later essays, he frequently shows himself very much an inhabitant of this world. The combination is a remarkable one, and it produces what appears to be this—worldly thoughts and descriptions somehow mysticized. The true inwardness of eating bread and cheese and pickled shallots and drinking a pint of stout would not be a surprising subject for this mystic man of the world.

"L'Intelligence des Fleurs" shows him experimenting for nearly four years in the hybridization of different kinds of sage; having his first "satisfying vision of happiness" in a country where nothing is cultivated but flowers for making scents ; and admiring "a certain magnificent oak" so much that he says it would not be out of place in any paradise or after-life imaginable. He is still, as in "Le Double Jardin," fundamentally at ease with himself and such of the world as he must or chooses to see. He preserves the same starry urbanity when he remarks that it would be "interesting to calculate" whether a sudden bloody revolution would involve more or fewer evils than a slow, nagging one ; and, having made the remark, he passes on to point out, in the same tones, that the human race now "seems to be in the decisive phase of its evolution" ; but let it always be borne in mind that Maeterlinck is personally a kindly and charitable man. Perhaps a new reason for his comfortableness is that he now perceives that we are not after all "miraculous, unparalleled, and marvellously incidental beings" in an alien earth, as we used proudly to think, but that in reality we follow " the same road as the soul of this great world," where we are quite in place. This marks almost a revolution in his thought, but he makes no comment whatever upon it. Observation of the ways and thoughts of flowers has taught him to believe this, and the lessons of the flowers may, he thinks, be as nothing compared with those to come from the mountains, the sea, and the stars :

" Ils nous permettent néanmoins de présumer avec plus d'assurance que l'esprit qui anime toutes choses ou se dégage d'elles est la même essence que celui qui anime notre corps. S'il nous ressemble, si nous lui ressemblons ainsi, si tout ce qui se trouve en lui, se retrouve en nous-mêmes, s'il emploie nos méthodes, s'il a nos habitudes, nos préoccupations, nos tendances, nos désirs vers le mieux, est-il illogique d'espérer tout ce que nous espérons instinctivement, invinciblement, puisqu'il est presque certain qu'il l'espère aussi ? Est-il vraisemblable, quand nous trouvons éparse dans la vie une telle somme d'intelligence, que cette vie ne fasse pas œuvre d'intelligence, c'est-à-dire ne poursuive une fin de bonheur, de perfection, de victoire sur ce que nous appelons le mal, la mort, les ténèbres, le néant, qui n'est probablement que l'ombre de sa face ou son propre sommeil ? "

No one who has followed Maeterlinck's development will fail to see that here is, or should be, a prodigious access of reason for optimism ; no one will fail to notice, and few will be surprised, that the new idea is one of those which are "purely ideas" to him. All now is right with the world. But what matters it? Maeterlinck is on another planet.

He is, however, as willing as ever to think of the case of mortals, and particularly of those to whom the old religions of the earth consciously mean nothing. He assumes, perhaps rashly, that we are in an exceptional position—*i.e.* that we are abandoning one religion and have no other before us —though it is by no means certain, first, that many pagans of the last three or four centuries before Christ were not in a similar position; and, second, that we are not really entering another religion half consciously, as pagan souls, *naturaliter Christianæ*, must often have done. He also exaggerates our "feverish elaboration" of a premature morality to take the place of religion. It is true that we discuss our morality more than ever, because we are more self-conscious; but in the morality that is really valid, that which controls our acts and our judgments of things near us, we are, with a difference, what men have been for some time, heirs of Christianity and of paganism. In spite of Nietzsche, we do not really ask ourselves if we are not dupes by practising a "noble morality" in a world which—as Maeterlinck still says—"obeys other laws"; or, if we ask this, we act without reference to the question, and as if it had never been put. Maeterlinck himself sees that we have, in our "mystic reason," a possession

17

perhaps equivalent to a religion.   What he means
by this may be gathered from any book of his
essays, from the first to the last ; but here in the
essay on our anxious morality he again makes it
clear :

"C'est dans notre raison, consciente ou non, que
se forme notre morale.   On pourrait, à ce point de
vue, y marquer trois régions.   Tout au bas, la
partie la plus lourde, la plus épaisse et la plus
générale, que nous appellerons le 'sens commun.'
Un peu plus haut, s'élevant déjà aux idées d'utilité
et de jouissance immatérielles, ce qu'on pourrait
nommer le 'bon sens,' et enfin, au sommet, admet-
tant, mais contrôlant aussi sévèrement que possible
les revendications de l'imagination, des sentiments
et de tout ce qui relie notre vie consciente à
l'inconsciente et aux forces inconnues du dedans
et du dehors, la partie indéterminée de cette même
raison totale à laquelle nous donnerons le nom de
'raison mystique.' "

He sees the "mystic reason" offered to the "good
sense" of a scientific age, here again perhaps
exaggerating the novelty of "good sense," which
must be a kind of wisdom used since very ancient
times by persons without imagination, and even by
those with it when they themselves were not
immediately concerned.   Good sense tends probably to advance by additions from the mystic
reason, and the difference between the good sense
of 1911 and 1811 gives this probability much support.   Maeterlinck himself believes in a spiritual
wave, with ebbs and flows, "which seems slowly to

overtake and conquer we know not what in space,"
but does not think that the average of goodness
was raised by the movements in the Middle Ages
when faith was strong with a certainty like that of
"our scientific certainties." And at last he pleads
for the preservation of a few "fancy pictures,"
herein reminding us of the poet's speech in Mr.
W. B. Yeats's " King's Threshold " :

> If you are a poet,
> Cry out that the king's money would not buy,
> Nor the high circle consecrate his head,
> If poets had never christened gold, and even
> The moon's poor daughter, that most whey-faced metal,
> Precious: and cry out that none alive
> Would ride among the arrows with high heart,
> Or scatter with an open hand, had not
> Our heady craft commended wasteful virtues.

If we are no longer to be saints and martyrs, says
Maeterlinck, we have need of their spirit, and he
ends in confidence :

"Ce ne sont point les religions qui ont formé
cet idéal ; mais bien celui-ci qui a donné naissance
aux religions. Ces dernières affaiblies ou disparues,
leurs sources subsistent qui cherchent un autre cours.
Tout compte fait, à la réserve de certaines vertus
factices et parasites qu'on abandonne naturellement
au tournant de la plupart des cultes, il n'y a encore
rien à changer à notre vieil idéal aryen de justice,
de conscience, de courage, de bonté et d'honneur.
Il n'y a qu'à s'en rapprocher davantage, à le serrer
de plus près, à le réaliser plus efficacement ; et,

avant de le dépasser, nous avons une longue et noble route à parcourir sous les étoiles."

In this way, as elsewhere, he advocates the instinct, the imagination, the unconsciousness, by means of the intelligence which he esteems so far beneath them ; he is, in fact, trying to persuade the intelligence to encourage its superior, to prove that there is a higher expediency in what may seem to it inexpedient. Nowhere is his use of the pure reason more remarkable than in the essay on immortality. He has not one profound intimation or conviction with which to support his argument. He begins by reminding us that nothing can perish. We are bound to survive, but can the manner of the survival be of any comfort or pride ? What we wish to survive is that part of us " which used to perceive phenomena " when we were alive. If that goes we shall not know that we are. Yet this desire he compares with that of a sick man to continue in his sickness lest he should not recognize himself. He asks us to think of a man who is blind, paralysed, and deaf, but dreading death with a great despair ; and to suppose that, by a miracle, he could suddenly see and hear the glory of the earth and move amidst it. " At what corner of his past" will this man "clutch to continue his identity " ? Yet something—" some sense or in-stinct"—would tell him that he was the man who was blind, paralysed, and deaf. The power by which he would know this is lost in sleep, in pain, in intoxication, in moments of self-forgetfulness.

In eternity should we not be loth, like Christopher Sly, "to fall into our dreams again"—so Maeterlinck asks; and he asks, too, if many would not be glad to accept a sleep of a hundred years with the certainty of awaking at the end of it. Yet between this and death there would be small difference. Also he reminds us that many do not despair when they see others, or think of themselves, in the abeyance of our mental and physical faculties in old age, or even when they consider the disintegration of the body. He then reminds us of some of the "irrefutable" proofs that something does continue in some cases for a time after death. Also, if we do not perish we have lived before, yet we do not remember it, and the uncertainty of it is indifferent to us. He suggests that there is another consciousness which may be part of us before and after life, etc. It is entered in moments when—

"Il demeure en nous quelque chose d'absolument désintéressé qui goûte le bonheur d'autrui. N'est-il pas également possible que les joies sans but de l'art, la satisfaction calme et pleine où nous plonge la contemplation d'une belle statue, d'un monument parfait, qui ne nous appartient pas, que nous ne reverrons jamais, qui n'excite aucun désir sensuel, qui ne peut nous être d'aucune utilité; n'est-il pas possible que cette satisfaction soit la pâle lueur d'une conscience différente qui filtre à travers une fissure de notre conscience mnémonique?"

This is his nearest approach to an intuition, that there may be an existence accessible, even during life, which is "more spacious" than that of our ordinary consciousness, as if we had—

> The cloudy winds to keep
> Fresh for the opening of the morning's eye.

Let us admit this possibility, and strive to know what it is in us that will survive. This is no more than Richard Jefferies' belief in "a whole world of ideas outside and beyond those which now exercise us"; to cultivate the soul because, so long as it lives, "it matters not if the entire material world disappears." Jefferies in a passionate, if imperfect, mystic ecstasy, prayed for "the deepest of soul-life, the deepest of all, deeper far than all this greatness of the visible universe, and even of the invisible." He, like Maeterlinck, hated asceticism. He, like Maeterlinck, thought that there were other alternatives than the sequence of cause and effect. He also exhorted men "to do their utmost to think outside and beyond our present circle of ideas." He also marvelled that until now the soul, "the keenest, the sharpest tool possessed by man," had been left uncultivated. He felt a sympathy in the universe when he wrote: "The sea thinks for me as I listen and ponder: the sea thinks, and every boom of the wave repeats my prayer"—a feeling which Maeterlinck does not reveal. His passionate autobiography has a force almost equalling a revelation: Maeterlinck's essay is a subtle and eloquent recommending of a cool possibility.

He treats another favourite subject with all his

usual adroitness and subtlety in an essay on the psychology of accident. It is an elaboration of the idea suggested by the fact that a child or a drunken man falls with less danger to himself than a sober man who tries to save himself by his intelligence. He believes that we are losing this admirable instinct, and that a workman has more chances than his educated employer if both are in the same physical disaster. Here again he proposes that by " special study " the instinct should be educated and restored. He makes no suggestion as to how this can come to pass. To educate the instinct by means of a power which is overcoming it, and is jealous of it, may be a difficult task ; and in the course of the essay a story is told to show how fatal may be this interference of the intelligence with the instinct. A cart full of women was rushing down a precipitous hill, apparently to certain ruin, and one woman thought to save at least her child by throwing it out. The cart fell over the precipice, but the women were all saved by the bushes on the face of the cliff : only the child was killed by its fall on the wayside. The instinct of the women saved them ; the intelligent forethought of the mother destroyed her child. Such is Maeterlinck's account of the matter, and very good it is ; but a few qualifications should be added. First, it was the venerable maternal instinct which interrupted the still older instinct of self-preservation, and caused the mother to throw out the child. Second, it might well have been expected that the child would fall right by instinct.

Third, if the woman had fallen over the cliff with the child in her arms, it is likely that the burden would have prevented her from acting perfectly according to instinct, and both would have perished.   At the conclusion of the essay he makes a statement which may be compared with his new view that man and nature have the same methods and aims.   He points out that, in an earthquake or a thunderstorm, or the fall of a tree, an animal rather than a man will be struck. This he oddly attributes first to man's reason and "more prudent instinct," and finally to the fact that nature "seems to be afraid of man," surrounding him "with a sort of manifest and unaccountable respect."   If this were not a mere bland extravagance, Maeterlinck's thought would have followed very different lines.   Compare with this another but more excusable extravagance, in a rhapsody of pure rhetoric, on the "Gods of War," viz. melinite, dynamite, panelastite, cordite, etc.   Thinking of these, he says that man has abdicated ; his reign is over; he is at the mercy of these "monstrous and enigmatic powers."   But, except De Quincey or Victor Hugo, perhaps no other could have written it.

The essay in praise of boxing must rank with that in praise of the sword for ingenuity.   It was written for the summer holidays, when it is fitting "to occupy ourselves with the aptitudes of our body, once more restored to nature."   He admits that, in writing of the sword, his subject carried him away into an injustice to the fist.   The fist is, he says, our natural weapon, like the bull's horns, and a wiser race would make it the only legal weapon, which would bring about "a sort of panic-stricken respect of human life." He paints a picture of a skilled boxer serene among enemies who cannot box: "The grossest insult cannot impair his indulgent smile," and if he is forced to use his power against "the most powerful brute," it is with a sense of shame and a regret for the "too-easy victory." This is by far the most genial and amusing thing Maeterlinck has ever written, but it leaves a doubt as to whether it was meant to be amusing. There is equal ingenuity in the essay on sundials, clocks, etc., and a graceful rhetoric which he has nowhere excelled. The following page is one of the best from his contemplative-descriptive writings:

"La pendule, le sablier, la clepsydre perdue donnent des heures abstraites, sans forme et sans visage. Ce sont les instruments du temps anémié de nos chambres, du temps esclave et prisonnier ; mais le cadran solaire nous révèle l'ombre réelle et palpitante de l'aile du grand dieu qui plane dans l'azur. Autour du plateau de marbre qui orne la terrasse ou le carrefour des larges avenues et qui s'harmonise si bien aux escaliers majestueux, aux balustrades éployées, aux murailles de verdure des charmilles profondes, nous jouissons de la présence fugitive mais irrécusable des heures radieuses. Qui sut apprendre à les discerner dans l'espace, les verra tour à tour toucher terre et se pencher sur l'autel mystérieux pour faire un sacrifice au dieu que l'homme honore mais ne peut pas connaître.

Il les verra s'avancer en robes diverses et changeantes, couronnées de fruits, de fleurs ou de rosée : d'abord celles encore diaphanes et à peine visibles de l'aube ; puis leurs sœurs de midi, ardentes, cruelles, resplendissantes, presque implacables, et enfin les dernières du crépuscule, lentes et somptueuses, que retarde, dans leur marche vers la nuit qui s'approche, l'ombre empourprée des arbres."

The long chapter on the intelligence of flowers is another exercise of the same kind. He says that he is merely going to recall "a few facts known to every botanist," but he proceeds to describe some of the adventures of plant-life in such a way that the description is an argument for the intelligence of the plants. One plant has "discovered," another has "calculated"; one is "restless," another is "thoughtless." The presumption of these words must be held unpardonable until it is believed, as well as stated in cold blood, that man's equipment and destiny are not singular among living things. Maeterlinck finds it consoling to observe that we follow the same road as the plants, "as the soul of this great world." The term "mystic" is not to be dwelt on too seriously, because it is now in an advanced stage of popular corruption. Yet the acceptance of science by a man to whom it is widely applied is remarkable. Maeterlinck is the first "mystic," though not the first mystical writer, to appear in the age of science; and he is all the more important because he really belongs to the age. He is not, however, always a mystic and a man of science at once, and there are times when he seems to be striving to look at scientific facts in a poetical manner. Thus some of his passages are simply science in fancy dress. Yet his descriptions can be masterly, more brief and precise at their best than those of Ruskin, with which alone they can be compared.

XVII

"L'OISEAU BLEU"

THE English translation of "L'Oiseau Bleu" appeared in 1909, before its original, and was soon afterwards charmingly performed at the Haymarket Theatre in London, with scenery which was for the most part brilliantly apt. The woodcutter's children, Tyltyl and Mytyl, lie in bed dreaming on Christmas Eve, but, appearing to wake, they get up and watch the party in the great house opposite, which they enjoy as if they were of it. There is a knock at the cottage door, and an old hunch-backed woman enters, rather like their neighbour, Madame Berlingot. She wants the Blue Bird for her little sick daughter, and Tyltyl and Mytyl are to find it for her. She is the fairy Bérylune, and gives Tyltyl a green hat and the magic diamond: "One turn, you see the inside of things. . . . One more, and you behold the past. . . . Another, and you behold the future." Tyltyl turns the diamond, and the fairy becomes a princess of marvellous beauty, and all things are resplendent. The Hours trip out of the tall grand-father's clock and begin to dance to delicious music.

The souls of the loaves, of the fire, of the dog, and
of the cat appear. The dog is enthusiastic at this
release, the cat circumspect. The soul of water
comes from the tap and fights with fire, and the
souls of milk, sugar, and light appear. At a knock
on the door, Tyltyl turns the diamond, and the
enchantment is gone. Fire, Bread, Water, Sugar,
Milk, Light, and Tylo the Dog and Tylette the
Cat remain to accompany the children. All go
out through the window, and Daddy and Mummy
Tyl, entering, believe their children asleep.

In the Fairy's palace all receive their dresses.
The Cat rebels. The Dog is for Man, and so
is Light, who is to lead the guest. First they visit
the Land of Memory, and see Granny and Gaffer
Tyl, who tell them : " Every time you think of us,
we wake up and see you." Tyltyl notices that the
old blackbird in the cage is quite blue, and Gaffer
agrees to give it to them. Their dead brothers
and sisters run out of the cottage, they play and
sup together, but a clock strikes and the two have
to go—the bird has turned black again. In the
Palace of Night the Cat asks Night to keep them
from finding the Blue Bird, " hidden here, among
the blue birds and the dreams . . . that die as soon
as they set eyes on the sun." The children, Bread,
Sugar, and the Dog timidly enter and find Night,
Sleep, and Death. In cave after cave they discover the Ghosts, the Sicknesses, the Wars, the
Shades and Terrors, Silence and the Mysteries,
the Stars, Perfumes of Night, Will-o'-th'-Wisps,
Fireflies, Transparent Dew, and at last a dream-

garden with many blue birds. The children take
away some of these, but when Light enters they
droop and die, and Tyltyl flings them down and
cries. In the Forest the Cat conspires with the
Trees against the children before they and the Dog
enter. When the diamond is turned the trees'
souls appear. A blue bird is perched on the Oak,
who denounces Man and calls on the Animals.
At the Cat's suggestion the Dog is bound up by
Ivy to the Oak because he has threatened it. None
of the trees will attack Tyltyl, and the war is
left to the Animals. The Dog and Light save the
children in the battle, and, Tyltyl turning the
diamond, the Forest is once more harmless. Light
says: "You see Man is alone against all in this
world."

After this sinister forest scene Maeterlinck has
introduced two most genial scenes at the suggestion
of Mr. Herbert Trench. "I believe we have the
Blue Bird this time," says Light, on approaching
the Palace of Happiness. Here they meet the
Luxuries—the Luxury of Being Rich, the Luxury
of Being a Landowner, the Luxury of Knowing
Nothing, the Luxury of Understanding Nothing,
and so on. But the Luxury of Being Rich tells
Tyltyl that the Blue Bird "is a bird that is not
good to eat, I believe. . . . At any rate, he has
never figured on our table. . . . That means that we
have a poor opinion of him. But don't trouble;
we have much better things. . . ." Tylo, Sugar,
and Bread give way to the temptations of the
Luxuries' table: one Luxury catches Light herself

round the waist. The turning of the diamond brings the tempted ones to their senses, and wipes out the glories of the Luxuries. For them are substituted the angelic beauty of the Happinesses. First the " Children's Happinesses " appear dancing and singing, but without the Blue Bird. Then come the Happinesses of Tyltyl's own home, though he does not recognize them They are the Happiness of Being Well, the Happiness of Pure Air, the Happiness of Loving one's Parents, the Happiness of Running Barefoot in the Dew, and many others. When Tyltyl asks them about the Blue Bird, they all burst out laughing at hearing that he does not know where the Bird is. The Happiness of Running Barefoot in the Dew has taken word to the Great Joys. They appear to the children—the Joy of Being Just, the Joy of Being Good, the Joy of Fame, the Joy of Under-standing, and such gentry. The Joy of Loving comes also, and " the peerless joy of Maternal Love "—in her Tyltyl sees the resemblance to his mother, " but you are much prettier." She wears a ring like Mummy Tyl, but with light flowing through it. " Doesn't it do any work like the one at home ? " asks Tyltyl.

" ' Why, yes,' says Maternal Love, ' it is the very same : did you never see that it becomes quite white and fills with light the moment it fondles you ? ' "

She tells him that " Heaven is wherever you and I kiss each other." These Joys kneel at the feet of Light because she is to teach them to see beyond themselves ; but not yet. They part from her with tears, but without the Blue Bird, and with only the slightest mention of it in the whole act, as is natural in a scene designed to consummate the daintily, solemnly, airy Christmas quality of the whole play.

Light now has to announce that a note from the Fairy Bérylune tells her the Blue Bird is probably in the graveyard, one of the dead is hiding it. She sends the children alone to the graveyard, and there, in the turning of the diamond, the gaping tombs give forth an efflorescence which makes a fairy-like garden, with dew on the flowers, murmuring wind, and bees and birds. " There are no dead," is the discovery.

The children are next taken by Light to the Kingdom of the Future, where the children are waiting to be born—playing, talking, dreaming, working at future inventions—and among them a child who is to wipe out injustice from the earth, and another who is to be Tyltyl's brother. The great opal doors open and Time appears calling those whose turn it is to be born, and of two lovers one is taken and another is forced to remain behind. The galley bearing them passes away ; the song of the glad and expectant mothers is heard. Time sees the children and is furious and threatening, but they slip away with Light, who has the Blue Bird under her cloak.

At the wall of their cottage the children part from Light and the rest. They are still without

ABBEY OF SAINT WANDRILLE : THE REFECTORY

the Blue Bird, because the one from the Future turned pink: " he changes colour when he is eyed." The Dog and the Cat quarrel again. The clock strikes and all flee, the Dog howling outside. The children are awakened by Mummy Tyl, who is frightened at their strange talk and adventures. She thinks she is to lose them, but Daddy Tyl thinks all is well. After a knock their neighbour Berlingot enters, and the children think her the Fairy Bérylune. Her little sick daughter wants Tyltyl's bird, and behold it is blue. He gives it and she goes away. " How lovely it all is!" he says, " and how glad I feel! " The neighbour returns presently with a beautiful little girl carrying Tyltyl's dove. But as Tyltyl is stroking the bird it escapes and flies away. The little girl sobs, but Tyltyl comforts her and says he will catch him again ; then, addressing the audience, he says : " If any of you should find him, would you be so very kind as to give him back to us? . . . We need him for our happiness, later on."

Compare " L'Oiseau Bleu " simply as a fairy play for children with any other books or plays for children—with " Peter Pan," with " Alice in Wonderland," with Mr. Walter de la Mare's " Three Mulla Mulgars "—and it will bear the comparison. It innovates less than " Alice " and no more than " Three Mulla Mulgars." The animals and inanimate things are personified and made to talk. All takes place during the sleeping hours, and it is " only pretending," for the two children might have been seen lying rightly in

18

their bed at any hour of the night. It is the night before Christmas Day. The children are the masters, with the help of a fairy of a thoroughly acceptable traditional kind. All these are conditions which cause less surprise fulfilled than if unfulfilled. Then Tyltyl is to be dressed like Hop-o'-my-Thumb in Perrault's tales, Mytyl like Grethel or Little Red Riding Hood, the Fairy Bérylune and neighbour Berlingot like " the poor woman in fairy tales," the Dog in a costume suggesting " John Bull," the Cat in that of Puss-in-Boots, though Maeterlinck might easily defend himself against any one who attacked him with his own objection to the use of ancient bogeys and fustian in modern plays. The reader, and still less the spectator, if he be acquainted with new as well as old fairy tales, children's books, pantomimes, etc., has no difficulties at the opening of the play and few at any other point. It satisfies the most rigid and the most indolent conventional standards by its total form and most of its detail. The Palace of Happiness is indeed an irrelevant intrusion, but it can be played so that the " angel forms" of the Joy of Doing Good and the other shadows appear as pretty and as little symbolical as ballet-girls. Upon the stage, the brilliant or fantastic or amusing dresses, and the various surprising and charming scenes, add yet a great deal more to the power of the play to conquer the eye and the fancy.

But Maeterlinck has not merely done consummately what many could have done somehow or very well. Here, for example, are Tyltyl and Mytyl looking out of their window at the rich children's party.

T. It's snowing! . . . There's two carriages, with six horses each! . . .

M. There are twelve little boys getting out! . . .

T. How silly you are! . . . They're little girls. . . .

M. They've got knickerbockers. . . .

T. What do you know? . . . Don't push so! . . .

M. I never touched you.

T. (*who is taking up the whole stool*). You're taking up all the room.

M. Why, there's no room at all! . . .

T. Do be quiet! I see the tree! . . .

M. What tree? . . .

T. Why, the Christmas tree! . . . You're looking at the wall! . . .

M. I'm looking at the wall because I've got no room.

T. (*giving her a miserly little place on the stool*). There! Will that do? . . . Now you're better off than I! I say, what lots and lots of lights!

M. What are those people doing who are making such a noise? . . .

T. They're the musicians.

M. Are they angry? . . .

T. No ; but it's hard work.

M. Another carriage with white horses! . . .

T. Be quiet! . . . And look!

M. What are those gold things there, hanging from the branches?

T. Why, toys, to be sure! . . . Swords, guns, soldiers, cannons. . . .

M. And dolls ; say, are there any dolls ? . . .

T. Dolls ? That's too silly ; there's no fun in dolls.

But these things, perfect as they are in their way, might have been by other clever writers. The humour can be quietly playful enough, as when the Fairy says she thinks it wrong of the rich children not to give Tyltyl and Mytyl some, and Tyltyl replies : " Not at all, they're rich "—or when the Cat tells the Oak that it does not throw off its rheumatism " because of the moss ; you put too much of it on your feet "—or in the assumed superiority of the little boy to the little girl all through, or of the similar superiority of Gaffer Tyl to Granny Tyl, or in the quarrels of Cat and Dog down to the time when the Dog asks the children : " Shall I do a wonderful trick for you ? Would you like me to kiss the Cat ? " Or when Mytyl asks Tyltyl what the dead eat and he says " Roots," she asks, " Shall we see them ? " Yet if this humour, taken altogether, can be called individual, it is not distinctive ; nor perhaps is the mere invention of the Land of Memory, the Kingdom of the Future, the Forest where the Animals strive against Man ; it is certainly far less so than the invention of several of the early plays. One reminder of the early plays there is in the third scene of the fifth act when the two unborn lovers are begging to be allowed to go together to earth, and one says, " I shall never see him again," and the other, " We shall be alone in the world." This echoed ex-

pression of the feeling of separation has been seen
to survive and to reappear again and again. No ;
as in " Monna Vanna," Maeterlinck has taken an
outline which might have been any one's, but this
outline he has filled with delicate and significant
fancy that is purely his own, and with thoughts
which are not only his own but are for the most
part to be found in his essays. If any one is inclined
to lay too much stress upon this serious side of the
book he should turn to the first act, where the
power of the diamond is explained. It will, says
the Fairy, open the children's eyes so that they can
see at once " the inside of things." The boy turns
the diamond, and among other souls appear those
of the loaves :

" The souls of the Quartern Loaves, in the form
of little men in crust-coloured tights, flurried and
all powdered with flour, scramble out of the bread-
pan and frisk round the table, where they are
caught up by Fire, who, springing from the hearth
in yellow and vermilion tights, writhes with laughter
as he chases the loaves."

And the Fairy tells the boy that they are " taking
advantage of the reign of truth to leave the pan in
which they were too tightly packed." This is
Maeterlinck's playful warning to those who are not
content that a Christmas fairy play should be that
above all things. It is as if, in an hour of un-
controllable and pyrotechnic high spirits, he had
taken his essays and vowed to turn them into something amusing. For the most part he has done

this with a zest and lightness which are as remarkable as the qualities of the essays themselves,
but, instead of writing of the wisdom of silent
children, he compares seven brothers and sisters to
a set of Pan's-pipes. He has once or twice relented,
and even so far forgotten his vow that he writes
as would better become the essayist. The in-
truded " Palace of Happiness " is a case in point.
It can only be effective on the stage by obliterating
whatever meaning it has and making it simply an
excuse for scenery and dress.

It is yet worth while to see how much of the
essays has not been completely transformed. Tylo,
the dog, for example, who, dressed as John Bull or
not, is probably the favourite character with English
audiences. Tylo does nothing which might not
have been foreseen by readers of Maeterlinck's
essays on the death of a little dog and on chrysanthemums. When his soul is free and can
speak, he at once jumps about with joy and
addresses the boy as " My little god " and cries,
" At last, at last we can talk ! . . . I had so much
to tell you ! Bark and wag my tail as I might,
you never understood. But now ! . . . Good
morning, good morning ! . . . I love you ! " The
Fairy was to tell the souls that all who accompany the children will die at the end of the
journey, and the Cat cries out at once that they
should return to the " trap "; but Tylo accepts the
condition. " I want to go with the little god ! I
want to talk to him all the time." When the
animals are left alone together, the Cat tells them

that their future is at stake, and that they must prolong the journey as much as possible. Tylo simply explains :

"'This is ridiculous ! . . . There is Man, and that's all ! . . . We have to obey him and do as he tells us ! . . . That is the one and only fact ! . . . I recognize no one but him ! . . . Hurrah for Man ! . . . Man for ever ! . . . In life and death, all for Man ! . . . Man is God ! ' "

In the forest scene Tylo's acts are as heroic as these speeches. Much of this scene is unmitigated philosophy from the essays. The Oak, for example, speaks for inhuman Nature to the assembled animals :

" The child you see before you, thanks to a talisman stolen from the powers of Earth, is able to take possession of the Blue Bird and thus to snatch from us the secret which we have kept since the origin of life. . . . Now we know enough of Man to entertain no doubt as to the fate which he reserves for us once he is in possession of this secret. That is why it seems to me that any hesitation would be both foolish and criminal. . . . It is a serious moment. The child must be done away with before it is too late."

Tylo breaks in upon this anarchism with gruff, abusive humour, calling the trees " Timbertoes " and the Ivy " You old ball of twine." But he is tied up, and the Oak continues :

"' This is the first time that it is given to us to judge Man and make him feel our power. . . . I

do not think that, after the harm which he has
done us, after the monstrous injustice which we
have suffered, there can remain the least doubt as
to the sentence that awaits him.' "

And all of them are, in fact, for death, and
immediate death. The Beech offers its highest
branch to hang the children on, and the Fir-tree
four planks for a coffin, and so on, the Lime
interrupting to oppose " such extremities." They
are alarmed at the knife, and make a very poor
fight against two small children and afterwards the
dog. When the Wolf tries to corrupt Tylo by
reminding him that Tyltyl's father drowned his
seven puppies, he retorts: " Quite right! And
a good thing too! . . . It was because they looked
like you!" When Light has saved the children
she tells them that the animals and trees are
" always like that; but we do not know it because
we do not see it. . . . Man is all alone against all
in this world." Not a word about vegetarianism,
though the sheep gives, as the reason of its hostility,
the fact that Tyltyl has eaten her brother, two
sisters, three uncles, an aunt, and a grandfather
and grandmother. Maeterlinck's cheerful confidence in the romance of Man is not prominent
in this scene alone. In the Palace of Night, Night
admits that Man has " captured a third of her
mysteries, that all her terrors are afraid, her
ghosts fled, and most of her sicknesses ill—
" almost all poorly and very much discouraged . . .
the doctors are so unkind to them." She asks:

"Must he absolutely know everything?" In the Kingdom of the Future the same is expressed with greater extravagance and not always so much humour. Maeterlinck's interest in machinery and invention leads to a whirl of "wheels, disks, fly-wheels, driving-wheels, pulleys, straps, and strange and as yet unnamed objects," where experimenters are at work, and Time, choosing those who are to be born, comments, "More doctors? . . . Where are the engineers?" The unborn children boast to Tyltyl of their inventions; and one shows a scented daisy as big as a table—"They will grow like that when I am on the earth"—and another a bunch of grapes as big as pears; one is to bring pure joy to the earth "by means of ideas which people have not yet had," and another is "to conquer death." There is a curious piece of cruelty also in this scene. A brother of Tyltyl's, who is to be born on next Palm Sunday, comes running up to the children with a bag. Tyltyl asks what is in it, and he tells them, "Three illnesses: scarlatina, whooping-cough, and measles." Tyltyl's comment might have been invented by Mr. Kenneth Grahame or any child: "Oh, that's all, is it?" But he continues: "And, after that, what will you do?" "I shall have you," says the unborn. "It will hardly be worth while coming," is Tyltyl's last word. It is cruel, to any one but a child, and it is admirable. The child is perhaps to be one of the doomed children of "Le Trésor des Humbles," but it has a reality which is lacking there. This is one of the passages where philosophy fails Maeterlinck

and reality breaks in. It is not the only un-
expected thing in the scene.   Among the children
who are to go off on Time's galley to the earth are
several who have forgotten the things they had
to bring—for each must bring something—and one
of them has forgotten " the box containing the two
crimes which I shall have to commit."   This need
not be taken as doctrine, unless the whole scene
is, but it is so consistent that I think it must.
" Life is right "—at least to the extent of being
unalterable, and Merlin was wrong when he
told Lancéor that Joyzelle could change the
future.

If Maeterlinck gives up, for the purposes of the
play, his suggestion that man may learn to change
the future, he returns to the belief that he makes
his own past. In " Le Temple Enseveli " he expressed this belief very cunningly.   The most
dangerous past, he said, is one inhabited by " too
dearly cherished phantoms," and against such
cherishing he urges that, if the dead were to return,
they would bid us dry our eyes and say that they
live only in our memories, but that we falsely
believe our regrets alone can touch them ; in truth
they are robbed yet again of life when we return
too often to their graves and allow them to " sadden
our ardour."   This is the language of old Gaffer
Tyl, whom the children meet in the Land of
Memory :

" ' Why don't you come to see us oftener ? . . . It
makes us so happy ! . . . It is months and months

now that you've forgotten us, and that we have seen nobody. . . .

"'We are always here, waiting for a visit from those who are alive. . . . They come so seldom ! . . . Well, every time you think of us, we wake up and see you again.'"

The scene in the graveyard, ending in Tyltyl's " There are no dead " is a continuation of the same thought, and the child has evidently read the essay on immortality, as Tylo has read that on the death of a little dog. If the Kingdom of the Future is not quite in keeping with holly and mistletoe, there can be no objection of the kind against the Land of Memory. In the book, and still more on the stage, it is full of concessions to amiability, and this scene at the supper-table is a charming example:

Tyltyl (half raising himself on his stool). I want more, more ! . . . (*He seizes the tureen, drags it towards him, and upsets it and the soup, which trickles over the table and down over their knees, and scalds them. Yells and screams of pain.*)

Granny Tyl. There ! . . . I told you so ! . . .

Gaffer Tyl (giving Tyltyl a loud box on the ear). That's one for you ! . . .

Tyltyl (staggered for a moment, next puts his hand to his cheek with an expression of rapture). Oh, that's just like the slaps you used to give me when you were alive ! . . . Grandad, how nice it was, and how good it makes one feel ! . . . I must give you a kiss ! . . .

Gaffer Tyl. Very well ; there's more where that came from, if you like them.

In this Land of Memory Gaffer Tyl wants to smoke, but has broken his pipe. Another piece of geniality is the pipe which is given to the soul of the Lime-tree to smoke in the Forest scene : he comes forward quietly smoking his pipe. These personifications of the trees may serve as examples of Maeterlinck's pretty anthropomorphic fancy. Tyltyl turns the diamond and—

" A long-drawn-out rustling shakes the leaves and branches. The oldest and most stately trunks open to make way for the soul which each of them contains. The appearance of these souls differs according to the appearance and the character of the trees which they represent. The soul of the Elm, for instance, is a sort of pursy, pot-bellied, crabbed gnome ; the Lime-tree is placid, familiar, and jovial ; the Beech, elegant and agile ; the Birch, white, reserved, and restless ; the Willow, stunted, dishevelled, and talkative ; the Fir-tree, tall, lean, and taciturn ; the Cypress, tragic ; the Chestnut-tree, pretentious, and rather dandified ; the Poplar, sprightly, cumbersome, and talkative."

The early plays of Maeterlinck are irregularly and incompletely symbolic, as life, nature, and biography are. " L'Oiseau Bleu " is more allegorical than symbolic ; in fact, few books are less symbolic, for the writer has been too self-conscious to allow his imagination to work in the manner which produces symbols. It is also far too lively a play to be systematically allegorical, and to call the Blue Bird happiness, and to claim the play as a picture of the quest for happiness, is to blind ourselves to many of the merits of a theatrical fairy story, and to substantiate the claim is to attempt an impossible and ungrateful task. By writing the new fourth act for Mr. Herbert Trench Maeterlinck shows his robust indifference to everything but the entertainment. He very nearly left the Blue Bird altogether out of this act. The Blue Bird, says the Oak, in one of the dangerously abstract speeches of the play, is "the great secret of things, and of happiness"; and again, to win the Blue Bird is "to snatch from us the secret which we have kept since the origin of life." Fairy Bérylune, says Light, has said that the Blue Bird is in the graveyard—"One of the dead is hiding it in his tomb"; but "there are no dead." Light again claims to have the Blue Bird when they leave the Kingdom of the Future, and when they are back again at the cottage she tells them that the Fairy is coming to ask for it. "But," says Tyltyl, "I haven't got the Blue Bird!" Whereupon Light seems to prevaricate, saying: "It seems likely that the Blue Bird does not exist or that he changes colour when he is caged." Nevertheless, in the cage is a blue bird found, instead of a common turtle-dove, and, by giving it to Madame Berlingot, Tyltyl cures her sick daughter: which causes no surprise in a fairy play, and more cannot be said. The Blue Bird has given an excuse for the play and continuity to the adventures, and that it should seem to mean something important is no more than was to be expected in a work by Maeterlinck. He has probably tricked us good-naturedly by playing with his liking for symbols. The Blue Bird means happiness, as the White Peacocks of "Serres Chaudes" meant ennui, and no more.

XVIII

A TRANSLATION of Maeterlinck's latest play, "Mary Magdalene," was published in 1910. The original has not yet appeared. Its chief characters are Mary Magdalene and her lover, Lucius Verus, a Roman military tribune. At the beginning of the play he is telling his friend, a master in philosophy, Annæus Silanus, that he has lost trace of her. She had not appeared to accept his love, though she was, as a courtesan, "not at all inexorable to the Roman knights." He still desires her, as he had never desired any other woman. Silanus tells him that she is now living not far away, in the retirement of a marble villa. She is to be his guest this day, and, as they are speaking, the sound of a double flute betokens her arrival. She has just lost some rubies and pearls, a Babylonian peacock and her *murænæ*, and she puts down the robbery to the wandering band of the Nazarene, whom she calls "a sort of unwashed brigand, who entices the crowds with a rude kind of sorcery, and, on the pretence of preaching some new law or doctrine, lives by plunder and surrounds himself

287

with fellows capable of everything." But Silanus
argues against this opinion, for the band has been
gathered for some time near his house and seems
"incapable of stealing more than a cup of water
or an ear of wheat." Their leader has a voice "of
a penetrating and peculiar sweetness." When
Silanus leaves Verus and Mary for a moment alone
together, she will only say that now she sells
herself "more skilfully, and dearer than before";
which Verus at first chivalrously disbelieves and
then accepts by saying, "If it is a question only
of rating you more highly, know, Magdalene, that
from this moment you are mine." Now other
Romans, Appius and Cælius, enter and relate how
they have been delayed by a multitude gathered
about a blind man newly healed by the Nazarene.
He is now staying with Silanus's neighbour, Simon,
lately cured by him of leprosy, and while they are
speaking together they hear the sound of a crowd
gathering. A silence follows and a voice saying,
"Blessed are the poor in spirit, for theirs is the
kingdom of heaven ! . . ." Mary, as if drawn by
the voice, goes down towards the speaker and will
not be stopped. But the crowd presently discovers
her and chases her back with cries of "The adulteress !
. . . stone her !" until the voice is heard saying,
"He that is without sin among you, let him first cast
a stone at her." The crowd retreats. Mary rejects
the support of Verus "with a harsh and fierce
gesture, and, staring in front of her, alone among
the others, who look at her without understanding,
slowly she climbs the steps of the terrace."

In the second act Verus visits her in her own villa. She seems to accept him, reminding him how she received many others in the old days, but him, "the comeliest, the purest," she tried to forget, and was shy with him. Verus is a little incredulous of his happiness, especially as he had lately been refused the house by her slaves. That was because she was still "tired and worn out" since the struggle with the crowd in Simon's garden. She asks if Verus knows where the Nazarene is. "His hours are numbered," says Verus. But Mary asks, "What has he done? . . . He brings a happiness that was not known before; and all those who come next to him are happy, it seems, like children at their awaking. . . . He fixed his eyes for but a moment on mine. . . . He seemed to choose me gravely, absolutely, for ever." Verus does not understand this, but is reassured by her sobs upon his breast and her saying that she will never see the Nazarene again. Nevertheless, she asks after him from Appius and Silanus, who between them tell the story of the raising of Lazarus from the dead. Appius is convinced that "this man, who has conquered death, which hitherto had conquered the world, is greater than we and our gods." While Silanus is questioning Appius's opinion that they ought to conform their lives to the teaching of the Nazarene, Mary hears a sound which she interprets : "He is coming." But it is Lazarus, not Jesus, who comes unopposed into their presence. Then Verus bids him go, but he says only : "Come. The Master calls you," to Mary. She at once steps towards him, willing to go "wherever he wishes." But Verus holds her back by force until he believes that she loves the Nazarene. She protests that she loves Verus, who bids her go with her "guide from the tombs." She goes out after Lazarus in silence.

In the third act Jesus has been arrested. The scene is the room in Joseph of Arimathæa's house, where the Last Supper took place. It is crowded with men and women miraculously healed by Jesus and others waiting to be healed, and Nicodemus, Cleophas, Levi the publican, Mary Cleophas, Martha the sister of Lazarus, and others. Martha has seen Jesus going into Caiaphas's palace, and she tells them they are going to persecute all Galileans; at which Cleophas says, "We are all Galileans"; but many deny it, and one says, "It is not well that we should be found together." They gossip miserably of what has happened to them, asking "Why does he not protect us?" and the like. Martha tells what she saw: how the Roman soldiers struck Jesus to make him walk faster. Mary Magdalene, she has heard, is mad with grief, and was "dashing her head against the walls in Annas' palace." Presently she enters with Joseph of Arimathæa, James, Andrew, and Simon Zelotes. Mary has to say that she has seen Verus and that he thought it possible to save him—"I do not know how. . . . He will explain to us. . . But, if he does not save him, we must." She is thinking of armed deliverance, and asks which of the men in the town have arms. Joseph of Arimathæa thinks Jesus "determined to be de-

stroyed" because he has confessed to being Son
of God and King of the Jews. Mary replies that
he has renounced his defence "to try your faith,
your strength, your love." She addresses the men
about her, telling them "even those whom he
raised from the dead are afraid." Nicodemus
and Joseph counsel moderation. And now Verus
arrives. She runs to him with outstretched arms
for help; he ironically says: "I have not come
to command this . . . foreign . . . troop." The
two are left alone. His attitude escapes Mary;
she thinks him willing to help Jesus. Verus has
the fate of the Nazarene in his hands, as the
guardian responsible for the Roman peace; but
he is not willing to save one whom he thinks a
rival except for a price, and it will mean exile,
if not death. The price is her body. Perplexed
and speaking what her lover does not merely fail
to understand but misunderstands, she refuses,
until at length he calls in the people and tells
them that she has refused to save Jesus. Joseph
cannot believe it, nor Mary, nor Martha, but the
rest cry out: "She has sold him. . . . Where is
the money? . . . Strumpet!" Joseph tries to get
her to speak, to consent to save Jesus. She remains
silent. Then a sound of tumult is heard and all
go to the windows, putting out the lamps to
avoid being seen. Outside are heard the cries:
"Crucify him! . . . Crucify him!" The onlookers
comment. The blind man of Jericho says, "It is
he!"; another, "He cannot walk any farther! . . .
He staggers!"; and the blind man again, "He has

fallen! . . . He is looking at the house." Once more Verus says, "I still promise you," and Mary, without looking at him, "without anger, simply in a voice from another life, full of peace, full of divine clarity and certainty, says, "Go!"

The whole play must have been written for the sake of this last act. The rest is either spectacles or eloquent speeches. Annæus Silanus has been a teacher of philosophy, and it is natural that he should speak like one. It is less natural that he should actually teach philosophy and occupy our ears with fair copies, presumably, of wise and elegant letters to be sent to his friends in Rome. As such a letter his opening speech would be charming, and Cicero would certainly have admired it had it been in Latin equal to Maeterlinck's French:

"'Here is the terrace, the glory of my little domain: it reminds me of my terrace at Præneste, which was the crown of my desires. Here are my orange-trees, my cypresses, my oleanders. Here is the fish-pond, the portico with the images of the gods: one of them is a statue of Minerva, discovered at Antioch. (*Pointing to the landscape on the left.*) And here you have the incomparable view over the valley, where spring already reigns. We hang midway in space. Admire the anemones streaming down the slopes of Bethany. It is as though the earth were ablaze beneath the olive-trees. Here I relish in peace the advantages of old age, which knows how to take pleasure in the past; for youth narrows the enjoyment of good things, by considering only those which are present.'"

Once, in fact, and speaking to Mary, he quotes the letter which Longinus sent him to console him for the death of his little child. The letter is given at length, with one brief interruption by Appius, and Mary's comment: "That would not have consoled me." This man begins a conversation in a manner which should have ended it:

"'It was said and it was written that, on this most propitious day, I should behold two marvels, not the lesser of which is to see thus promptly reunited two lovers who, according to love's ancient custom, should have fled from each other the more obstinately the more they yearned to meet.'"

Only too well had his pupil, Verus, learnt his lessons, and, when Mary is sobbing on his breast, telling him she still loves him in spite of the Nazarene, he says to her:

"'Come, I know these tears that well at the same moment from our two hearts in our one joy. . . . But here, between the columns of the vestibule, come the greatest ornaments of that beautiful Rome which we shall soon astonish with our love. . . . I am right: it is our good Silanus, accompanied by the faithful Appius; led by the immortal gods, they descend the marble steps to hallow with their fraternal presence the first smiles of a happiness born under their eyes.'"

Whenever Mary appears these Romans at once begin to compose elegant orations, beginning: "Venus has left Cyprus and soars above Jeru-

salem," and so on ; and, in one place, three of them
vie in phrases.   This may be archæologically correct, and, if the aim of these two acts be to depict
the ceremonious side of Roman life, they do so
very effectively, though narrative and description,
without pretension of drama, would have done it
still more effectively.   Some of the stage directions
combine with these statuesque speeches to give, in
reading the play, the effect of narrative.   For
example :

"An incomparable silence, in which it seems as
though the birds and the leaves of the trees and
the very air that is breathed take part, falls with
all its supernatural weight upon the country-side ;
and in this silence, which weighs upon the people
on the terrace above, there rises, absolute sovereign
of space and the hour, a wonderful voice, soft
and all-powerful, intoxicated with ardour, light,
and love—distant and yet near to every heart and
present in every soul."

In the second scene of the second act the story
of the raising of Lazarus is told in a manner which
would be even more admirable if it were frankly
Maeterlinck's and not put into the mouths of
Appius and Silanus alternately—a method explained but hardly justified by the different effects
of the miracle on the two different temperaments.
Appius begins to speak ; Mary asks a question ;
Silanus answers it, and continues the narrative.
Mary again interrupts, and now Appius takes up
the story, only to surrender it to Silanus after the

next interruption. Sometimes not even this device is used, and Silanus says:

"'He has not left Simon's house. The swaying multitude is waiting for him in the orchard and along the roads; for, after the first long minutes of stupor, reaction set in and a general alacrity followed.'"

And Appius continues the sentence:

"'Which was as extraordinary as the miracle itself!'"

Nor is this more transparent than the fact that Silanus, as Marco does in "Monna Vanna" and Merlin in "Joyzelle," talks like Maeterlinck, or, in one place, makes Longinus talk like him, in the words:

"'I assure you that, of those whom we have loved, much remains to us after death has removed them. The time that is past is ours; and I see nothing of which we are more certain than of that which has been.'"

The resemblance is closer and unquestionable when Silanus says, while Mary is going into the orchard to hear Jesus: "Women sometimes have thoughts which wise men do not understand"; and when Verus tells Mary that in their separation: "While you were calling me, I called you also with all the deep and wonderful voices of my heart."

If in the first two acts these Romans explain themselves too much and too professionally, Mary Magdalene explains herself too little.   At first she talks much like the Romans, thus :

" ' I at first suspected some Tyrian workmen who are fitting up one of the rooms in my villa with those movable panels which are changed at every course, so that the walls may harmonize with the dishes covering the table.' "

But when she is first " irresistibly drawn " by the voice of Jesus, Maeterlinck leaves everything to the actress who plays the part.   Silence is a more profound form of speech than words, but it must use words to express itself upon the stage, or at least in the printed book.   Between the moment when she goes down towards the voice and the sound of the voice that saved her with the words, " He that is without sin . . ." she says nothing at all. We have to explain to ourselves how this supercilious prostitute should leave her powerful Roman friends and go down to listen to the man whom she had thought a noisome and thieving vagabond. Certainly a prose sketch like the " Portrait of a Lady " would have done all that these words do, the short speeches and the lengthy stage directions, *i.e.* to produce a picture of a beautiful and luxurious woman, languidly proud but still young, silenced and solemnized by the voice of a wandering religious Jew saying, " Blessed are the poor in spirit."   There is, however, one important indication near the beginning of the play : Verus tells

Silanus that Mary had repulsed him with "a harsh gentleness" mingled with "a certain incomprehensible dread," and that "she seemed to have suffered a great sorrow, for which she has already, I hear, consoled herself more than once." But in the second act the emotion of the first seems to have turned all to love of Verus: she now realizes that Verus was her destined lover long before. She is at once "glad and light-hearted and yet more shattered than if all the misfortunes that hover in the skies were about to burst over me." She feels a danger, she knows not what it is. The name of the Nazarene comes up again, but still she wants to fly from this danger, from this land where she suffocates. She begins to fear that the life of the Nazarene is in danger, and tells Verus that he owes him her life and their happiness. Verus suspects at once, but she quiets him with a sobbing "I love you." The story of Lazarus compels her soon afterwards to think again of the Nazarene, and she hardly speaks during the long narration except in brief questions, one of them, when Mary Cleophas is mentioned as one who never leaves the master, being "Is she young?" As a short story, this might have ranked with Flaubert's "Hérodias." But only at the end of it does the drama begin, to be seriously retarded by the apparent necessity of making perfectly pictorial the scene where Lazarus comes to call Mary. Things are seen to happen, but how remains a mystery. Surely the method of the short story may be said to prevail in the third scene, where,

for example, the slaves of Mary Magdalene form up
to block the way of Lazarus ; " but," says the stage
direction, " at the approach of the man risen from
the dead, who seems unaware of their presence,
they fall back silently, one after the other." Here,
as in the scene where Mary first hears Jesus, she
hardly speaks. Maeterlinck's object has been to
produce a living picture for the stage, a tableau,
where as few words as possible are used and the
condition of silence is approached. In many
places the characters show themselves fond of clear
visual images, like Maeterlinck, and willing to
express them in words, as when Verus asks
Silanus if he means " The villa with the wide white
steps leading to a semicircular colonnade adorned
with statues." Verus introduces the medium of
speech where Mary is giving way ; as he says
himself, " Roman reason does not waver, like the
rest, at the first foul breath that issues from a
tomb." He commands Lazarus to let his master
know that " his life, which will not be a long one,
after what he has done, lies wholly in this hand
which drives you hence." Mary still struggles to
go, until Verus bids her " Go, since you love him."
" No, No ! . . . I love you, but he . . . it is a
different thing," she tries to explain. Instead of
this silence, so different from the " gracious silence "
of Virgilia, an earlier dramatist would have let the
words as nearly as possible tell the audience what
in real life the woman could hardly have told her
lover : such is the ancient convention of dramatic
poetry. But here Mary remains inarticulate. In

the greater part of the play she represents the
silence of the spirit's profundity in contrast with
the Roman eloquence of the intellect. She goes
out after Lazarus ; and Appius, after a long pause,
exclaims, " We have this day seen more than one
thing that we had not seen before " ; and Silanus :
" It is true, Appius, and this is as surprising as the
resurrection of the dead."   In this scene, as in the
next act, Verus is much like Guido Colonna and
Mary like Monna Vanna. Both men are honourable
men, dignified, high-minded men of rigid and
customary views. They are protective, and still
more possessive, towards their women, and begin
by assuming that the women will not think or
question or be troubled in their benignant shade.
The women try to convince them that their
proposed independence in one matter does not
imply severance and indifference.   The men
protest that they must have all or nothing, and at
once. The women sadly and decidedly go their
way under the anger and contumely of the men.

The first scene of the third act is a less stately
but still finer picture, and it is not a tableau with
accessory words, but drawn, like " Les Aveugles,"
in simplicity, yet intense without monotony, and
restlessly alive instead of lulled in a sleepy submission of numb despair. They are crowded mutter-
ing and whispering together in the candle-lit room
after the news of Jesus' arrest :

A Man cured by a miracle. It is not well that
we should be found together. . . .

Nicodemus. Where will you go?

A Man cured by a miracle. No matter where. . . . We shall be safer than here. . . .

Another. They do not know us. . . . I have never been seen with him. . . .

A Woman. Nor I either : he just simply healed me. . . . I was bowed together, and he made me straight. . . .

A Man. I saw him only once : it was when he said to me, " Arise, and take up thy bed, and go thy way into thine house." I am he whom they let down through the roof upon a bed. . . . Now I walk like other men. . . . (*He turns to the door and goes out, followed by those cured by miracles who spoke before him.*)

A Sick Man. They are right. . . . We are not known either. . . . I came to be healed of a dysentery. . . . I have not had time to touch him. (*He also makes for the door.*)

Martha. Are you not ashamed ? . . .

The Sick Man (*stopping on the threshold*). Of what ? . . . It serves no purpose that those whom he has healed should perish because of him. *He goes out.*)

Another Man cured by a miracle. He can do nothing for us, because he can do nothing for himself : and we can do nothing for him.

Now at length Mary—she has been " mad with grief," says Martha, and they fear that she will bring misfortune—is thoroughly alive. She comes in upon the crowd of the skulking and the timid, an imperious, distracted woman, barefooted and in torn garments. She can think only of an armed attempt at deliverance, " if Verus does not deliver

him." If only she had had five or six more when
they took him to Caiaphas—only two soldiers and
two sergeants from the Temple! "We save those
whom we love," she tells Joseph of Arimathæa;
"we listen to them afterwards." She speaks easily
now, dominating the room with her boldness and
her scorn. Joseph tries to silence her by bidding
her reflect that if he heard her. . . . "Well," she
says:

"'Well, if he heard me, it would be as on the day
when that one among you whom you all resemble
reproached me with anointing his feet with too
costly an ointment! . . . Have you forgotten what
he said? . . . Whom did he declare to be right? . . .
You have understood nothing! . . . For months
and years you have lived in his light; and not one
of you has the least idea of what I said, because
I loved him—I who did not come until the eleventh
hour, I whom he drew from lower than the lowest
slave of the lowest among you all!'"

She runs to Verus as trustfully as Monna Vanna
returning to Guido. She thinks that he is going
to lead her and the timid to rescue their master.
When he is alone with her he sarcastically refers
to her company of "cripples, vagrants, and evil-
smelling sick people." However, "that no longer
concerns me," he adds. He knew what was hap-
pening, and was biding his time. "How good and
generous you are!" says Mary. It seems to her
as if Rome herself were protecting them, and "that
your arms, which can do all things, cannot abandon
him." But if Verus is "good and generous," it is

" in his own manner," he says. She continues to misunderstand him, and when she begins a sentence with, " There is no excuse for a moment's hesitation ; it would be monstrous, . . ." he has to pervert it by repeating it and adding, " Shall I, to snatch a favoured rival from a well merited death, for the second time lose the only woman whom I love or can love ? " He thinks that if he saves Jesus that man will drag her down to the depths of " folly and wretchedness." If Jesus perishes, then she may " return to the light," and " many roads, as you well know, lead to Rome." She cannot believe that he will destroy Jesus in revenge for the supposed injury. There must be something else. Verus is perfectly articulate :

" ' Have you not understood that it is you I want, you alone, and all of you ; that I have wanted you for years ; and that this is my hour ? . . . It is not beautiful, I know, and it is not as I dreamt it ! . . . But it is all I have, and a man takes what he can to make his life ! . . . We stand here face to face with our two madnesses, which are more powerful than ourselves, and cannot recede ; we must come to an understanding ! . . . The more you love him, the more I love you ; the more you wish to save him, the more I wish to destroy him ! We must come to an understanding ! . . . You want his life, I want mine ; and you shall have his life ; but I shall have you, before he escape his death. . . . Is it understood ? . . . Are we agreed ? . . . Say No, if you dare, and let his blood be upon her who has brought him to this pass, and who is destroying him twice over ! ' "

Her awakening is like Monna Vanna's when she understands her husband and lies for Prinzivalle, and unlies it again with at first hesitating speech, then calm and resolved: the meanness and brutality of Verus must have had something to do with her refusal. Verus's "madness" does not prevent him from reminding her that "a few days ago" she "would not have needed so much urging." Also what he wants, or what he is willing to accept with a measure of content, is not her love, not any kind of life with her, but her body simply. He says: "Since you love him so well, is his life not worth a slight displeasure, which but lately would not have inspired you with such a horror?" He is not too "mad" for a bargain: the thought of a bargain that would gain anything is impossible to her ecstasy. Even Verus is impressed by her "mad and terrified eyes" as he is saying these things. Yet he can still claim to be making a great sacrifice to love—a claim which awakens a sudden outburst from Mary. As Vanna bids Guido look in her eyes to see her truth, so Mary bids Verus "Look at me with clearer eyes, and you shall perhaps see all that I perceive without being able to tell you!" "If I bought his life," she says, "at the price which you offer, all that he wished, all that he loved, would be dead."

She says that what Jesus has given to them is much more than his life, and lives more in their hearts than in him. It is not a question of defiling herself, but of defiling his "salvation," and the source whence all purity and happiness and all life will spring. And thinking that she does not even yet love him as he should be loved, she passes into an ecstasy and says: "Verus, Verus, have pity; I cannot bear it. . . . I am falling! . . . Do with me what you will!" The man catches her in his arms, saying, "I knew." "No," she says, regaining strength at his touch and springing back, "you did not know." Still again she implores him, and she will be his slave all her life. Then he summons the crowd to make them hate her, and she tries to stop him, saying, "This is not worthy of you!" And so, furiously and vilely, he betrays her to them. When at last he goes out after her final silence and her final "Go!" when Christ, who had fallen before that "Go!" was spoken and looked up at the window, rises to his feet, Verus goes out with his eyes fixed on Magdalene, "who remains motionless, as though in ecstasy, and all illumined with the light of the departing torches."

Another sublime tableau! Nor are the words unworthy: they do not merely help the picture; they are heard rising out of silence at the call of events developing before our eyes. The awakening of Mary, her wavering but never doubtful struggle to see the truth and to express it convincingly to Verus, is suggested with the subtlest fidelity to feeling. But, though Mary speaks freely and at some length, her language is not always quite satisfying. It is too abstract, it is too much like what Maeterlinck would use if he were writing about her instead of putting words into her mouth.

Her words are not those of religious passion so much as of a metaphysician describing religious passion. And even so they are inadequate, and I do not understand her when she says : " My God ! . . . Is it not Thou alone whom I defile to-day in defiling Thy salvation, Thou, the very source whence the source of all purity and of every happiness and of every life will spring ? " Such phrasing comes rather from the defiled stream of common religion than from the high sources ; it is at most a second best, and not pure imaginative speech, though it cannot prevent Mary Magdalene from appearing in these last scenes a very moving figure of a woman of pleasure burning and flaming unquenchably with religion. In the earlier scenes, also, such is the prestige of her tradition, she cannot fail to be impressive when the right actress plays her part. The other characters are little more than background, and are treated with an exterior care and even polish. Verus is a Roman, and he is a gentleman ; so much is certain : yet Maeterlinck does him perhaps less than justice in making him confuse his last desperate attempt to gain something with the " madness " of love itself. Silanus, who is not carried so far, is in this same exterior manner ; in another play, or, better still, an imaginary portrait, his character would have earned the applause of the elegant, especially where he refuses to be disturbed, like Appius, by the raising of Lazarus :

" ' By awaking a dead man, in the depth of his

20

grave, he shows us that he possesses a power greater than that of our masters, but not a greater wisdom. Let us await everything with an even mind. It is not difficult, even for a child, to discern that which, in men's words, augments or increases the love of virtue. If he can convince me that I have acted wrong until to-day, I will amend, for I seek only the truth. But, if all the dead who people these valleys were to rise from their graves to bear witness, in his name, to a truth less high than that which I know, I would not believe them. Whether the dead sleep or wake, I will not give them a thought unless they teach me to make a better use of my life.' "

He in his kind is nearer perfection than Mary in hers. But it is a different method, and the two together, though so often admirable, make a play worthy of deep respect, yet an exercise, a study, in the legend of Mary Magdalene, not a full and sufficient creation ; and it is a little disconcerting to see the hard classic grace more surely handled than the romance of a woman who might have summed all that Maeterlinck has divined of the soul's beauty.

XIX

CONCLUSION

MAETERLINCK is now nearly fifty, and it is twenty years since his poems, "Serres Chaudes," and his first play, "La Princesse Maleine," appeared. The poems, as their title declared, were of a hot-house type obscurely struggling towards the free air. They were the vapours and bad blood of youth, more unconventional than sincere, expressed in the manner of the symbolists, but with a personal music which at its best seemed about to turn them into poems without words. They were interesting then only to symbolists, and to-day only to those interested in the symbolists and in Maeterlinck. Two or three scenes of "La Princesse Maleine" had qualities which proved to be enduring, and they dominated his work for six or seven years. These characteristic scenes, and still more those of the succeeding plays, represent with a numbed and melancholy intensity the littleness of men, lost, ignorant, and powerless amidst the forces of Nature and their own kind. Mary Magdalene, in his last play, found her choice difficult for "a poor creature born on this earth," and throughout these plays men and women—children, very old or blind persons, doomed lovers—are poor creatures born on this earth and living out a great torture upon it which Maeterlinck turns into a delicate music of grey and purple. They are curious, exceptional, beautiful works, having all the intensity which youth is apt to give to the one or two qualities which in its own opinion distinguish it, to the exclusion of others often more profound and lasting. But as Maeterlinck had written these plays for six or seven years in spite of the applause given to him for the superficial Shakespearean element in " La Princesse Maleine," so, though he had afterwards won applause for their proper qualities as they were seen in books and on the stage, he advanced to the different perfections of " Alladine et Palomides," " Intérieur," " Pelléas et Mélisande," and " Aglavaine et Sélysette," and then wrote no more of the kind.

The longer speeches of the plays, especially those spoken by the old men, and the introductions which he wrote to volumes of Emerson and Ruysbroeck, had gradually been revealing a philosopher who was not content to let his tragic marionettes embody his conceptions. " Aglavaine et Sélysette " was even a little overburdened by the reflections of the characters. But in the same year as this play came his first volume of essays, " Le Trésor des Humbles," which made it clear that he had found another way of expressing himself, and that he was willing to address the

MAURICE MAETERLINCK

public directly as a philosopher. He appeared as
a follower of Emerson and the mystics whose chief
business was to proclaim the mystery of life, the
greatness of little things, the beauty of all common
things except common standards, as the advocate
of new standards or none at all, in the conduct and
criticism of life. This he did in the gentlest and
most refined prose. It was a philosophy of the
infinitely little, of *la nuance*, the passionate evan-
gelical extension to life of Verlaine's doctrine for
poetry:

> Car nous voulons la nuance encor.
> Pas la couleur, rien que la nuance.
> Oh ! la nuance seule fiance
> Le rêve au rêve et la flute au cor !

It encouraged charity and toleration, more anxious
sympathy and more hesitating decisions in life.
The feeling of the plays for the "poor creature
born on this earth" was not insistent, but it was
strong, and it helped to explain the melancholy
and consumptive fragility of the work with all its
hopefulness. The next book, "La Sagesse et la
Destinée" marked a great increase of confidence
and some strength in the essayist, though he still
regarded man as the destined victim, if not of
Jupiter and Jehovah, yet of unknown and more
inexorable gods, nameless, or known as Destiny
and Nature. Gradually the thought has grown
that man can achieve the most difficult things by
realizing that he is alone, and can depend only on
himself, by refusing to settle down under crude

codes in civil and private life, by more widely
acknowledging mystery, yet more ardently striving
to conquer it instead of denying it, by seeking to
understand and enlarge the powers which affect
our lives more deeply and more obscurely than
reason can do.   As this thought has developed the
thought of Nature's hostility has declined, and
once at least it has been renounced : it has been
revived in " L'Oiseau Bleu," chiefly for its
picturesqueness.   The cardinal, indefinite mysteries
of life which gave gloom to the early plays
have obsessed him less and less, and he has
tended to touch only upon those which are definite,
and will listen to a declaration of war from
the human intelligence—such as luck, instinct,
accident.

The plays, and even the early essays, had
something of a mute, resigned, religious gloom.
This gave way before a freer acceptance of modern
life, its science, its political interest, its progress
by means of legislation, machinery, invention, and
the enlightenment of the many.   Between " Le
Trésor" and " La Sagesse " he met, says André
Gide, " life and Nietzsche."   He came, and he has
since come still farther, out from the North's
impressive twilight into the certain light and
warmth of the South.   He came to see man, not as
a poor little emmet under the eyes of gods, but as
a majestic and subtle being, with " a long, noble
road before him under the stars."   He has thrown
off all the religious trappings, but has respected what
mysteries they covered, and though he accepts no

mystery, new or old, as such, he is aware that there is still, and must always be, mystery on the right hand or on the left. He explains nothing, but he is afraid of nothing, and unashamed of being baffled. He is a materialist in his attitude only towards what is known. Nature, that once seemed a hostile or indifferent mystery, has become chiefly the provider of pleasure to the senses of a buoyant and curious observer, and his descriptions are among the best of his work in their eloquence and precision.

His descriptions, reflections, character-studies, narratives, rhapsodies, criticisms, all now fall easily into the kindly and popular form of essays. But during his fourteen years as an essayist he has written six plays. He has become a dramatist with a strong sense of the pictorial, and a master of theatrical effect. His plays have been for the most part in harmony with his essays, and he might have written them to illustrate the essays, except that he has not—unless in "Aglavaine et Sélysette"—touched modern life, but has always brushed aside his belief in a new, quiet drama, which is to replace the ostentatious and sounding old drama, and has chosen legendary or ancient characters, or such as are no more than personifications. But with his stage skill and inexhaustible fancy he can seldom succeed in being dull, while in " L'Oiseau Bleu " he has produced a Christmas masterpiece which some yet hold to be a philosophy. He has only failed to create a human character.

He has extraordinary facility, adroitness, exuberance, and versatility. He is an experimental botanist, an apiarist of long standing, an automobilist capable of driving himself, a mystic moralist, a playwright, a critic of letters, a topical writer. Above all, he is an artist who handles with equal skill incorporeal and corporeal things. No one can be harder and more clear in depicting a scene or a flower. No one can be more light and vaporous in treating an abstract subject, and he thus softens his impression by seeming to speak of things unrelated to experience but also contrives an entrance for his perfectly free speculations into minds which could not receive them in a more vital form. This same easiness, perhaps, has proved incompatible with the creation of a human character in his plays. His detached, even, and quite uncontroversial manner make him a valuable auxiliary of liberal thought. He is insidious and insinuating, but, except for those who can honestly follow his flights from beginning to end, he is not bracing, and probably fosters a combination of tolerance and enlightened inactivity. So free is he in this mild boldness that he might seem, at times, to be careless and aimless if he were not so obviously an optimist content with the lines of modern civilization and the future towards which they lead. It is the freedom, perhaps, of a high-spirited metaphysical subtlety rather than of mystic intuition. And undoubtedly he has a verbal fertility and skill which might take a few phrases like De Musset's " Le mélodrame est bon où Margot

a pleuré," and " Cette rêverie qui ne pense à rien,"
and William Morris's—

> (Lips) that work
> As though her soul had learned
> Deep things she has never heard of,

and make out of them his philosophy of women
and children—" the silent child is wiser than Marcus
Aurelius speaking." Yet, if it were not for this
sometimes defective, heady exuberance we should
never have had essays like that on sundials, or
perhaps much of " Le Trésor des Humbles," where
there is a kind of courage of timidity which is
beyond braver men. He has less of this than
he began with, and he is now an idealist whose
ideal is the development of the human spirit as it
is definitely promised by to-day, chiefly by science.
He is confident in the future, and not troubled
as to the methods of reaching it. Things are too
mysterious to be judged here, and he is content
to acknowledge that what is had to be and is
right—to show how it is right is part of his task.
His thought may be said to be based on the future,
as Tolstoy's is based on a definite epoch in the past
and Ibsen's on the present ; but he is nearer to
Ibsen in that he sees truth rising, if at all, out of
the crucible of things as they are ; he is for evolution, and not revolution. He is one who advocates
more than he originates, whose chief gifts are
subtlety in amplifying and eloquence in expressing
ideas, who is thus more a rhetorician than a

mystic, though he deals in mystical ideas. He is an apostle of the mystical rights of men, who extends into the moral and spiritual world the doctrine of the freedom and equality of all men.

INDEX

315

Printed in the United Kingdom
by Lightning Source UK Ltd.
9772100001B/8